Creative Problem Solving

in School Mathematics

2nd Edition

Dr. George Lenchner

A Handbook For Teachers, Parents, Students, And Other Interested People.

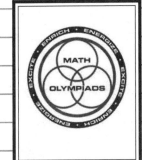

About the Author

Dr. George Lenchner (1917-2006) was the Director of Mathematics for the Valley Stream Central High School District, and Consultant to the three associated Elementary School Districts in Long Island, NY. He was the founder of the Nassau County Interscholastic Mathematics League (Mathletes) in 1955. He also organized the Mathematical Olympiads for Elementary and Middle Schools (MOEMS) in 1979 and served as its Executive Director until his retirement in 1996. He then served MOEMS as its Executive Director Emeritus until 2006.

Dr. Lenchner was the author of many mathematics textbooks and articles appearing in national publications. He brings to this book over 50 years of experience as a mathematics teacher, supervisor, teacher-trainer, and creator of problems. Harvard University has honored him for Outstanding and Distinguished Secondary School Teaching.

Publisher

Mathematical Olympiads for Elementary and Middle Schools, Inc., Bellmore, NY 11710
Web site: *www.moems.org*   Telephone: 866-781-2411

Consultant

Richard S. Kalman

Layout, Graphics, and Cover Design

Richard Kalman, MOEMS
Cover photograph by Christine Matthesen, taken at Shore Road School, Bellmore, NY

Printer

Tobay Printing Company, Inc., Copiague, NY

First Edition, printed in U.S.A., first published in New York, N.Y. 1983.
Revised and expanded edition, printed in U.S.A., published in Bellmore, N.Y. 2005, 2008, 2010, 2013.

ISBN No. 978-1-882144-10-5
Library of Congress Control Number: 2005927296

Contents

INTRODUCTION

About the Author ii
Preface vii

PART A. TEACHING PROBLEM SOLVING 1

1. WHAT IS PROBLEM SOLVING? 2
2. USING A FOUR-STEP METHOD 3
   2.1 Understanding the Problem 3
   2.2 Planning How To Solve The Problem 4
   2.3 Carrying Out The Plan 4
   2.4 Looking Back 5
3. CHOOSING PROBLEMS 7
4. EVALUATING PROBLEMS 8
5. PRESENTING PROBLEMS 9
   5.1 The Chalkboard 9
   5.2 The Overhead Projector 9
   5.3 Duplicated Sheets 10
   5.4 Oral Presentation 10
6. HELPING STUDENTS 11
7. USING CALCULATORS AND COMPUTERS 11

PART B. SOME PROBLEM SOLVING STRATEGIES 13

1. DRAWING A PICTURE OR DIAGRAM 14
2. MAKING AN ORGANIZED LIST 16
3. MAKING A TABLE 18
4. SOLVING A SIMPLER RELATED PROBLEM 20
5. FINDING A PATTERN 22
6. GUESSING AND CHECKING 24
7. EXPERIMENTING 26
8. ACTING OUT THE PROBLEM 28
9. WORKING BACKWARDS 29
10. WRITING AN EQUATION 31
11. CHANGING YOUR POINT OF VIEW 33
12. MISCELLANEA 35

PART C. SOME TOPICS IN PROBLEM SOLVING 37

1. NUMBER PATTERNS 38
1.1 Addition Patterns 38
1.2 Multiplication Patterns 42
1.3 More Addition Patterns 44
1.4 Unusual Patterns 46
1.5 Patterns And Sums 49

2. FACTORS AND MULTIPLES 52
2.1 Factors 52
2.2 Factors and Primes 54
2.3 Greatest Common Factor (GCF) 57
2.4 Least Common Multiple (LCM) 60

3. DIVISIBILITY 65
3.1 Divisibility By 2, 5, 10, and 100 65
3.2 Divisibility Principle For Sums And Differences 67
3.3 Divisibility by Powers of 2 68
3.4 Divisibility by 3 and 9 70
3.5 Divisibility by 11 71
3.6 Combined Divisibility 74
3.7 Divisibility by 7, 11, and 13 75

4. FRACTIONS 77
4.1 Unit Fractions 77
4.2 Complex Fractions 79
4.3 Extended Finite Fractions 81
4.4 Fractional Parts 82

5. GEOMETRY AND MEASUREMENT 84
5.1 Squares and Rectangles 84
5.2 Triangles 87
5.3 Circles 89
5.4 Perimeter 92
5.5 Circumference 94
5.6 Area of Rectangles and Squares 96
5.7 Area of Circles 98
5.8 Geometric Patterns 101

6. TRAINS, BOOKS, CLOCKS, AND THINGS 103
6.1 Motion Problems 103
6.2 Book Problems 105
6.3 Work Problems 107
6.4 Clock Problems 109
6.5 Related Problems 111

7. LOGIC 115
   7.1 Cryptarithms 115
   7.2 Certainty Problems 118
   7.3 Venn Diagram Problems 120
   7.4 Whodunits 124

SOLUTIONS

PART D. SOLUTIONS TO PART A PROBLEMS 132

SOLUTIONS TO PART B PROBLEMS 134

   1. DRAWING A PICTURE OR A DIAGRAM 134
   2. MAKING AN ORGANIZED LIST 135
   3. MAKING A TABLE 137
   4. SOLVING A SIMPLER RELATED PROBLEM 139
   5. FINDING A PATTERN 139
   6. GUESSING AND CHECKING 141
   7. EXPERIMENTING 142
   8. ACTING OUT THE PROBLEM 142
   9. WORKING BACKWARDS 143
  10. WRITING AN EQUATION 144
  11. CHANGING YOUR POINT OF VIEW 145
  12. MISCELLANEA 146

PART E. SOLUTIONS TO PART C PROBLEMS 150

   1. NUMBER PROBLEMS 150
   1.1 Addition Patterns 150
   1.2 Multiplication Patterns 151
   1.3 More Addition Patterns 152
   1.4 Unusual Patterns 153
   1.5 Patterns and Sums 156

   2. FACTORS AND MULTIPLES 160
   2.1 Factors 160
   2.2 Factors and Primes 161
   2.3 Greatest Common Factor 162
   2.4 Least Common Multiple 164

   3. DIVISIBILITY 166
   3.1 Divisibility by 2, 5, 10, 100 166
   3.2 Divisibility Principle for Sums and Differences ... 167
   3.3 Divisibility by Powers of 2 169
   3.4 Divisibility by 3 and 9 170
   3.5 Divisibility by 11 172
   3.6 Combined Divisibility 173
   3.7 Divisibility by 7, 11, and 13 173

4. *FRACTIONS* *176*
    4.1 Unit Fractions 176
    4.2 Complex Fractions 179
    4.3 Extended Finite Fractions 180
    4.4 Fractional Parts 181

5. *GEOMETRY AND MEASUREMENT* *183*
    5.1 Squares and Rectangles 183
    5.2 Triangles 184
    5.3 Circles 185
    5.4 Perimeter 187
    5.5 Circumference 190
    5.6 Area of Rectangles and Squares 192
    5.7 Area of Circles 195
    5.8 Geometric Patterns 198

6. *TRAINS, BOOKS, CLOCKS, AND THINGS* *200*
    6.1 Motion Problems 200
    6.2 Book Problems 201
    6.3 Work Problems 203
    6.4 Clock Problems 204
    6.5 Related Problems 206

7. *LOGIC* *209*
    7.1 Cryptarithms 209
    7.2 Certainty Problems 211
    7.3 Venn Diagram Problems 212
    7.4 Whodunits 216

PART F. APPENDICES **221**

APPENDIX 1: BASIC INFORMATION 222
APPENDIX 2: ANGLE-MEASURES IN POLYGONS 227
    Solutions 234
    Notes 237
APPENDIX 3: PYTHAGOREAN THEOREM 238
    Solutions 246
APPENDIX 4: WORKING WITH EXPONENTS 249
    Solutions 254
APPENDIX 5: JUSTIFYING SOME DIVISIBILITY RULES ... 257
    Solutions 262
APPENDIX 6: SEQUENCES AND SERIES 264
    Solutions 273

PART G. INDEX **279**

Preface

Creative Problem Solving in School Mathematics is a problem solving handbook for teachers of mathematics, parents, students, and other interested people. Although it was written primarily for elementary and middle schools, part of the material in the book is also appropriate at the secondary level.

The writing of this book was inspired by an in-service course designed for elementary and middle school teachers. The purpose of the course was to acquaint the participating teachers with rich and exciting problem solving experiences related to the core mathematics of the school curriculum. The teachers found that solving interesting and significant mathematical problems enhanced their interest and curiosity in mathematics, and they learned that by approaching problem solving creatively in the mathematics classroom they could similarly arouse the interest and curiosity of their students.

The basic text of Creative Problem Solving in School Mathematics consists of three parts. Part A is a brief discussion of teaching techniques that have been found to be especially effective in the introduction of problem solving strategies. Part B highlights some strategies that are commonly used in school mathematics and provides some practice problems for each strategy. In Part C, problem solving is examined in relation to many standard topics of the school mathematics curriculum, and the discussion of each topic is followed by a comprehensive set of related practice problems. At the end of the book, six appendices provide additional material that supplement the topics in Part C. An index is also included.

The purpose of Creative Problem Solving in School Mathematics is to help teachers and parents improve each student's ability to solve problems. However, it is a well-known saying that we learn by doing. Therefore, this book affords teachers, parents, and students an opportunity to learn more about problem solving strategies by trying out some new approaches and new techniques for themselves. Through these experiences it is hoped that they will be able to bring to their classrooms and homes some fresh insights and ideas.

Richard Kalman, Executive Director of MOEMS, voluntarily created and supervised every element of the production of the book. In addition, he supplied many suggestions relative to content and problems. The result is an unusually attractive appearance and a professional book of the highest order.

I wish to recognize my good friend and distinguished colleague, Lawrence J. Zimmerman, for his significant contributions to this book. His excellent advice and recommendations enriched the content of this book beyond expectations.

Finally, I gratefully acknowledge the thoughtful contributions of Gilbert W. Kessler, Wendy Hersh, and Elliott Bird, whose input enhanced several sections of the book, and of Curt Boddie, Michael Carlson, Sandy Cohen, Grant Duffrin, John Lufrano, Betty Minson, Lori Nimmo, Cheryl Novick, Eric O'Brien, and Dot Steinert for their diligent and careful reviewing of the manuscript.

George Lenchner

January, 2005

Teaching Problem Solving

Part A

1. **What is Problem Solving?**

2. **Using a Four-Step Method**

3. **Choosing Problems**

4. **Evaluating Problems**

5. **Presenting Problems**

6. **Helping Students**

7. **Using Calculators and Computers**

Teaching Problem Solving

1. What is Problem Solving?

It seems that everyone concerned with mathematics education today talks about problem solving. Professional organizations recommend that problem solving become the focus of school mathematics; curriculum guides list problem solving skills as key objectives at all levels; and it is difficult to find a meeting of educators that doesn't have at least one problem solving session on its agenda. However, we should be careful not to think of this interest in problem solving as just another "bandwagon." The ultimate goal of school mathematics at all times is to develop in our students the ability to solve problems.

Some teachers believe that the ability to solve problems develops automatically from mastery of computational skills. This is not necessarily true. Problem solving is itself a skill that needs to be taught, and mathematics teachers must make a special effort to do so.

Since we will be using the word "problem" repeatedly, let's begin by agreeing on its meaning. Any mathematical task can be classified as either an exercise or a problem. An EXERCISE is a task for which a procedure for solving is already known; frequently an exercise can be solved by the direct application of one or more computational procedures. A PROBLEM is more complex because the strategy for solving may not be immediately apparent; solving a problem requires some degree of creativity or originality on the part of the problem solver.

Let's look at an example: Suppose you are talking with your class about a collection of coins that consists of three nickels, two dimes, and one quarter. Before continuing, pause a moment to jot down some questions you might ask. Did you list any of the following?

1. How many coins are in the collection?
2. What is the total value of the collection in cents? in dollars?
3. Which of the sets of different types of coins has the greatest value? the least value?
4. How many different amounts of money can be made using one or more coins from this collection?
5. How many different combinations of one or more coins can be made using the coins in this collection?
6. How many other combinations of nickels, dimes, and quarters have the same value as the given collection?

(*Solutions are on page 132.*)

Notice that the first three questions listed have a quality different from the last three in that they can be solved by simple inspection or by using a computational algorithm. We consider the first three to be exercises. For the last three, no routine process of solving is applicable; the person faced with these questions must determine an appropriate strategy for solving before actually proceeding to solve. We classify these questions as problems.

2. Using a Four-Step Method

Problems can be solved in a variety of ways, and no one of these ways is appropriate to the solution of all problems. However, students often find it helpful to have at least a general framework within which they can organize their efforts. In his classic book *How to Solve It*, George Polya outlined the following four steps as a guideline for successful problem solving.

♦ **Understanding the problem (2.1)**
♦ **Planning how to solve the problem (2.2)**
♦ **Carrying out the plan (2.3)**
♦ **Looking back (2.4)**

Originally proposed in the 1940s, this four-step method has withstood the test of time. Let's examine it step-by-step, considering how each step might be implemented in the mathematics classroom today.

2.1 Understanding the Problem

Before your students ever set pencil to paper, encourage them to *think* about the problem at hand. Allow them to ask you questions as long as their questions concern the problem itself. At this point, you should decline to answer any questions related to the process of solving the problem.

If your students seem to have no questions, you may wish to be the one who queries. Your questions may prompt their questions. Here are some examples:

♦ Does the problem give you enough information? too much information?

♦ What is the question you are being asked?

♦ What should your solution look like?

Some of the difficulties that students experience in understanding a problem are related to the language of the problem. If you think that language may be a barrier to their understanding, ask your students questions that will pinpoint the source of the difficulty. You may also find it an effective technique to ask a student to restate the problem in his or her own words. Either process helps to identify vocabulary that is unfamiliar and to reveal any areas of ambiguity in the statement of the problem.

Even when you feel sure that your students understand the problem at the outset, you will find that an ambiguity occasionally surfaces after they have begun working. For example, if a problem refers to a person's work for one week, the actual number of workdays in a week may be unclear. If this type of difficulty arises, it should be discussed and clarified before your students work on the remainder of their solution.

2.2 *Planning How To Solve The Problem*

Once students understand the problem situation that they are facing, it is time for them to decide on a plan of action to follow in solving the problem. That is, they must choose a reasonable problem-solving *strategy*. The strategies appropriate to solving mathematical problems are many and varied, but the following are some of those commonly used:

♦ Drawing a picture or diagram

♦ Making an organized list

♦ Making a table

♦ Solving a simpler related problem

♦ Finding a pattern

♦ Guessing and checking

♦ Experimenting

♦ Acting out the problem

♦ Working backwards

♦ Writing an equation

For any given problem, strategies such as these may be used singly or in combination. Also, you will find that different problem solvers use different strategies in solving the same problem.

It is important to realize that we often cannot expect students to use strategies that are unfamiliar to them. Just like other skills, problem-solving skills are learned. Therefore, students need to be exposed to a wide variety of problems so that they can try out new strategies and practice using them. In Part B of this book we will take a closer look at the strategies listed above and at some suggested practice problems for each strategy.

2.3 *Carrying Out The Plan*

Carrying out the problem-solving plan is often confused with the plan itself. The difference, though, is that in carrying out the plan the problem solver finally sets pencil to paper, implementing the planned strategy to arrive at the answer to the problem.

Although students often are able to work on their own at this point, the teacher remains essential to the problem solving process. Since carrying out the plan frequently involves arithmetic calculations, be ready to provide help and guidance if your students are having computational or logical difficulties. If solving the problem involves two or more steps, remind students to check their work at the end of each step before proceeding. Should students find that their planned strategy is not effective, suggest that they consider changing their point of view.

There is a tendency to emphasize the third step, carrying out the plan, almost to the exclusion of the other steps in the problem solving process. Remember that the careful consideration of *each* step develops the student's perception of problem solving and helps the student realize that computation is just a part of a broad and powerful process.

2.4 Looking Back

Students often believe that they are "done" with a problem when they have an answer — any answer — and that looking back on what they have done is unnecessary. The result is that they omit an important part of the problem solving process.

Tell your students always to look back and consider the *reasonableness* of their answers; encourage or require them to write an answer in the form of a complete sentence. This should result in their review of the statement of the problem and of the question being asked. It should also help in the detection of a possible error. If the answer does make sense, encourage students to make one final check for computational accuracy.

Students should be taught to pause and reflect not only on the answer to a problem, but also on how they arrived at the answer. Whenever possible, take time to discuss the strategy or strategies that were used in solving a given problem. If different students used different strategies, compare and contrast the strategies with regard to their relative efficiency and simplicity. This focus on strategies may lead some students to relate the problem at hand to similar problems solved in the past, thereby strengthening their accumulated body of experiences in solving problems.

One worthwhile way to look back on a problem is to consider how it might be extended. This usually entails changing the question asked, the numerical information given, or a condition of the problem. Let's look at an example:

A wooden cube that measures 3 cm along each edge is painted red. The painted cube is then cut into 1-cm cubes as shown at the right. How many of the 1-cm cubes do not have red paint on any face?

Before you read on, pause first to solve the problem. Did you realize that there is only one 1-cm cube in the middle that does not touch the surface of the original 3-cm cube? Therefore, there is only one 1-cm cube that does not have red paint on its surface.

Now look back on your work in solving this problem. Do you have any ideas for extending the problem? If so, jot them down.

Did you list any of these?

1. How many 1-cm cubes have red paint on just 1 face?

2. How many 1-cm cubes have red paint on just 2 faces?

3. How many 1-cm cubes have red paint on just 3 faces?

4. Do any 1-cm cubes have red paint on 4 or more faces?

5. How many 1-cm cubes would not have red paint on any face if the original cube measured 4 cm along each edge?

6. How many 1-cm cubes would not have red paint on any face if the original cube measured 5 cm along each edge?

7. Are there any patterns among the results for the 3-, 4-, and 5-cm cubes?

(*Solutions are on page 133.*)

There are of course other questions that could be asked in extending just this one problem, and perhaps you had some of these on your list. How do you know how far to carry these extensions with a class? The answer is to let your students' interest and enthusiasm be your guide. You may not wish to extend every problem, but by all means do so when a problem has captured the curiosity and imagination of your students. Be aware that ideas for appropriate extensions often come from the students themselves in the form of "What if …" or "Suppose …" questions. However, always be sure that all students in your class understand the original problem and its solution before proceeding to an extension with them.

3. Choosing Problems

Equally important as knowing *how* to teach problem solving is knowing *what* problems to use with your students. Many sources are available to you. Start with your textbook, which probably contains a fairly sound collection of routine word problems related to the topic you are currently teaching. Use these problems as they occur, but also consider how you might adapt or extend them to meet your classroom needs and your students' interests. Also look for related *nonroutine* problems; such problems may be found in special sections of your textbook or teacher's guide, in professional publications, in contest problems, at many web sites, in puzzle books, and so forth.

Students themselves can be a valuable resource when you encourage them to create their own problems. Although this activity usually is highly motivational in itself, you might add to your students' enthusiasm by using their problems as a bulletin board display. Also invite your students to share in the fun of solving each other's problems. You will probably find that problem *creating* helps to sharpen students' problem-*solving* skills.

As you go through this book, consider how you might use the problems contained in it with your students. You probably will find that some problems are appropriate for your classroom just as presented. For other problems, you may think of changing one or more conditions to make them simpler or more complex as needed to meet the abilities of your students. Perhaps some problems will inspire you to invent similar other problems. Remember throughout that one of the best sources of problems is you, the creative and imaginative teacher.

Interesting and challenging problems should:
♦ stimulate students' interest and enthusiasm for problem solving in mathematics,

♦ broaden their mathematical intuition and develop their insight,

♦ introduce them to important mathematical ideas, and consequently

♦ provide opportunities to experience the fun, satisfaction, pleasure, and thrill of discovery associated with creative problem solving.

4. Evaluating Problems

It is especially important when choosing a problem from a source other than your textbook or teacher's guide that you evaluate the problem to determine if it is a good problem for your students. Sometimes a problem that seems appropriate at first glance reveals itself to be inappropriate upon closer inspection: it may be too easy or too difficult, too routine or too involved, too simple or too time-consuming, and so on. How can you determine if a problem is a good problem? You may find the following set of guidelines to be helpful.

A good problem is sufficiently interesting and challenging to make the reader want to solve it. If students are not interested in a problem, they usually are not interested in its solution. Many students are motivated to solve problems that deal with their everyday experiences or that in some way spark their curiosity. Many students are also attracted to problems of the nature of puzzles or brainteasers.

A good problem can be approached through a variety of strategies. Although each of these strategies may be effective in carrying out the task of solving the problem, students generally benefit from the opportunity to consider several approaches from the viewpoint of relative directness and efficiency. It also is worthwhile to students to realize that, for any given problem, different approaches may be more effective for different people.

A good problem can be extended to related or other problems. After solving a problem it is a valuable experience for students to consider new problems or to recall past problems that require a similar approach. Problem solving skills are strengthened when students can generalize as a result of their accumulated problem solving experiences.

A good problem should be at the appropriate skill level for your students' abilities. Before you ask your students to solve a nonroutine problem, it is important that you solve it yourself to determine the skills necessary for its solution. If the solution requires much more mathematical background than your students presently have, either adapt the problem to their level or put it aside for future use. Be sure that the language is appropriate for your students' reading level; if possible, replace any vocabulary that is too difficult and shorten any sentences that are too lengthy. As a rule of thumb, most of your students should be able to understand the problem when you present it and should feel comfortable attempting the solution.

Students need not only to develop their *ability* to solve problems, but also to develop their *confidence* in this ability. If they are to become good problem solvers, we must present good problems to them.

5. Presenting Problems

There are many ways to present problems other than to simply refer your students to a written problem in a textbook or workbook. Different techniques have different advantages, and their proper use can be a tremendous aid to both you and your students. Let's look at some of these techniques and consider how you might use them in your classroom.

5.1 The Chalkboard

Writing a problem on a chalkboard or whiteboard is perhaps the most traditional technique. Such a display is easily seen, and the problem is readily available for reference throughout the problem solving process. When using this technique, though, you may find it helpful to try to write the problem on the chalkboard before class or when your students are engaged in some other activity; students sometimes become restless, impatient, or disinterested when they have to wait for a problem to be written.

Since the chalkboard technique seems to invite worthwhile classroom discussion, an interesting variation is occasionally to leave a blank or blanks in the problem in the place of an important word or piece of data. You might also try providing all the data, but omitting the final question. Then have your students suggest appropriate words, data, or questions. Involving students in the creation of problems often enhances their understanding of the solution of problems. You may find that it also prompts some lively and thought-provoking class discussions.

Another advantage of the chalkboard is that a problem can be left on display for more than one day. You might even wish to keep a special section of the chalkboard reserved for an especially challenging "Problem of the Week" for which an immediate solution is not expected.

5.2 The Overhead Projector

Another technique for presenting a problem is to write it on a transparency for use on an overhead projector or use presentation software. If you have a projector available, you will find that with it you can use most of the ideas recommended for the chalkboard.

The overhead projector does have some advantages over the chalkboard. For example, using a transparency can eliminate concern about finding an appropriate time to prepare the display of a problem since you can prepare a transparency at the same time that you are planning your lesson. You may also find that it takes you less time to write a problem on a transparency, especially if the problem involves a graph, diagram, or geometric figure. Furthermore, once you have prepared a transparency of a problem, there is no need to erase it. This means that you can store the problem in a file and have it immediately available for use when you need it again.

When presenting a problem with the overhead projector, you may of course project the entire problem at once. At times, though, you may wish to present a problem line-by-line, using a piece of opaque paper to mask those parts of the transparency that you do not yet want your students to see. This method of presentation serves to temporarily focus your students' attention on each of the individual components of a problem and you may find it helpful in pinpointing any sources of difficulty in their understanding of the problem.

5.3 Duplicated Sheets

Sometimes you may prefer to present a problem by duplicating it onto individual sheets so that each student receives a copy. Besides the fact that duplicated sheets can save you precious class time, you will also find that some students simply find it easier to refer to a problem this way. Duplicated sheets also eliminate the possibility of student error in copying a problem from the chalkboard or overhead projector.

Used properly, a duplicated sheet can be a valuable instructional aid. For example, if you are teaching your students how to deal with problems that contain too much information, having the problems at hand gives students the opportunity to physically cross out extraneous information and highlight essential information. When your students are working with problems that require a chart or graph, it sometimes is helpful to use the duplicated sheet to supply a partially completed chart or graph beside the problem.

When you expect your students to work directly on a duplicated sheet, be sure to leave enough blank space for necessary computations or diagrams. You may also want to consider providing answer blanks, since they can save you time in helping your students by making their answers easier to locate.

5.4 Oral Presentation

Presenting a problem by reading aloud is a useful technique that provides needed practice in screening out extraneous information. It also helps to sharpen students' listening and note-taking skills.

Before you present a problem orally, explain to your students that you will read the problem a given number of times — perhaps three. The first time, instruct them to just listen. The second time they may take notes, but stress the fact that their notes should contain just the information that is important to solving the problem. The third time, students should listen to make sure that their notes are accurate and that they understand the question. Using their notes, your students should then be able to proceed with solving the problem.

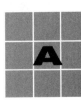

6. Helping Students

How much help should you give your students in their problem solving efforts? Too much help will leave them with little or nothing to do. Too little help may result in frustration and lack of progress. The right amount of help is such that it allows your students to experience the challenge of a problem and the pleasure of discovering its solution.

Whenever possible, give your students the opportunity to work on a problem independently. If they have trouble getting started, do not tell them which strategy to use; try to ask questions that will lead them to choose an appropriate strategy. Be aware that some students mistakenly believe successful problem solvers are those who are able to immediately determine a strategy for solving and carry it out. Help your students to realize that they may need to test several strategies before an appropriate one is found. When students understand that it is all right to experience some difficulty in this process, they are more likely to approach problem solving with interest and enthusiasm.

When your students have arrived at an answer for a problem, encourage them to whisper in your ear; if answers are blurted out, other students may feel that the challenge is gone and may be deterred from continuing to work on the solution. Respond to a whispered answer by saying "Correct," "Close," "Try again," or something similar. Try to avoid expressions such as "No," "Wrong," or "No Good," which tend to discourage students. Always remember to give your students praise — it is still an excellent motivation.

7. Using Calculators and Computers

Some students are blocked from carrying out their problem-solving plan by their weakness in computational skills. Calculators and computers can help overcome this obstacle for many students. Used properly, they make it possible for students to spend less time on computation and more time on the other steps of the problem solving process.

The availability for calculators and computers has opened up a broader range of problems to students. For example, you may find that your students are more inclined to attempt problems that involve large numbers if they have access to a calculator or computer. Because calculators and computers can be used to store and retrieve information, your students also may feel more comfortable attempting problems that involve large amounts of data.

The speed and accuracy of calculators and computers can bring a wider variety of problems within the reach of a greater number of students. However, the danger is that students can become overly dependent on these devices. Be sure that your students are aware of the fact that calculators and computers do not solve problems — people do.

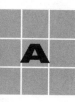

Some Problem Solving Strategies

Part B

1. **Drawing a Picture or Diagram**

2. **Making an Organized List**

3. **Making a Table**

4. **Solving a Simpler Related Problem**

5. **Finding a Pattern**

6. **Guessing and Checking**

7. **Experimenting**

8. **Acting Out The Problem**

9. **Working Backwards**

10. **Writing an Equation**

11. **Changing Your Point of View**

12. **Miscellanea**

Some Problem Solving Strategies

B

1. Drawing a Picture or Diagram

If a problem is not illustrated, sometimes it is helpful to draw your own picture or diagram. A visual representation of the situation may reveal conditions that may not be obvious when you just read the problem. If the situation is not easily pictured, a simple diagram using symbols to represent the situation may help clarify the problem for you. Pictures and diagrams are also useful for keeping track of the various stages of a multi-step problem and often reveal a useful strategy.

1.1 The Tournament

The eight teams of the City League will determine this season's champion with a single-elimination tournament. That is, a team will be out of the tournament after one loss. How many tournament games will the championship team have to play?

One good way to approach this problem is to diagram the progress of the tournament. Use symbols such as an × to represent a team and a bracket (⟩) to represent a game played.

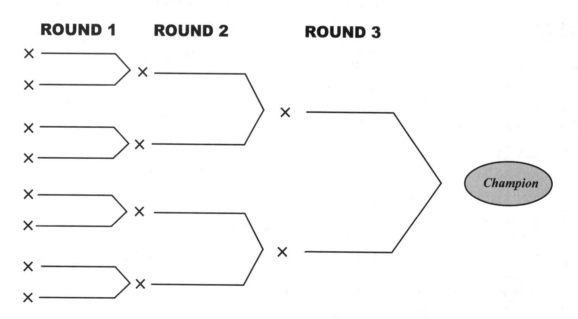

Answer: **The championship team will have to play three tournament games in all.**

1.2 Rod Measures

The lengths of three rods are 6 cm, 9 cm, and 11 cm.
How can you use these rods to measure a length of 14 cm?

Sketch diagrams of various placements for the rods to help you arrive at the solution most quickly. Here are three such possibilities.

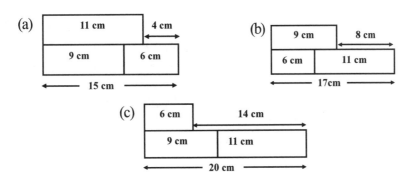

Answer: **Diagram (c) shows how to place the rods to measure a length of 14 cm.**

★ *Problems* ★

1. How many tournament games will the champion have to play if there are 16 teams competing in a single-elimination tournament?

2. How can you use four rods that measure 2 cm, 5 cm, 7 cm, and 9 cm to measure a length of 1 cm?

3. Making cuts across the diameter, a lumberjack can cut a log into 4 pieces in twelve minutes. How long would it take to cut a log of the same size and shape into 6 pieces?

4. Three containers have capacities of 3, 5, and 9 liters. How can you use these containers to measure exactly 7 liters of water?

5. Assuming that each corner must be tacked, what is the least number of tacks that you need to display 4 rectangular pictures of the same size and shape so that they can all be seen?

6. If the number of competitors is odd in any round of a tournament, then one of the competitors is given a "bye" which means that the competitor does not compete in that round. No competitor may have more than one bye in a tournament. What is the maximum number of games a champion will have to play if nine competitors are enrolled in a single-elimination tournament?

(Solutions are on pages 134-135.)

2. Making an Organized List

A useful problem solving strategy is organizing information into some type of list, a technique that may serve a variety of purposes. When a problem requires you to generate a large amount of data, a list may help you account for all possibilities and avoid repetitions.

2.1 Bull's Eye!

Three darts are thrown at the target shown below. Assume that each of the darts lands within one of the rings or within the bull's eye. How many different point totals are possible?

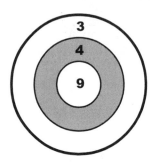

Notice that, since we are interested in *totals*, the *order* in which the darts hit the target does not matter. There are many ways to organize a list of the possible totals. For our list, let's focus on the number of darts that might hit the bull's eye.

3 Darts Hit Bull's Eye	2 Darts Hit Bull's Eye	1 Dart Hits Bull's Eye	0 Darts Hit Bull's Eye
$9 + 9 + 9 = 27$	$9 + 9 + 4 = 22$	$9 + 4 + 4 = 17$	$4 + 4 + 4 = 12$
	$9 + 9 + 3 = 21$	$9 + 4 + 3 = 16$	$4 + 4 + 3 = 11$
		$9 + 3 + 3 = 15$	$4 + 3 + 3 = 10$
			$3 + 3 + 3 = 9$

Answer: **Ten different point totals are possible.**

2.2 Words, Words, Words!

How many different three-letter "code words" can you make using the letters *P*, *Q*, and *R* if repetition of a letter is not permitted?

Identify all the possible code words by using a special type of organized listing called a TREE DIAGRAM, as shown on the next page. This is a listing technique that is helpful because the lines of the "tree" visually account for all possibilities. Notice that, in this problem, the order of the letters *does* make a difference.

TREE DIAGRAMS:

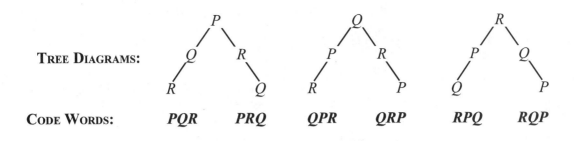

CODE WORDS: **PQR**   **PRQ**   **QPR**   **QRP**   **RPQ**   **RQP**

B

Answer: **Six different code words using the letters *P*, *Q*, and *R* can be made if repetition of a letter is not permitted.**

★ *Problems* ★

1. Suppose that the three regions of a target like the one pictured on page 16 are assigned point values of 3, 5, and 7. How many different point totals are possible if three darts are thrown and each lands somewhere on this target?

2. Suppose that *four* darts are thrown at the target described in problem 1. How many different point totals are possible if each lands on this target?

3. How many different three-letter code words can you make using the letters *P*, *Q*, and *R* if repetition of the letters is permitted?

4. Ken has a white shirt, a tan shirt, a pair of brown pants, a pair of black pants, a pair of blue pants, a plaid sport coat, and a tweed sport coat. How many different three-piece outfits can he make if each outfit consists of one shirt, one pair of pants, and one coat?

5. A domino has two square spaces on its face. Each of the two square spaces is marked with 1, 2, 3, 4, 5, or 6 dots, or it is left blank. A complete set of dominoes consists of one domino for each of the possible combinations of these markings. How many dominoes are in a complete set?

6. Some antique domino sets have each of the two square faces of a domino marked with 1, 2, 3, 4, 5, 6, 7, 8, or 9 dots, or left blank. How many dominoes are in a complete set of this type?

(*Solutions are on pages 135-137.*)

3. Making a Table

When a problem involves data that has more than one characteristic, an effective problem solving strategy is to organize the data into a table. A table displays data so that it is easily located and understood, and missing data becomes obvious. If you are not given the data for a problem and must generate it yourself, a table is an excellent device for recording what you have done so you don't repeat your efforts. A table also can be an invaluable aid in detecting significant patterns.

3.1 Take a Chance!

Suppose that you roll two number cubes, each of which has faces numbered from 1 through 6. What is the probability of rolling a sum of 8 in the uppermost faces?

To solve this problem you need to determine not only how many different numerical sums are possible, but also in how many ways it is possible for the two number cubes to form the sums. A table such as the one at the right helps to produce the data and display it in an organized manner.

Can you see that there are 36 possible ways the number cubes could land when you roll them? Of these 36 possibilities, there are 5 possibilities that have a sum of 8.

		First Cube					
	+	1	2	3	4	5	6
Second Cube	1	2	3	4	5	6	7
	2	3	4	5	6	7	8
	3	4	5	6	7	8	9
	4	5	6	7	8	9	10
	5	6	7	8	9	10	11
	6	7	8	9	10	11	12

Answer: **The probability of rolling a sum of 8 is 5 chances out of 36 chances, or $\frac{5}{36}$.**

3.2 Barnyard Brainstorming

I know that there are 18 animals in the barnyard. Some are chickens and the rest are cows. I counted 50 legs in all. How many of the animals are chickens and how many are cows?

Let's make a table that displays *some* of the ways that there could be 18 animals. Counting 2 legs for each chicken and 4 legs for each cow, we'll also calculate the total number of legs.

Number of chickens	0	1	2	3	4	5	...	?
Number of cows	18	17	16	15	14	13	...	?
Number of legs	72	70	68	66	64	62	...	50

Examining the data in the table, a pattern emerges. Reading from left to right, each time we "exchange" one cow for one chicken, there are 2 fewer legs in the total. Therefore, to reduce 72, the first number of legs, to 50, we must "exchange" 11 of the 18 cows for chickens since this will give us $11 \times 2 = 22$ fewer legs than 72 or a total of 50 legs.

***Answer:* There are 7 cows and 11 chickens in the barnyard.**

★ *Problems* ★

1. Suppose that you roll two number cubes, each of which has faces numbered from 0 through 5. What is your probability of rolling a sum of 8?

2. Suppose that you roll two triangular pyramids, each of which has equilateral faces numbered from 1 through 4.

   a. Make a table of the possible sums of the two faces that rest on the surface.
   b. What is the probability of rolling a sum of 5?

3. This week a carpenter made some three-legged stools and some four-legged chairs. The total number of stools and chairs was 30, and the carpenter used 103 legs in all. How many chairs did the carpenter make?

4. Using one or more coins, how many different amounts of money can be made from a collection of coins that consists of four pennies, one nickel, and one dime?

5. The toll for an automobile crossing a certain bridge is 50 cents. The machines in the "exact change" lanes accept any combination of coins that total exactly 50 cents, but they do not accept pennies or half dollars. In how many different ways can a driver pay the automobile toll in an "exact change" lane?

6. A collection of thirty coins consists of dimes and quarters and has a total value of $4.35. How many of each type of coin are in this collection?

(Solutions are on pages 137-138.)

4. Solving a Simpler Related Problem

When faced with a problem that appears difficult or complicated, you may find it helpful to first solve one or more similar problems that have simpler conditions. Sometimes the solutions of simpler problems may lead to the solution of the more difficult problem. At other times, solving a *series* of simpler problems may lead you to a pattern that provides a basis for solving the original problem.

4.1 Lucky Sevens

The houses on Main Street are numbered consecutively from 1 to 150. How many house numbers contain at least one digit 7?

You could of course examine each house number from 1 to 150, but this entails more work than is necessary. Let's see how you might separate this problem into two simpler problems.

How many house numbers contain the digit 7 in the ones place? This occurs once in every set of 10 consecutive numbers. For houses numbered 1 to 150, there are 15 distinct sets of 10 consecutive numbers, so 15 house numbers contain the digit 7 in the **ones** place.

How many house numbers contain the digit 7 in the tens place? There are 10 such numbers, from 70 to 79. However, note that we already counted 77 among the house numbers with the digit 7 in the ones place, so we will only add 9 of these numbers to our total.

Answer: **For houses numbered from 1 to 150, there are 15 + 9 = 24 house numbers that contain at least one digit 7.**

Note that, for young students, solving a simpler problem sometimes involves substituting *more manageable numbers* into the problem until they are able to determine an appropriate procedure for solving the more general problem.

4.2 Operation Diamond

Britney's calculator has a special ◊ key that obeys two rules:

Rule 1: If the display shows a one-digit number, pressing the ◊ key replaces the display with twice its value.

Rule 2: If the display shows a two-digit number, pressing the ◊ key replaces the display with the sum of the two digits.

Suppose Britney enters the value 1 on the calculator and then presses the ◊ key repeatedly. What does the display show after she presses the ◊ key 50 times?

To solve this sort of problem you should generate enough numbers to see if a pattern exists. After Britney enters a 1, the ◊ key produces, in succession, displays of 2, 4, 8, 16, 7, 14, 5, 10 — and then 1 again. Therefore if the ◊ key is pressed repeatedly, the sequence of nine numbers 1, 2, 4, 8, 16, 7, 14, 5, 10 is displayed repeatedly. Thus 10 becomes the 9th, 18th, 27th, 36th, and 45th number in the extended sequence.

Britney entered "1" and then pressed the ◊ key fifty times. Therefore, 51 displays appeared. The 51st display is the 6th display of the nine number sequence after the 45th display of 10.

Answer: **The display shows 7 after she presses the ◊ key 50 times.**

★ *Problems* ★

1. Suppose that the houses on Main Street are numbered consecutively from 1 to 150. How many house numbers contain at least one digit 9? 4? 1?

2. Suppose Britney enters the value 3. How many times must she press the ◊ key in order to next show the value 3 again?

3. Suppose Britney enters the value 7 and then presses the ◊ key 100 times. How many times will the display show 5?

4. Britney's calculator also has a special ✪ key that increases each display by 3. Suppose she enters a value of 2 and then presses the ✪ key repeatedly. What value is displayed if she presses the ✪ key
   a. 3 times? b. 5 times? c. 10 times? d. 100 times?

(*Solutions are on page 139.*)

5. Finding a Pattern

One of the most frequently used problem solving strategies is that of recognizing and extending a pattern. As we shall see, there are many times that this is used as a strategy in conjunction with other problem solving strategies. For this discussion, though, we will look at some problems that can be solved by identifying a pattern in given data and simply applying that pattern to the problem situation.

5.1 Odds and Ends

What is the sum of the following series of numbers?

$$1 + 3 + 5 + \cdots + 97 + 99$$

At first this may seem like a fairly tedious exercise in addition. Rather than proceeding with this lengthy calculation, though, we'll first consider the sums of a few simpler series of numbers related to the given series, list the data, and look for a pattern.

SERIES	SUM
1	1
1 + 3	4
1 + 3 + 5	9
1 + 3 + 5 + 7	16
1 + 3 + 5 + 7 + 9	25

The above table of simpler series has a pattern. Did you observe that each line of entries in the "Series" column is a simpler series of consecutive odd numbers, each beginning with 1; the entries in the "Sum" column are consecutive perfect-square numbers beginning with 1? To relate the series to its sum, notice that the sum of the first odd number is 1; the sum of the first 2 odd numbers is $2^2 = 4$; the sum of the first 3 odd numbers is $3^2 = 9$; the sum of the first 4 odd numbers is $4^2 = 16$; and the sum of the first 5 odd numbers is $5^2 = 25$. Notice that the sum of each of the odd number series beginning with 1 is equal to the square of the number of terms in the series.

Now we extend this pattern, assuming that it continues. The series $1+3+5+\cdots+97+99$ contains the first 50 odd numbers. Therefore, its sum is $50^2 = 2500$.

Answer: $1 + 3 + 5 + \cdots + 97 + 99 = 2500$

5.2 Connect the Dots

Fifteen points are placed on a circle. How many straight line segments can be drawn by joining all the points in pairs?

B

A good way to search for a pattern is to try simpler related cases and arrange the results in a table. Draw a circle. Place the 1st point on the circle. No line segment is determined because it takes two points to determine a line segment. Place the 2nd point on the circle and connect it to the 1st point thus determining the first line segment. Place the 3rd point on it and connect it to each of the first 2 points. This determines 2 new line segments, for a total of 3 segments. Place the 4th point on it and connect it to each of the first 3 points. This determines 3 new line segments, for a total of 6 segments. Continue until enough data is accumulated as in the table below. Notice that the 15th point adds 14 new segments to the total of segments.

Number of points on circle	1	2	3	4	5	6	...	15
Number of new segments	0	1	2	3	4	5	...	14
Total number of segments	0	1	3	6	10	15	...	?

The total number of line segments determined by 15 points is the sum of the counting numbers 1, 2, 3, ... , 14 shown in the second line of the table.

***Answer:* 105 segments can be drawn by joining 15 points on a circle in pairs.**

(See pages 111-114 for further discussion of this topic.)

★ *Problems* ★

1. What is the sum of each of the following series of numbers?
   a. $1 + 3 + 5 + \cdots + 997 + 999$ b. $2 + 4 + 6 + \cdots + 98 + 100$

2. If $1^2 + 2^2 + 3^2 + \cdots + 9^2 + 10^2 = 385$, what is the sum of $2^2 + 4^2 + 6^2 + \cdots + 18^2 + 20^2$?

3. What is the units digit of the product when one hundred 7s are multiplied?

4. What is the remainder when the product of one hundred 5s is divided by 7?

5. Ten people enter a room one at a time. Each new entrant shakes hands with each person already in the room. How many handshakes occur?

6. January 1, 1941 fell on a Wednesday. On which day of the week was January 1, 1942?

7. The first four statements are true. Complete the fifth statement without computing.

   a.
   $$\begin{array}{rcl} 1 \times 8 + 1 &=& 9 \\ 12 \times 8 + 2 &=& 98 \\ 123 \times 8 + 3 &=& 987 \\ 1{,}234 \times 8 + 4 &=& 9{,}876 \\ 123{,}456{,}789 \times 8 + 9 &=& \boxed{} \end{array}$$

   b.
   $$\begin{array}{rcl} 3 \times 37{,}037 &=& 111{,}111 \\ 6 \times 37{,}037 &=& 222{,}222 \\ 9 \times 37{,}037 &=& 333{,}333 \\ 12 \times 37{,}037 &=& 444{,}444 \\ \boxed{} \times 37{,}037 &=& 999{,}999 \end{array}$$

8. Under which letter will 101 appear? Assume all the counting numbers are entered in alternating directions, as indicated.

A	B	C	D	E	F
			1	2	3
9	8	7	6	5	4
10	11	12	13	14	15
21	20	19	18	17	16

   ... and so on.

(Solutions are on pages 139-141.)

6. Guessing and Checking

An effective way to solve certain problems is to make a reasonable guess of the answer, then check the guess against the conditions of the problem. Sometimes your first guess will yield the correct answer, and the other times you will have to go through many guesses before you succeed. However, even when your guess is "incorrect," you make progress in solving the problem by eliminating one possible answer, thus obtaining other information that may lead to the correct answer. This method is also known as "Guess, check, and revise."

6.1 Triangle Sums

Arrange the counting numbers from 1 to 6 in the circles at the right so that the sum of the numbers along each side of the triangle is 10.

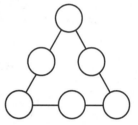

A few guesses should lead you to the conclusion that there are only three ways to obtain the sum of 10: $1 + 3 + 6$, $1 + 4 + 5$, and $2 + 3 + 5$. Since each of the numbers 1, 3, and 5 appears in two of these sums, each of the numbers 1, 3, and 5 must be placed in the circles at the corners of the triangle. The numbers 2, 4, and 6 can be placed in the appropriate remaining circles on the sides of the triangle.

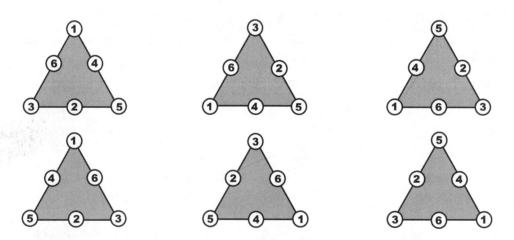

Answer: **Any one of the above six arrangements is correct.**

Note that all six are variations of the same basic arrangement.

6.2 Four!

How can you use four 4s to create an expression that has a value equal to 1?

Although this may sound impossible at first, remember that you have available to you a wide range of arithmetic operations: addition, subtraction, multiplication, division, square root, raising to a power and so on. Try various operations, such as $4 + 4 = 8$, $4 - 4 = 0$, $4 \times 4 = 16$, $4 \div 4 = 1$, $\sqrt{4} = 2$, and $4! = 4 \times 3 \times 2 \times 1$. Observe that the sum of $4 - 4$ and $\frac{4}{4}$ is $0 + 1$ and is an answer.

Answer: **The expression $4 - 4 + \frac{4}{4}$ has a value equal to 1.**

Note that there are many *different* correct answers. The following are a few of these.

$$\frac{44}{44}, \quad \frac{4 \times 4}{4 \times 4}, \quad \frac{4 + 4}{4 + 4}, \quad \frac{4 + 4}{\sqrt{4} \times 4}, \quad 4^{\frac{(4-4)}{4}}, \quad \frac{4! - 4}{4} - 4$$

★ Problems ★

1. Arrange the counting numbers from 1 to 6 in the circles pictured on page 24 so the numbers along each side of the triangle add to each of the following sums.
   a. 9   b. 11   c. 12

2. Arrange the counting numbers from 1 to 7 in the circles at the right so that the sum of the numbers along each line is 10.

3. A MAGIC SQUARE is a square grid of distinct numbers in which the sum of the numbers along each row, column, and major diagonal is the same number. Arrange the counting numbers from 1 to 9 in the 3 by 3 grid at the right to form a magic square.

4. Use four 4s to create an expression that has a value equal to each of the following numbers.
   a. 0   b. 2   c. 3   d. 4   e. 255

5. Replace each ▇ with an operation symbol to make the following a true statement:
   1 ▇ 2 ▇ 3 ▇ 4 ▇ 5 ▇ 6 ▇ 7 ▇ 8 ▇ 9 = 100

6. When a certain landowner died, this L-shaped plot of land was left to be shared among four children. The only stipulation of the will was that the land must be separated into four congruent plots. Show how this can be done.

(Solutions are on page 141.)

7. Experimenting

Problems involving geometric configurations or spatial relationships are sometimes solved by experimenting with a physical model in which concrete objects may be manipulated.

7.1 Bowling Pin Blues

The bowling pins shown at the right have been arranged incorrectly, with the triangle pointing away from the bowler. Can you make the triangle point toward the bowler by repositioning exactly three pins?

Many people find it difficult to visualize the movement of the pins to new positions while simultaneously "erasing" the old positions. You may find that the most direct method of solving this problem is to duplicate the arrangement with ten small objects such as coins, as shown at the right. Then try various movements of the objects.

Answer:

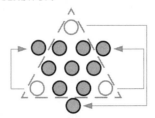

Repeat the above diagram of the 10 shaded circles with the corner circles unshaded, as shown at the left. Move the 3 unshaded circles to the new locations and shade the new locations as shown. The new configuration points to the bowler as required.

7.2 Toothpick Puzzler

The figure at the right shows twelve toothpicks arranged to form three squares. How can you form five squares by moving only three toothpicks?

This problem involves not only a rearrangement of the given objects, but also some careful observation of geometric relationships. For a number of people, the simplest approach is to gather twelve toothpicks, arrange them as shown above, and experiment.

Answer:

Notice that one of the squares is formed by the outer boundary of the arrangement. There was no requirement that each of the five squares must be congruent to each of the others.

★ *Problems* ★

1. Six shrubs are planted as shown below at the left. Show how you could transplant exactly two shrubs to get the arrangement at the right.

2. Sixteen toothpicks are arranged as shown. Remove four toothpicks so that exactly four congruent triangles remain.

3. Show how to arrange these shapes to form a rectangle.

4. Moving two adjacent coins at a time, rearrange the top row to look like the bottom row in exactly four moves. The coins you move must stay together and remain in the same order.

5. Describe how to fold this "map" so that the numbered sections lie on top of one another in order from 1 to 8.

3	4	2	7
6	5	1	8

(Solutions are on page 142.)

8. Acting Out The Problem

There may be times when your students experience difficulty in visualizing a problem or the procedure necessary for its solution. In such cases, they may find it helpful to physically act out the problem situation. They might use items that *represent* the people or objects. Acting out the problem may itself lead them to the answer, or it may lead them to find another strategy that will help them find the answer. Acting out the problem is a strategy that is very effective for young students.

8.1 Trading Stamps

Suppose that you buy a rare stamp for $15, sell it for $20, buy it back for $25, and finally sell it for $30. How much money do you make or lose in buying and selling this stamp?

Many people erroneously conclude that you make $15. To see why this answer is wrong, it may help to act out the problem with a friend, using slips of paper to represent the money and the stamp.

Let your friend have the stamp, while you start with a certain amount of money in your "pocket," such as $50. (Your friend will need some money too, but there is no need to keep track of that amount.) Pay your friend $15 for the stamp; you have $50 − $15 = $35 remaining. Now trade the stamp for $20 from your friend; you have $35 + $20 = $55. Trade again, this time paying your friend $25 in exchange for the stamp; you have $55 − $25 = $30 remaining. Finally, trade the stamp for $30 from your friend; the transaction is finished, and you have $30 + $30 = $60 in your "pocket." The amount of your profit is the difference between this amount and the amount of money in your "pocket" at the beginning.

Answer: **In buying and selling the stamp, you made $60 − $50 = $10.**

8.2 Evens Up

A class of 32 students counted off by ones beginning with the number 1. Each student who counted an even number stood up. Then the students who were still seated counted off by ones again. Each student who counted an even number this time also stood up. After the second counting was completed, how many students remained seated?

For young students especially, solving this problem with pencil and paper may make it seem more difficult than it actually is. Acting out the problem in the classroom can help your students realize that the solution is not all that complicated. Since half of the 32 numbers are even numbers, half of the 32 students stand up on the first counting; this is 16 students. On the second counting, half of the *remaining* 16 students stand up; this is 8 students.

Answer: **After the second counting, 8 students remain seated.**

★ *Problems* ★

1. Suppose that you buy a rare stamp for $15, sell it for $20, buy it back for $22, and finally sell it for $30. How much money did you make or lose in buying and selling this stamp?

2. A class of 27 students counted off by ones beginning with the number 1. Each student who counted a number that was a multiple of 3 stood up. Then the students who were still seated counted off by ones again. Each student who counted a number that was a multiple of 3 stood up. This procedure was repeated one more time. After the third counting was completed, how many students were standing?

3. An old-fashioned toaster can toast just one side of each of two slices of bread in exactly one minute. How can it toast both sides of three slices of bread in three minutes?

4. There is a duck in front of two ducks, a duck behind two ducks, and a duck between two ducks. What is the least number of ducks that there could be in this group?

(*Solutions are on pages 142-143.*)

9. Working Backwards

Some problems involve a sequence of actions: the final result of the action is known, and you are asked to determine the beginning conditions of the problem. An effective way to solve this type of problem is to consider the actions in reverse order.

9.1 Money Wise

Ashley gave Ben and Chris as much money as each had. Then Ben gave Ashley and Chris as much money as each already had. Then Chris gave Ashley and Ben as much money as each had. Then each of the three people had $24. How much money did each have to begin with?

This problem has four stages:
1. Ashley gives Ben and Chris as much money as each has.
2. Ben gives Ashley and Chris as much money as each has.
3. Chris gives Ashley and Ben as much money as each has.
4. Each now has $24.

The only amount of money that is known is in the fourth stage, which is the final outcome. Therefore, try starting your solution there and working backwards. Consider the stages in reverse order, making a table (see page 30) of how much money each of two recipients had been given in each of stages 3 through 1.

As you work backwards, keep two facts in mind. Each time a person gives each of the others "as much money as each had," each of the others will have had *half* as much money as in the succeeding stage. Also note that the total amount of money can be computed from the final stage (3 × $24 = $72), and this total must remain the same throughout each stage of the problem.

STAGE	ACTION	Ashley	Ben	Chris	SUM
4	Each ends with $24.	$24	$24	$24	$72
3	Chris gave Ashley and Ben half of what each will have in stage 4.	$12	$12	$48	$72
2	Ben gave Ashley and Chris half of what each will have in stage 3.	$6	$42	$24	$72
1	Ashley gave Ben and Chris half of what each will have in stage 2.	$39	$21	$12	$72

Notice that the amount for the donor in stages 3, 2, and 1 is determined by subtracting the sum of the two amounts received by the recipients in each of the stages 3, 2, and 1 from $72.

Answer: **To begin with, Ashley had $39, Ben had $21, and Chris had $12.**

9.2 Inverse Flow

What number belongs in the *START* circle of this "flow chart?"

START ? → DIVIDE BY 2 → SUBTRACT 5 → MULTIPLY BY 8 → END 32

To find the starting number, the most direct procedure may be to begin with the *ending* number and work backwards. Use the inverse of each of the operations along the way.

START ? ← MULTIPLY BY 2 ← ADD 5 ← DIVIDE BY 8 ← END 32

9 × 2 = 18 ← 4 + 5 = 9 ← 32 ÷ 8 = 4

Answer: **The number in the *START* circle is 18.**

★ Problems ★

1. I went into a store and spent half of my money and then $20 more. I went into a second store and spent half of my remaining money and then $20 more. Then I had no money left. How much money did I have when I went into the first store?

2. What number belongs in the **START** circle of this "flow chart"?

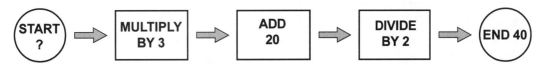

3. At the end of one school day a teacher had 17 crayons left. The teacher remembered giving out 14 of all her crayons in the morning, getting 12 crayons back at recess, and giving out 11 crayons after lunch. How many crayons did the teacher have at the start of the day?

4. I have a Magic Money Box that will double any amount of money placed in it and then add $5 to the doubled amount. Today I placed a certain amount of money in the box. The box then gave me a new amount, which I placed back into the box. This time the box gave me $43. How much money did I first place in the Magic Money Box?

5. A cooperative farm has three subdivisions, A, B, and C; the subdivisions lend equipment to each other as needed. In the beginning A lent B and C as many reapers as each then had. Several months later B lent A and C as many reapers as each then had. The following spring C lent A and B as many reapers as each then had. Each subdivision then had 16 reapers. How many reapers did each have to begin with?

(*Solutions are on page 143.*)

10. Writing an Equation

Algebra involves the use of a mathematical "shorthand" to represent different quantities and the relationships among them. Usually letters of the alphabet or other symbols are used as variables to represent unknown quantities in the problem, and the conditions of the problem are represented by an equation or inequality. Solving the equation or the inequality leads to the solution of the problem.

10.1 Name that Number!

The triple of what number is sixteen greater than the number?

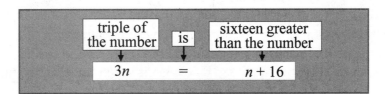

Let's use the variable n to represent the unknown number. We can then translate the problem into one simple equation.

(*For each equation the conditions and operations are stated.*)

Given:	1)	$3n = n + 16$
Subtract n from both sides:	2)	$3n - n = n + 16 - n$
Simplify both sides:	3)	$2n = 16$
Divide both sides by 2:	4)	$n = 8$

Answer: **The number is 8.** (Check: the triple of 8 is 24, and 24 is 16 greater than 8.)

10.2 A Weighty Question

Two apples weigh the same as a banana and a cherry. A banana weighs the same as nine cherries. How many cherries weigh the same as one apple?

This time we have three unknown quantities, so we'll need to use three variables. Let's choose a, b, and c to represent the weights of one apple, one banana, and one cherry, respectively. We can then translate the given information into *two* equations.

Two apples weigh the same as a banana and a cherry. $\quad 2a = b + c$

A banana weighs the same as nine cherries. $\quad b = 9c$

Although it may seem that we have too many variables and equations, you may recall that, in algebra, one expression may always be replaced by an equal expression. Since $b = 9c$, we can substitute $9c$ for b in $2a = b + c$. Then we can solve the resulting equation for a, the weight of one apple in terms of c.

Substitute $9c$ for b:	1)	$2a = 9c + c$
Simplify the right side:	2)	$2a = 10c$
Divide both sides by 2:	3)	$a = 5c$

The last equation gives an expression for the weight of one apple in terms of the weight of one cherry.

Answer: **One apple weighs the same as five cherries.**

★ Problems ★

1. Find each of the following numbers:
   a. Four times a number is twelve greater than the number.
   b. Five times a number decreased by one is twice the number increased by eleven.
   c. A number multiplied by two is the same as two decreased by the number.
   d. One-third of a number increased by eleven is seven less than the number.

2. Three pears weigh the same as a quince. A quince weighs as much as eighteen raspberries. How many raspberries weigh the same as a pear?

3. I have twice as many nickels as quarters. The total value of all my nickels and quarters is $4.20. How many quarters do I have?

4. Ten years from now Sophia's age will be three times her present age. How old is Sophia now?

5. Find four consecutive numbers such that the sum of the first three numbers is twelve more than the fourth number.

(Solutions are on pages 144-145.)

11. Changing Your Point of View

Occasionally you may find that you are blocked in your attempts to solve a particular problem. Sometimes this type of difficulty arises from developing a "mind set". That is, you may have decided that there is only one way to approach the solution, or perhaps you made an incorrect assumption about the given information. If you reach this point, it often helps to read the problem once again and try to change your point of view.

11.1 Chain Links

You have four pieces of chain with three links apiece. A jeweler will charge you $2 to open a link and $3 to close a link. How can you have the four pieces joined to form a continuous-chain bracelet for only $15?

Many people are baffled by this problem because they think of the four pieces of chain as fixed units, as shown above. If one link at each of the four "corners" of this arrangement is opened, then closed, the total cost would be $20.

Obviously, a change of approach is needed. Consider cutting one piece of three links into three separate pieces, and the solution becomes apparent.

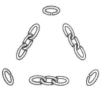

Answer: **Open all three links of one piece of chain. Use these three links to join the ends of the remaining pieces, as shown below. The cost to open and close just three links is $15.**

11.2 Connect the Dots

Show how to draw four continuous line segments through the nine dots shown at the right without lifting your pencil from the paper.

Nearly everyone who attempts this problem becomes frustrated by assuming that the line segments must lie within the confines of the 3 by 3 array. Avoiding this unnecessary restriction opens the door to the solution shown below.

Answer:

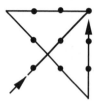

★ **Problems** ★

1. You have six sticks of equal length. Without altering the sticks in any way, show how to arrange them end-to-end to form exactly four equilateral triangles.

2. Show how to plant ten apple trees in five rows with only four trees in each row.

3. Every day a commuter takes a train that arrives at her station at precisely 6:00 p.m. She is met at the station by her husband, who also arrives at precisely 6:00 p.m. He always drives the same route to the station and never varies his speed. One day the commuter takes an earlier train and arrives at the station at precisely 5:00 p.m. She decides to begin walking home along her husband's usual route. They meet, she gets into the car, and they drive home. They arrive home precisely ten minutes earlier than usual. How long had the commuter been walking?

4. The 303 members of the chess club are planning a single-elimination tournament to determine a regional champion. How many tournament games will have to be played?

5. The measure of a radius of this circle is 10 cm. Point *O* is the center. If *OPQR* is a rectangle, what is the measure of segment PR?

6. Show how to place twenty-seven sheep into four pens so that there is an odd number of sheep in each pen.

(*Solutions are on pages 145-146.*)

12. Miscellanea

In addition to our listed strategies, there are many other strategies for solving problems, too many to list. The following problems may involve one or more unlisted strategies which may also be combined with one of our listed strategies.

12.1 Fruitful Thinking

Three apples and two pears cost 78 cents. But two apples and three pears cost 82 cents. What is the total cost of one apple and one pear?

Some people experience difficulty with this type of problem because they try to find the cost of one apple and the cost of one pear. Notice that this is not necessary: you only need to find the *combined* cost of an apple and a pear. Therefore, consider combining the given information to obtain the fact that *five* apples and *five* pears must cost 78¢ + 82¢, or $1.60. Therefore, one apple and one pear must cost only one fifth as much; $\frac{1}{5}$ of $1.60 is 32¢.

Answer: **The cost of one apple and one pear is 32¢.**

12.2 Network News

The first figure below shows the NET for a certain number cube. That is, this figure shows how the number cube would look if it were a box and could be "unfolded." One of the figures below the net is a drawing of this number cube. Which one is it?

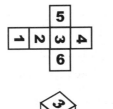

     A   *B*   *C*

Consider if it is possible to eliminate any of the possible answers. In Figure *A*, the numbers 2 and 3 are positioned incorrectly in relation to one another; the same is true of the numbers 3 and 5 in Figure *C*. This leaves Figure *B* as the only possibility. Upon careful examination, we note that the numbers 2, 3, and 6 in Figure *B* are positioned exactly as in this net.

Answer: **Figure *B* is the drawing of the number cube for this net.**

★ **Problems** ★

1. Five oranges and a banana cost 87¢. An orange and five bananas cost 99¢. What is the total cost of two oranges and two bananas?

2. Nine coins look exactly alike, but you know that one of them is counterfeit and weighs slightly less than the others. The only equipment that you have available is a balance scale like the one pictured at the right. How can you find out which is the counterfeit coin by making just two weighings on this scale?

3. The six faces of a cube are marked with the following patterns.

Here are three different views of the cube.

Which pattern appears on the face that is directly opposite each of the following faces?

a.   b.   c.

4. The native inhabitants of a certain island country have a strange characteristic: those who are swimmers always tell the truth. But those who are nonswimmers always lie. Suppose that you visit the island and meet a group of three people who are native inhabitants. You ask the first person, "Are you a swimmer?" The answer is unintelligible. The second person immediately says, "That was 'Yes.' I am a swimmer, too." The third person says, "They are both lying." Is each of these three people a swimmer or a nonswimmer?

5. ***For the Adventurous***
   What whole numbers should appear on the twelve faces of two number cubes so that the probabilities that the top two faces show any sum from 1 to 12 inclusive are exactly the same?

   (Solutions are on pages 146-148.)

Some Topics in Problem Solving

C

Part C

1. Number Patterns

2. Factors and Multiples

3. Divisibility

4. Fractions

5. Geometry and Measurement

6. Trains, Books, Clocks, and Things

7. Logic

37

Some Topics In Problem Solving

---

1. Number Patterns

1.1 Addition Patterns
Dollars and Sense

The symbol used for a dollar in United States currency is most commonly drawn as an uppercase **S** with 1 vertical stroke through it. The stroke separates the **S** into 4 parts, as shown at the right.

Sometimes the dollar symbol is drawn as an uppercase **S** with 2 vertical strokes through it. These 2 strokes separate the **S** into 7 parts.

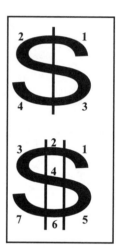

Suppose that the symbol could be drawn with 100 vertical strokes. Into how many parts will the S be separated?

One way to solve this problem is to actually draw the dollar symbol with 100 strokes, then count the parts. However, the drawing would be far too complicated, your counting could be inaccurate, and the entire process would be lengthy. The following is an alternate approach.

Consider the fact that we already know the number of parts for 1 and 2 strokes. It would not be difficult to gather some data for other simple problems, such as those associated with 3, 4, and 5 strokes. In a situation like this, a very effective strategy is to look for a pattern. Let's see if one emerges as we organize the data for these simpler problems into a table.

FIGURE	$	$	$	$	$
Number of strokes	1	2	3	4	5
Number of parts	4	7	10	13	16

If you study the data in the table, you will find that there is a simple pattern; the difference between two consecutive numbers of parts is always 3. How can you use this pattern to determine the number of parts for 100 strokes?

The constant difference of 3 means that each time a new stroke is drawn, the number of parts increases by 3. If you wish you could start at 16, the last entry in the table, and add 3s until you reach the entry for 100 strokes. However, this is a process that could become very time-consuming. Instead, let's rewrite each number of parts on the table as a number of 3s added to the original 4 parts.

FIGURE	$	$	$	$	$
Number of strokes	1	2	3	4	5
Number of parts	4	7	10	13	16

4   (4 + 1 × 3)   (4 + 2 × 3)   (4 + 3 × 3)   (4 + 4 × 3)
+3   +3   +3   +3

Do you see that the number of 3s being added is always one less than the number of strokes? Therefore, for 100 strokes you would have to add ninety-nine 3s to the original 4 parts. This is equivalent to $4 + 99 × 3$, or $4 + 297 = 301$.

Answer: **If the dollar symbol is drawn with 100 vertical strokes, the S will be separated into 301 parts.**

Although we have solved the dollar-symbol problem, let's take this opportunity to look at the problem in more general terms.

In mathematics, a SEQUENCE is a set of numbers that is ordered, usually according to some rule. In our problem, the number of parts into which the strokes separate the symbols is an example of a sequence. These numbers can be written using SEQUENCE NOTATION, in which numbers are separated by commas.

4, 7, 10, 13, 16, …

Each number in a sequence is called a TERM of the sequence. The position of a term in the sequence — 1ˢᵗ, 2ⁿᵈ, 3ʳᵈ, 4ᵗʰ, 5ᵗʰ, and so on — is called the ORDER of the term.

A sequence is an ARITHMETIC *(a rith MET ik)* SEQUENCE if the difference between any two consecutive terms is the same constant number. The sequence in our problem is arithmetic, since we have identified in it a constant difference of 3.

In an arithmetic sequence, an interesting fact surfaces when the order of each term is multiplied by the constant difference between terms. The chart on page 40 compares the numbers of parts in the dollar-symbol problem with the products obtained by multiplying the order of each term by 3.

Figure	$	$	$	$	$
order → **Number of strokes**	1	2	3	4	5
term → **Number of parts**	4	7	10	13	16
order of term × 3 →	3	6	9	12	15

Do you see that each term is one greater than 3 times its order? A relationship such as this provides a RULE for the sequence. If you can determine a rule for a sequence, you can then find the value of any term of that sequence.

How do all these facts relate to the solution of our problem? We have already identified the "number of parts" as a term of a sequence and the "number of strokes" as the order of that term. Therefore, in trying to determine the number of parts for 100 strokes, we are looking for the value of the 100th term of the sequence 4, 7, 10, 13, 16, ... According to the rule, the 100th term of this sequence is one greater than 3 times 100. This gives us $3 \times 100 + 1$, or $300 + 1 = 301$. We have arrived at the same solution as before using a method that may be considered more direct.

☆ **Problems** ☆

1. Into how many parts will the **S** be separated if the dollar symbol is drawn with the number of vertical strokes given below?
   a. 6   b. 10   c. 75   d. 200

2. The symbol used for a cent in United States currency is most commonly drawn as a lowercase c with 1 vertical stroke through it (¢). The stroke separates the c into 3 parts.
   a. Into how many parts is the c separated if the cent symbol is drawn with 2 vertical strokes? 3? 4? 5?
   b. Use sequence notation to write a pattern for the number of parts into which the c is separated.
   c. Do the numbers of parts form an arithmetic sequence? If it is, write a rule for the sequence.
   d. Into how many parts is the c separated if the cent symbol is drawn with 100 vertical strokes?
   e. How many vertical strokes are drawn through the c if it is separated into 165 parts?

3. Write the next three terms of each of the following arithmetic sequences.
   a. 3, 7, 11, 15, 19, ...
   b. 6, 7, 8, 9, 10, ...
   c. 2, $2\frac{1}{2}$, 3, $3\frac{1}{2}$, 4, ...
   d. 5, 5.3, 5.6, 5.9, 6.2, ...

4. What is the 50th term of each sequence in problem 3?

5. Consider the arithmetic sequence 2, 7, 12, 17, 22, … Which term of the sequence is 102?

6. In a certain arithmetic sequence, the first term is 5 and the tenth term in 68. List the first ten terms of the sequence.

7. The following figure shows a rubber band wrapped twice around the blade of a pair of scissors. If the rubber band were now cut, 4 pieces would be formed. How many pieces would be formed if the rubber band were wrapped 50 times around the blade before being cut?

8. Under which letter would the number 999 appear if each of these patterns were continued?

a.

A	B	C	D	E	F	G
1	2	3	4	5	6	7
8	9	10	11	12	13	14
15	16	…				

b.

A	B	C	D	E	F	G
	2		3		4	
8		7		6		5
	9		10		11	
					…	12

9. If the 1st day of a certain month is a Tuesday, what day of the week is the 21st day of that same month?

10. If the 1st day of a certain year is a Friday, what day of the week is February 19th of that same year?

11. What is the date of the 100th day of any year that is not a leap year?

12. When the rule for the sequence 4, 7, 10, 13, 16, … was discussed on page 40, it was said that "each term is one greater than 3 times its order." A shorthand way to state this rule using a variable is to describe the nth term as $(3 \times n) + 1$. However, when we first discussed this sequence in relation to the dollar-symbol problem on page 39, we said that "the number of 3s being added [to the original 4 parts] is always one less than the number of strokes." A shorthand way to state this rule is to describe the nth term as $4 + 3 \times (n - 1)$. Show that these two shorthand statements of the rule are equivalent.

(Solutions are on pages 150-151.)

1.2 *Multiplication Patterns*
An Odd Job

Suppose that you receive a very unusual job offer. You are told that your pay for the first day will be only 10 cents. Each working day after that your pay will be twice as much as it was the day before. What would your pay be at the end of a month on the job? (Consider one month to be 21 working days.)

Pause to estimate what you think the answer will be. Because the starting pay is only ten cents, many people guess that the most you could be making at the end of a month is just a few dollars. But what really happens? Let's begin by making a table of the pay for each day of the first week (5 working days).

Day	1	2	3	4	5
Pay (in cents)	10	20	40	80	160

From the table above you see that the pay on the 5th day would be 160 cents, or $1.60. This still isn't very much money, but notice that it is already 16 times as much as the pay for the 1st day. Let's go on to calculate the pay for the 21st day. However, let's first examine the table to see if there is a pattern that may be helpful. You know from the statement of the problem that the basic pattern is one of doubling, or multiplying by 2s. In the table below, you see that the pay can also be shown as the product of the beginning pay of 10 cents multiplied by a number of 2s.

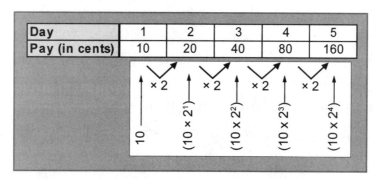

Notice that exponents were used as a shorthand way to show the number of times that 10 cents is multiplied by 2. Do you see that the exponent of 2 is always one less than the number of the day? Therefore, on the 21st day you would multiply the beginning pay of 10 cents by 2^{20} (which represents the product of twenty 2s). This may be written as 10×2^{20}, or you may compute the standard form if a calculator is available. The surprise in this problem is how rapidly the numbers become very large: $10 \times 2^{20} = 10 \times 1,048,576 = 10,485,760$.

Answer: **On the 21st working day your pay would be 10,485,760 cents, or $104,857.60.**

Let's pause to look at this multiplication pattern in more general terms, as we did with the addition pattern on pages 38-40.

As before, we encounter a set of numbers ordered according to a specific rule. Therefore, this set of numbers forms a sequence, and we can label our data according to the basic definitions associated with a sequence.

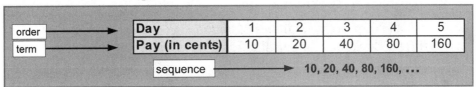

order → term →	**Day**	1	2	3	4	5
	Pay (in cents)	10	20	40	80	160

sequence ⟶ **10, 20, 40, 80, 160, ...**

Recall that an arithmetic sequence is obtained by the addition of a constant number, resulting in the same difference between consecutive terms. The sequence shown above is obtained by the *multiplication* by a constant non-zero number, which results in the same *quotient* between consecutive terms. This type of sequence is called a GEOMETRIC SEQUENCE.

Like an arithmetic sequence, any geometric sequence has a rule. In this case, we have already observed that the terms can be written as $10, 10 \times 2^1, 10 \times 2^2, 10 \times 2^3, 10 \times 2^4, ...$ Therefore, the rule of this sequence is that each term is the product of 10 multiplied by 2 raised to an exponent that is one less than the order of the term.

Although it may not seem so, this rule applies even to the first term, giving us 10×2^0. In mathematics, any number (except 0) with the exponent of 0 is defined as being equal to 1. Consequently, $10 \times 2^0 = 10 \times 1$. This in turn is equal to 10, which is indeed the first term of the sequence.

★ *Problems* ★

1. Consider a different job offer. You are told that your pay for the first day will be 5 cents. Each day after that your pay will be three times as much as it was the day before.
    a. What will your pay be on the 2nd day? 3rd? 4th? 5th?
    b. Use sequence notation to write the pattern of pay for this job.
    c. Is the sequence formed by the pay for this job a geometric sequence? If it is, write a rule for the sequence.
    d. What would the pay be on the 10th day?

2. Write the next three terms of each of the following geometric sequences.
    a. 2, 6, 18, 54, 162, ...
    b. 3, 15, 75, 375, 1875, ...
    c. $\frac{2}{3}, \frac{4}{9}, \frac{8}{27}, \frac{16}{81}, \frac{32}{243}, ...$
    d. 5000, 500, 50, 5, 0.5, ...

3. What is the 20th term of each sequence in problem 2? You may give your answer in exponent form.

4. Consider the geometric sequence 4, 12, 36, 108, 324, ... Which term of the sequence is 8748?

5. In a certain geometric sequence, the 1st term is 2 and the 5th term is 1250. List the 1st five terms of this sequence.

6. A sheet of paper is torn in half and the pieces are placed on top of one another. These pieces together are torn in half, and the new pieces are placed on top of one another. Suppose that this process continues through 20 such tears. If the original piece of paper was 0.001 in. thick, how high is the final pile of pieces of paper?

7. An amoeba is a microscopic organism that reproduces itself in three minutes. One amoeba is placed in a jar, and in three hours the jar is filled. How long did it take for the jar to be half full?

(Solutions are on pages 151-152.)

1.3 More Addition Patterns
The Grapefruit Pyramid

The citizens of Hartville are creating a grapefruit pyramid as the central exhibit of this year's county fair. They plan to make the pyramid ten layers high. Each layer will have the shape of an equilateral triangle, so that each grapefruit above the bottom rests on three grapefruits below it. How many grapefruits will they need for the bottom layer?

One way to solve this problem is to draw a picture of the bottom layer and simply count the grapefruits. It may be hard to visualize though, and the drawing could be inaccurate. Instead, let's take a look at some of the *top* layers to examine a pattern that may be helpful.

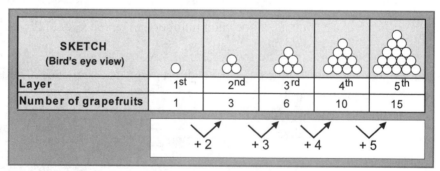

Although the difference between successive numbers of grapefruits is not constant, there is a steady increase taking place. This time, it is the differences themselves that are constantly increasing by 1. Therefore, the pattern of differences can be continued to find the number of grapefruits in the 10th, or bottom, layer.

Answer: **They will need 55 grapefruits for the bottom layer.**

Notice that the number of grapefruits in the tenth layer is the same as the sum of all the counting numbers from 1 through 10: $1 + 2 + 3 + \cdots + 10$. We shall say more about such sums in Section 1.5.

The numbers of grapefruits in the layers of the pyramid form another type of sequence, which is neither arithmetic nor geometric.

★ *Problems* ★

1. Suppose that the grapefruit pyramid is constructed as described with 20 layers each in the shape of an equilateral triangle. How many grapefruits are in each of the following layers?
   a. 12th   b. 15th   c. 18th   d. 20th

2. Suppose that the grapefruit pyramid is constructed with 100 layers each in the shape of a *square*, so that each grapefruit above those in the bottom layer rests on *four* grapefruits below it. How many grapefruits are in each of the following layers?
   a. 12th   b. 15th   c. 50th   d. 100th

3. Each of these sequences has a pattern of successive differences which increase by a constant. Write the next three terms of each sequence.
   a. 2, 5, 9, 14, 20, ...   b. 2, 5, 10, 17, 26, ...
   c. 3, 7, 13, 21, 31, ...   d. 2, 7, 16, 29, 46, ...

4. Write a rule for each sequence. (*Hint*: Compare each term with the perfect square of its order.)
   a. 2, 5, 10, 17, 26, ...   b. 0, 3, 8, 15, 24, ...
   c. 2, 8, 18, 32, 50, ...   d. 2, 6, 12, 20, 30, ...

5. What is the 12th term of each sequence in problem 4?

6. The numbers in the triangular grapefruit pyramid (1, 3, 6, 10, 15 , ...) are sometimes called the TRIANGULAR NUMBERS, since each number can be represented by an array of objects in the shape of an equilateral triangle.

1st   2nd   3rd   4th

Similarly, the numbers of the square pyramid (1, 4, 9, 16, 25, ...) are called the SQUARE NUMBERS or PERFECT SQUARES, as illustrated below.

1st   2nd   3rd   4th

These numbers were so named over 2500 years ago by Greek mathematicians who were searching for a link between arithmetic and geometry.

a. Use these figures to help you list the next 6 PENTAGONAL NUMBERS.

b. Use these figures to help you list the next 6 HEXAGONAL NUMBERS.

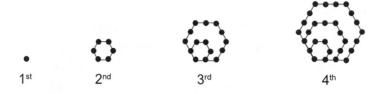

c. Use these figures to help you list the next 6 RECTANGULAR NUMBERS.

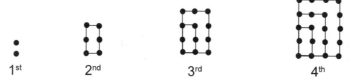

(Solutions are on pages 152-153.)

1.4 Unusual Patterns
About Face!

What could be the next number of this pattern?
1, 4, 9, 61, 52, 63, …

At first you may feel that there has been a mistake. Like many people, you may think that number patterns are supposed to consistently increase or decrease. The consistency of a pattern though, lies in the rule that is being followed. To discover the rule for this pattern, you may find that you need to change your point of view.

Let's start by examining the numbers to see if there is any element that is familiar. Did you recognize the first three numbers as the first three perfect squares? Perhaps you did, but then abandoned this line of thinking when you saw the next three numbers. Look again. Are the next three numbers related in any way at all? Let's make a table to compare the six given numbers with the first six perfect squares.

Given numbers	1	4	9	61	52	63
Perfect-square numbers	1	4	9	16	25	36

When the sets of numbers are placed side-by-side, one possible pattern that emerges is a simple reversal of the digits of the perfect squares. The first three numbers appear the same, of course, because a single-digit number reads the same way backward and forward. Other patterns may also yield these same six terms, but this pattern seems clearest.

Answer: **Since the next perfect square is 49, the next number of the given pattern is 94.**

You may find that unusual patterns such as these provide some of your most challenging problem solving experiences, because the list of ways to create these patterns is almost endless. Sometimes you may have an insight that reveals the rule of the pattern to you immediately, and at other times the rule may elude you. A good way to become adept at working with these patterns is to try to solve many of them.

★ *Problems* ★

1. What could be the next two numbers in each of the following patterns?
   a. 3, 6, 9, 21, 51, 81, …
   b. 0, 4, 8, 21, 52, 65, …
   c. 15, 26, 40, 16, 37, 58, …
   d. 5, 2, 6, 3, 9, 6, …

2. Sometimes the rule for a pattern is not numerical. What could be the next item in each of the following patterns?
   a. O, T, T, F, F, S, S, …
   b. **M, S2, 83, M4**, …

3. The number sequence 1, 1, 2, 3, 5, 8, 13, … has been given the special name of the **FIBONACCI SEQUENCE**.
   a. What is the rule of the Fibonacci Sequence?
   b. List the next three terms.
   c. Choose any three consecutive terms of the Fibonacci Sequence. Square the middle term and multiply the two outer terms. Compare the results. Repeat this process with other groups of three consecutive terms. What is the pattern?
   d. Choose any four consecutive terms of the Fibonacci Sequence. Multiply the two middle terms, and then multiply the two outer terms. Compare the results. Repeat this process with other groups of four consecutive terms. What is the pattern?

4. When a single-stalk plant such as corn sprouts new leaves, it follows an upward spiraling pattern so that the new top leaves do not shade the older bottom leaves. The 2nd leaf sprouts $\frac{1}{2}$ of the way around the stalk from the 1st leaf, the 3rd leaf sprouts $\frac{2}{3}$ of the way

around the stalk from the 2ⁿᵈ leaf, the 4ᵗʰ leaf sprouts $\frac{3}{5}$ of the way around the stalk from the 3ʳᵈ leaf, the 5ᵗʰ leaf sprouts $\frac{5}{8}$ of the way around the stalk from the 4ᵗʰ leaf, and so on. Following this pattern, how far around the stalk from the 8ᵗʰ leaf will the 9ᵗʰ leaf sprout?

5. A curious biological fact is that a male bee has only one parent, a mother, whereas a female bee has both a mother and a father. How many 2ⁿᵈ generation ancestors (grand-parents) does the male bee have? 3ʳᵈ generation ancestors (great-grand-parents)? 4ᵗʰ? 5ᵗʰ? 10ᵗʰ?

6. The figure below shows a special number pattern called **PASCAL'S TRIANGLE**. Pascal's Triangle is a triangular array composed of the coefficients in the expansion of $(a + b)^n$ for $n = 0, 1, 2, 3, \ldots$, where a and b are any numbers. The number of a row or diagonal is counted from the top down. The first seven rows and diagonals are shown.

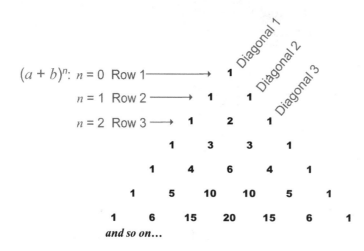

a. What rule holds for this pattern?
b. List the numbers in the 8ᵗʰ row.
c. What are the next three numbers in the 1ˢᵗ diagonal? 2ⁿᵈ? 3ʳᵈ? 4ᵗʰ?

7. A person named Pascal lives in the town pictured at the right. The streets are arranged in an orderly grid and are all either one-way south or one-way east, as shown.

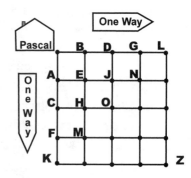

a. How many different routes are there from Pascal's house to location *A*? *B*? *C*? *D*? *E*? *F*? *G*? *H*? *J*? *K*? *L*? *M*? *N*? *O*?
b. How many different routes are there from Pascal's house to location *Z* on the other side of town?

8. The first figure below shows an example of a special type of number pattern called a NUMBER BRACELET.

a. What rule works for this pattern? (*Hint:* Some number patterns are formed by eliminating certain digits.)

b. Use this rule to fill in the missing links of the bracelet shown in the second figure.

c. Complete the bracelet that is begun in the third figure. (*Note:* There are 60 links in this bracelet.)

(*Solutions are on pages 153-156.*)

1.5 PATTERNS AND SUMS
A Child Prodigy

Karl Friedrich Gauss (1777-1855) was one of the world's greatest mathematicians. There is a story that, when Gauss was a nine-year-old schoolboy, the teacher of his class assigned the rather tedious task of finding the sum of all the counting numbers from 1 to 100 inclusive. To the teacher's surprise, Gauss arrived at the correct answer within seconds. What is the sum?

How do you think Gauss performed the calculations so quickly and accurately? We can't be sure, of course, but one possibility is that he noticed this pattern.

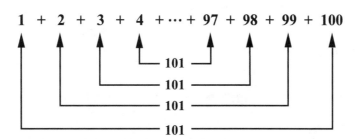

Do you see that the numbers pair to form sums of 101? How many such pairs are there? There are 50 in all, and so the sum is simply $50 \times 101 = 5050$.

It is also possible that Gauss used a strategy involving some very simple algebra, with a variable like *S* representing the unknown sum.

$$
\begin{array}{rl}
S &= 1 + 2 + 3 + \cdots + 98 + 99 + 100 \\
S &= 100 + 99 + 98 + \cdots + 3 + 2 + 1 \\
\hline
2S &= 101 + 101 + 101 + \cdots + 101 + 101 + 101
\end{array}
$$

Notice that the order of the addends was reversed in the second line. The third line was obtained by vertical addition, giving us the fact that $2S$ equals 100 sums of 101, or $100 \times 101 = 10,100$. To find the sum, solve for S in the resulting equation.

$$2S = 10,100$$
$$\frac{2S}{2} = \frac{10,100}{2}$$
$$S = 5050$$

Answer: **The sum of all counting numbers from 1 to 100 is 5050.**

★ Problems ★

1. Find the sum of all the counting numbers inclusive within the indicated limits.
   a. from 1 through 10
   b. from 1 through 50
   c. from 1 through 75
   d. from 3 through 12
   e. from 5 through 90
   f. from 15 through 55

2. Your New Year's resolution is to put 1¢ into your savings on the 1ˢᵗ day of the year, 2¢ on the 2ⁿᵈ day, 3¢ on the 3ʳᵈ day, 4¢ on the 4ᵗʰ day, and so on for all 365 days of the year. How much money in all will you have put into your savings by the end of the year?

3. In the game of bowling, ten pins are set up in a four-row triangular arrangement, as shown. Imagine a "super" bowling game in which a similar triangular arrangement contains forty rows of pins. What would be the total number of pins in this arrangement?

4. Draw two straight lines across this clock face so that the sum of the numbers in each region formed is the same.

5. For each of the following, distribute the eggs so that you have a different number of eggs in each basket.
   a. $\frac{1}{2}$ dozen eggs in 3 baskets
   b. $6\frac{1}{2}$ dozen eggs in 12 baskets
   c. 3 dozen eggs in 9 baskets
   d. 4 dozen eggs in 9 baskets

6. The indicated sum of the terms of an arithmetic sequence is called an arithmetic series. Find the sum of each of the following finite arithmetic series.
   a. $1 + 3 + 5 + \cdots + 97 + 99$ b. $1 + 5 + 9 + \cdots + 93 + 97$
   c. $1 + 5 + 9 + \cdots + 145 + 149$ d. $2 + 5 + 8 + \cdots + 95 + 98$

7. Last night there was a party, and the host's doorbell rang 20 times. The first time the doorbell rang, only one guest arrived. Each time the doorbell rang after that, two more guests arrived than had arrived on the previous ring. How many guests in all arrived at the party?

8. Rearrange the numbers in the "×" shown at the right so that the numbers on each of the two diagonals have the same sum.

9. Suppose that you have a secret. One Sunday, you tell your secret to a friend. On Monday, your friend tells your secret to 2 other friends. On Tuesday, each of the friends who heard your secret on Monday tells it to 2 other friends. If this procedure continues from day to day, how many people in all will have been told your secret by the end of the following Sunday? Assume that no one is told your secret more than once. (*Hint*: make a table and look for a pattern.)

(*Solutions are on page 156-159.*)

**For further development see "Sequences and Series"
in Appendix 6 on pages 264-277.**

---

2. Factors And Multiples

In the following sections, the word number refers to a natural number.

2.1 Factors
A Card Trick

A magician places twenty cards numbered in order from 1 to 20 face down on a table. She calls up 20 people from the audience. She instructs the first person to blindfold her and then turn over every card, the second person to turn over every second card, the third person to turn over every third card, the fourth person to turn over every fourth card, and so on. After the twentieth person finishes, she asks several people to call out the number of a card, and she tells them correctly whether the card is face up or face down. How does she know?

When a problem involves a lot of data, it is often a good strategy to start by solving a simpler related problem. In this case the table below examines what would happen if there were just 12 cards and 12 people.

Card Numbers

People	1	2	3	4	5	6	7	8	9	10	11	12
1	U	U	U	U	U	U	U	U	U	U	U	U
2		D		D		D		D		D		D
3			D			U			D			U
4				U				U				D
5					D					U		
6						D						U
7							D					
8								D				
9									U			
10										D		
11											D	
12												D

U = card up;   D = card down

Let us begin by examining what happened to card 12. The entries in the 12-column of the table show that the 12-card was turned over by persons 1, 2, 3, 4, 6, and 12. Each of these six numbers divides 12 exactly. Such numbers are called FACTORS.

Definition: The FACTORS OF A GIVEN NUMBER are those numbers which divide the given number exactly, including 1 and the given number itself. Observe that 1 is a factor of every natural number (counting number).

Notice that the six factors of 12 can be paired so that the product of each pair is 12, namely 1×12, 2×6, and 3×4. The six factors also resulted in card 12 being turned over six times and ending face-down. When a number has an even number of factors, the card will end face down.

The main diagonal of the table on page 52 shows that 1, 4, and 9 ended face-up. What do these three numbers have in common? 1 has just itself as a factor; 4 has 1, 2, and 4 as factors; 9 has 1, 3, and 9 as factors. Each of these numbers has an odd number of factors. You may recognize these numbers as the first three PERFECT SQUARES (also called square numbers, or perfect-square numbers). They and their successors may be written as 1×1, 2×2, 3×3, 4×4, 5×5, …, $n \times n$, and so forth.

Definition: A PERFECT SQUARE *is any number $n \times n = n^2$ where n is any natural number.*

Notice that 16 has five factors: 1, 2, 4, 8, and 16. We can pair four of the factors so that their product is 16: 1×16 and 2×8, but 4 must be paired with itself, 4×4. Every perfect square, like 16, has one factor that must be multiplied by itself to produce the perfect square.

Since perfect square card numbers will be turned over an odd number of times, they will end face-up. All other numbers will be turned over an even number of times and will end face-down.

Answer: **The magician knew that after all 20 people turned over the 20 cards, those cards numbered with the perfect square numbers less than 20 (that is, 1, 4, 9, and 16) were face-up and all other cards were face-down.**

★ *Problems* ★

1. In a table structured for 20 people and 20 cards numbered from 1 through 20, which people will turn over card 18?

2. List the factors for 36. Pair each factor with a different factor so that their product is 36. Which factor cannot be paired with a different factor?

3. List all the ways that 90 can be expressed as the product of two factors.

4. Suppose the magician has 100 people turn over 100 cards numbered from 1 through 100. Which card numbers will end face-up?

5. If the table is extended for 300 columns and 300 rows, which of the numbers between 200 and 300 will have an odd number of factors?

6. How many numbers from 1 through 1000 are perfect squares?

7. Between what pair of successive squares does the number 132 lie?

8. What year in the 21st century is a perfect square?

9. How many perfect squares are between 2000 and 3000?

10. If a number written in standard form ends in one or more zeros, then those zeros are called TERMINAL ZEROS. Find the number of terminal zeros in each of the following products when expressed in standard form.
   a. 700×80
   b. $80 \times 400 \times 30$
   c. 500×600
   d. $5 \times 10^1 \times 10^2 \times 10^3$

11. ***For The Adventurous***
   A recent census form included a space for residents to record the ages of all children in the household. One resident wrote, "I have three children. The product of their ages is 72. The sum of their ages is the same as our house number." The census worker who had to process the form phoned this resident to complain that this was not enough information. "I'm sorry," replied the resident. "I forgot to mention that my oldest child likes chocolate pudding." The census worker thanked the resident and hung up the phone. How old were the children? (Hint: list all the ways that 72 can be expressed as a product of three natural numbers.)

   (*Solutions are on pages 160-161.*)

2.2 *Factors and Primes*
The Card Trick Revisited

Revisit the table in section 2.1. Before reading ahead, answer the following question: Which card numbers were turned over just two times? You should have gotten 2, 3, 5, 7, and 11. Such numbers are called PRIME NUMBERS.

Definition: A PRIME NUMBER *is a number greater than 1 which has only 1 and the prime number itself as distinct factors.* (Note: 1 is not a prime number.)

Suppose that 1000 people turn over 1000 cards numbered from 1 through 1000 according to the procedure described in Section 2.1. How many people turn over card 432?

From our discussion in Section 2.1, we know that each card is turned by those people whose numbers are factors of the turned card numbers. Therefore, determining how many people turned one card is equivalent to counting all the factors of the card number. In the case of a large number such as 432, the process of listing its factors may be tedious and sometimes inaccurate. The key to counting all the factors of a large number lies in finding its prime factors.

Let us first consider a number whose prime factorization consists of one factor repeatedly multiplied such as $16 = 2 \times 2 \times 2 \times 2 = 2^4$. We call $2 \times 2 \times 2 \times 2$ the PRIME FACTORIZATION OF 16. We read 2^4 as "2 to the 4th power" or as the "4th power of 2." We also call 2^4 a PRIME POWER FACTORIZATION.

> ***For further development see "Working With Exponents"***
> ***in Appendix 4 on pages 249-256.***

The factors of 16 are 1, 2, 4, 8, and 16 which can also be expressed as 1, 2^1, 2^2, 2^3, and 2^4. Do you see a relationship between the prime power factorization and the number of factors it has? Observe that number of factors is 5, one more than the exponent in the prime power factorization.

RULE 1: If *p* is a prime number, then p^n has *n*+1 factors including 1 and p^n itself.

Example 1: How many factors does 7^{35} have?
    The factors of 7^{35} are: 7^1, 7^2, 7^3, ... , 7^{33}, 7^{34}, 7^{35}, and 1.
        Answer: 7^{35} has 36 factors.

We can now extend the above idea to find the number of factors of 432. A convenient way to find the prime factorization is to make a factor tree like the one below which shows that $432 = 2^4 \times 3^3$, the product of two Prime Power Factorizations.

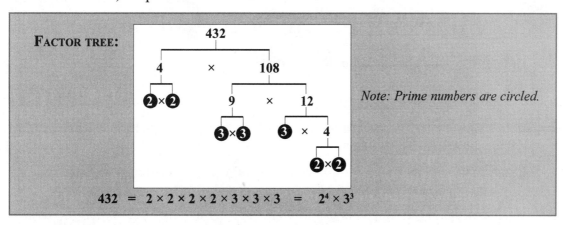

FACTOR TREE:

Note: Prime numbers are circled.

$$432 = 2 \times 2 \times 2 \times 2 \times 3 \times 3 \times 3 = 2^4 \times 3^3$$

On page 53 we saw that 2^4 has 5 factors and, from rule 1, we know that 3^3 has 4 factors. How do we combine these numbers to find the total number of factors?

RULE 2: If $N = p^a \times q^b \times r^c \times ...$ where *p*, *q*, *r*, ... are different primes and *a*, *b*, *c*, ... are exponents, then *N* has $(a + 1) \times (b + 1) \times (c + 1) \times ...$ different factors.

Let us now apply rule 2 to find the number of factors of 432. Since $5 \times 4 = 20$, 432 has a total of 20 factors.

Answer: Card 432 was turned by 20 people.

Example 2: How many factors does 720 have?
    Use a factor tree as above to obtain $720 = 2^4 \times 3^2 \times 5^1$.
    The bases are 2, 3, and 5, and their respective exponents are 4, 2, and 1.
Then the number of factors is (❹+ 1) × (❷+ 1) × (❶+ 1) = $5 \times 3 \times 2 = 30$.
        Answer: 30 factors are contained in 720.

We can also use the prime power factorizations shown on page 54 to determine exactly *which* people turned card 432. This may be done by listing all factors of 2^4 and 3^3 in the multiplication table below with the five factors of 2^4 in the first row and the four factors of 3^3 in the first column.

×	1	2	4	8	16
1	1	2	4	8	16
3	3	6	12	24	48
9	9	18	36	72	144
27	27	54	108	216	432

The entries of the table are the 20 factors of 432. Therefore Card 432 was turned by twenty people with assigned numbers:

1, 2, 3, 4, 6, 8, 9, 12, 16, 18, 24, 27, 36, 48, 54, 72, 108, 144, 216, and 432.

★ Problems ★

1. How many factors does each of the following numbers have?
   a. 64   b. 81   c. 125   d. 343
   e. 400   f. 648   g. 875   h. 540

2. If the magician has 20 people turning 20 cards, which card numbers between 12 and 20 will be turned exactly two times?

3. If our table was structured for 50 people and 50 cards numbered from 1 through 50, which card numbers between 20 and 50 have exactly 2 different factors?

4. What is the largest prime number less than 100?

5. The number 13 is a prime number. If its digits are reversed, 13 becomes 31 which is also a prime number. Name four other pairs of "reversible" two-digit prime numbers.

6. Which has more factors, 72 or 96?

7. List all the ways that 24 can be expressed as a product of three natural numbers if the order of the numbers does not matter.

8. Find three consecutive numbers whose product is 15,600.

9. A convenient way to express the product of all the counting numbers from 1 to 5 inclusive is 5! (read as "five factorial"). Thus $5! = 5 \times 4 \times 3 \times 2 \times 1$. Find the number of terminal zeros in each of the following when expressed in standard form.
   a. 7!   b. 10!   c. 18!   d. 25!

10. Evaluate each of the following:
    a. $5! \div 2^3$ b. $7! \div 4!$ c. $6! - 5!$

11. The product of two natural numbers is 100,000 but neither factor contains zero as a digit. What are the two factors?

12. List all numbers less than 100 which each have exactly 6 factors.

13. ***For The Adventurous***
    The mathematician Christian Goldbach (1690-1764) made two guesses about natural numbers that no one has been able to prove as either true or false. These guesses are called **GOLDBACH'S CONJECTURES**. The first conjecture is that every even number greater than 2 can be written as the sum of two prime numbers. The second conjecture is that every odd number greater than 5 can be written as the sum of three prime numbers.
    a. What two prime numbers have a sum of 6? 10? 28?
    b. What three prime numbers have a sum of 7? 9? 21?

    (Solutions are on pages 161-162.)

2.3 Greatest Common Factor (GCF)
Checkers, Anyone?

A set of 36 red checkers and 60 black checkers is to be arranged into piles. Each pile may contain only red or only black checkers. All piles, both red and black, must contain the same number of checkers. What is the greatest number of checkers that each of the piles can have?

There are many methods for finding the GREATEST COMMON FACTOR of two or more numbers.

Method 1. Listing of Factors
   Factors of 36 (red):   1, 2, 3, 4, 6, 9, 12, 18, 36
   Factors of 60 (black):   1, 2, 3, 4, 5, 6, 10, 12, 15, 20, 30, 60
   Common factors: 1, 2, 3, 4, 6, 12

   Answer: **The greatest number of checkers that can be in each pile is 12.**

Definition: The GREATEST COMMON FACTOR *(GCF) of two or more given numbers is the greatest number that divides each of the given numbers exactly.* We will write the greatest common factor of 36 and 60 in the convenient form GCF(36,60).

Method 2. Testing for the GCF of Two or More Numbers
   Take the factors of the smaller number(s) in order from the largest factor to the smallest factor. The first common factor of the smaller numbers to divide the larger number exactly is the GCF of the two numbers.

   Example 1: Find GCF(36,60)
      The smaller number of the two numbers is 36.
      Factors of 36 : 36, 18, 12, 9, 6, 4, 3, 2, 1
      The first factor of 36 to divide 60 exactly is 12.
         Answer: GCF(36,60) = 12

Example 2: Find GCF(36,60,90)
    The smaller numbers of the three numbers are 36 and 60.
    Factors of 36: 36, 18, 12, 9, 6, 4, 3, 2, 1
    Factors of 60: 60, 30, 20, 15, 12, 10, 6, 5, 4, 3, 2, 1
    Common factors of 36 and 60: 12, 6, 4, 3, 2, 1
The first common factor of 36 and 60 to divide 90 exactly is 6.
       Answer: GCF(36,60,90) = 6

Method 3. Prime Power Factorizations

    Since a factor may be overlooked in the methods described above, the method of Prime Power Factorizations may be preferable. First identify the factors that are common to two (or more) numbers. The GCF is the product of the *least power* of each prime that is present in all of the factorizations. Note: If a prime is not present in all of the factorizations, it is not to be considered in the GCF.

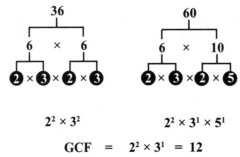

$$2^2 \times 3^2 \qquad\qquad 2^2 \times 3^1 \times 5^1$$

$$\text{GCF} \ = \ 2^2 \times 3^1 \ = \ 12$$

    The primes present in both above factorizations are 2 and 3. Their least powers are 2^2 and 3^1.
       Answer: GCF(36,60) = $2^2 \times 3 = 12$

Method 4. Euclid's Algorithm

    Another interesting method for finding the GCF of two numbers is associated with Euclid. This method consists of a series of divisions as shown below in two examples. The GCF of the two numbers is the divisor in the last division with 0 remainder.

    Example 3: Find GCF(36,60)

Divide the greater number by the lesser number: Divide the previous divisor by the remainder: Repeat the process until the remainder is 0:

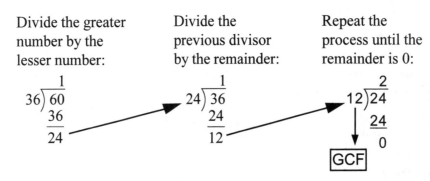

      Answer: GCF(36,60) = 12

Example 4: Find GCF(391,713)

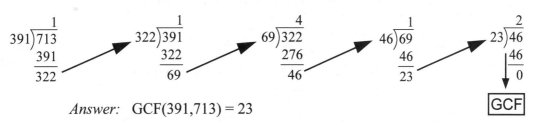

Answer: GCF(391,713) = 23

Example 4 shows how helpful this procedure, sometimes referred to as Euclid's Algorithm, can be in finding the GCF of two large numbers.

Method 5. The Difference of Two Numbers

If two distinct numbers are each exactly divisible by the difference of the two numbers, the difference is the GCF of the two numbers.

Example 5: Find GCF(48,60)
Each of 48 and 60 is exactly divisible by their difference 12.
Answer: GCF(48,60) = 12

Example 5 is related to a special case of a theorem in Number Theory. The general case of the theorem states that the largest number that divides any two different given natural numbers leaving the same remainder is the difference of the two given numbers. In the above example, the remainder is zero which also satisfies the conditions of the theorem.

> **See Appendix 5, page 260 for a proof of the theorem described above.**

Method 6. Complete Factorizations

Example 6: Find GCF(36,60,90)
Factor each of the three numbers completely.
$36 = ❷ \times 2 \times ❸ \times 3$
$60 = ❷ \times 2 \times ❸ \times 5$
$90 = ❷ \times ❸ \times 3 \times 5$
The three factorizations have just 2×3 in common.
Answer: GCF(36,60,90) = $2 \times 3 = 6$

★ *Problems* ★

1. Each of the following sets of red and black checkers is to be arranged into piles. Each pile may contain only red or only black checkers. All piles, both red and black, must contain the same number of checkers. What is the greatest number of checkers that each pile can have?
   a. 18 red, 30 black   b. 84 red, 56 black
   c. 12 red, 60 black   d. 21 red, 10 black

2. What is the GCF of each of the following pairs of numbers? Use Euclid's algorithm if other methods are not convenient.
   a. 54 and 144   b. 38 and 95   c. 629 and 2257

3. To find the lowest terms of a given fraction, divide both the numerator and the denominator by their GCF. Use Euclid's Algorithm if other methods are not effective.
   a. $\dfrac{54}{72}$ b. $\dfrac{119}{391}$ c. $\dfrac{679}{1261}$ d. $\dfrac{1921}{2599}$

4. A North American fellowship conference is attended by 96 students from the United States, 72 from Canada and 48 from Mexico. What is the greatest number of discussion groups that can be formed so that the students from each country are distributed equally among all the groups? How many students from each country will be in each group?

5. Two numbers are said to be RELATIVELY PRIME (or CO-PRIME) if the pair of numbers has no common factor other than 1. Three or more numbers are said to be RELATIVELY PRIME IN PAIRS (or CO-PRIME PAIRWISE) if each pair that can be formed is relatively prime, and RELATIVELY PRIME MUTUALLY if the entire set has no common factor other than 1. Which of the following sets of numbers are relatively prime pairwise?
   a. 27, 64   b. 112, 175   c. 18, 35, 75   d. 13, 45, 56

6. What is the remainder when 3^{10} is divided by 5? (*Hint:* Solve some simpler problems and look for a pattern.)

7. ***For The Adventurous***
   A rectangular kitchen floor is covered by square tiles. A straight line is drawn from one corner to the corner that is diagonally opposite.
   a. How many tiles does the line cross if the floor measures exactly 2 tiles by 3 tiles? 4 tiles by 6 tiles? 6 tiles by 9 tiles? 8 tiles by 12 tiles? (*Note*: A tile is considered to be crossed if the line intersects it only at a corner.)
   b. How many tiles does the line cross if the floor measures exactly 24 tiles by 40 tiles?
   c. State a rule for finding the number of tiles that the line crosses for any pair of whole-number dimensions of the kitchen floor.
   d. Use your rule to determine how many tiles the line crosses if the floor measures exactly 54 tiles by 96 tiles.

   (*Solutions are on pages 162-164.*)

2.4 Least Common Multiple (LCM)
Broadway Bound

The choreographer of a big Broadway musical has requested that the producer hire enough chorus dancers so that, for various scenes, the dancers can be arranged in groups of 4, 6, or 9 dancers with none left over. What is the least number of dancers that the producer must hire?

We need to find the LEAST COMMON MULTIPLE of 4, 6, and 9. Many methods exist for determining the least common multiple of two or more numbers.

Method 1. Listing Multiples of Given Numbers
Multiples of 4:   4, 8, 12, 16, 20, 24, 28, 32, **36**, 40, ...
Multiples of 6:   6, 12, 18, 24, 30, **36**, 42, ...
Multiples of 9:   9, 18, 27, **36**, 45, ...
    The Least Common Multiple of 4, 6, and 9 is 36.
Answer: **The producer must hire 36 dancers.**

Definition: The LEAST COMMON MULTIPLE *(LCM) of two or more given numbers is the smallest common multiple that each of the given numbers divides exactly.*

We will write the Least Common Multiple of 4, 6, and 9 in the convenient form LCM(4,6,9). In Method 1, LCM(4,6,9) = 36.

A special case occurs if the numbers are RELATIVELY PRIME IN PAIRS. See page 60, problem 5 for the definition of *relatively prime* (or *co-prime*).

If two numbers are relatively prime as in the case of 8 and 15, then their LCM is just their product, so that LCM(8,15) = 8 × 15 = 120. The same is true for any set of numbers which are relatively prime in pairs, such as 4, 5, and 9. Thus since GCF(4,5), GCF(5,9), and GCF(4,9) each equal 1, LCM(4,5,9) = 4 × 5 × 9 = 180.

Method 2. Multiples of the Greatest Given Numbers.
Example 1: Find the LCM of 18, 12, and 8.

Multiples of 18	Divisible by 12?	Divisible by 8?
18	No	No
36	YES	No
54	No	No
72	**YES**	**YES**

Each of the multiples of 18 is divided by each of the smaller numbers 12 and 8 until both quotients are whole numbers.
        Answer: LCM(18,12,8) = 72

Method 3. Prime Power Factorizations
The preceding methods are sometimes time-consuming and subject to errors, omissions, and the like. A more direct approach consists of finding the Prime Power Factorization of each number. The LCM is then the product of the greatest power of each prime that appears in any of the factorizations.

On page 62 we will extend the procedure in the preceding problem to find LCM(18,12,8).

$$18 = 2^1 \times 3^2 \qquad 12 = 2^2 \times 3^1 \qquad 8 = 2^3$$

The primes present in the above factorizations are 2 and 3. The greatest powers of these primes that appear are 2^3 and 3^2.

Answer: LCM(18,12,8) $= 2^3 \times 3^2 = 72$

Method 4: The LCM Algorithm

After describing the process, we will use two examples to show how the following algorithm is used to find the LCM of two numbers and then the LCM of three numbers.

Process For Finding LCM(*A*,*B*)

1. Construct a table whose columns have the following headings: Line Number, Prime Factor, Factors of *A*, Factors of *B*. Examples 2 and 3 illustrate this process.

2. Find any prime, *p*, that is a factor of either of the original numbers. List that prime on line (1) under "Prime".

3. Look at the numbers, *A* and *B*, that are on the previous line in the last two columns. If *p* does not divide the number exactly, repeat that number onto line (1) in the same column. If *p* does divide the number, do the division and put the quotient onto line (1) in the same column.

4. Repeat this process as follows: Find any prime, *q*, that is a factor of either of the two numbers in the last two columns of line (1). List that prime on line (2) under "Prime." [Note: *q* may be the same prime as *p*.]

5. Look at each of the numbers that are on the previous line in the last two columns. If *q* does not divide the number exactly, repeat that number onto line (2) in the same column. If *q* does divide the number exactly, do the division and put the quotient onto line (2) in the same column.

6. Continue to repeat this process until each of the numbers in the last two columns equals 1. Then the LCM of the two original numbers will be the product of the primes listed in the table under "Primes".

Example 2: Find LCM(15,18)

Line	Prime Factors	Factors of 15	Factors of 18
(1)	2	15	9
(2)	3	5	3
(3)	3	5	1
(4)	5	1	1

Answer: LCM(15,18) $= 2 \times 3 \times 3 \times 5 = 90$.

Example 3: Find LCM(45,75,175).

Line	Prime factors	Factors of 45	Factors of 75	Factors of 175
(1)	5	9	15	35
(2)	3	3	5	35
(3)	3	1	5	35
(4)	5	1	1	7
(5)	7	1	1	1

Answer: LCM(45,75,175) $= 5 \times 3 \times 3 \times 5 \times 7 = 1575$.

★ *Problems* ★

1. What is the LCM of each of the following sets of numbers?
   a. 6 and 10   b. 24 and 54   c. 108 and 126   d. 6, 8, and 15

2. What is the least number of dancers that a producer must hire if the choreographer wants to arrange them in groups of 4, 5, or 6 with none left over?

3. At the Fourth of July parade, the local scout troop found that they could arrange themselves in rows of exactly 6, exactly 7, or exactly 8, with no one left over. What is the least number of scouts in the troop?

4. I have a collection of pennies that can be arranged in piles that each contain exactly 9 pennies. My pennies can also be arranged in piles that each contain exactly 10 pennies, exactly 11 pennies, and exactly 12 pennies. What is the least number of pennies that can be in my collection?

5. Complete the calculations for each set of numbers. Then answer the questions.

    $16 \times 20 = ?$ $18 \times 48 = ?$

    GCF of 16 and 20 = ?   GCF of 18 and 48 = ?

    LCM of 16 and 20 = ?   LCM of 18 and 48 = ?

    GCF × LCM = ?   GCF × LCM = ?

    a. State a rule to describe the relationship between the product of two numbers and their GCF and LCM.

    b. Use your rule to describe a method for finding the LCM of two numbers if you already know their GCF.

    c. The GCF of 36 and 60 is 12. Show how to use your method to find the LCM of 36 and 60.

6. If a certain number is divided by 2, 3, 4, or 5, the remainder is 1 in each case. What is the least number greater than 1 that satisfies these conditions?

7. If a certain number is divided by 2, 3, 4, or 5, the respective remainders are 1, 2, 3, and 4. What is the least natural number that satisfies these conditions?

8. A banquet hall has just two sizes of tables. One size seats exactly 5 people and the other size seats exactly 8 people. At tonight's banquet, exactly 79 people will be seated at less than one dozen tables and there will be no empty places. How many tables of each size will there be at the banquet?

9. ***For The Adventurous***

    If a number is divided by 3, 4, 5 or 6, there will be a remainder of 1 in each case. If the number is also exactly divisible by 7, what is the smallest value that the number could have?

    (*Solutions are on pages 164-165.*)

3. Divisibility

In the following sections the word **number** refers to a natural number.

3.1 Divisibility By 2, 5, 10, and 100
One for the Books

> **The pages of a certain book are numbered consecutively from 1 to 300.
> How many page numbers contain the digit 5 and are also divisible by 5?**

A number is DIVISIBLE by another number if their quotient is a whole number and the remainder is zero.. You may recall that there are "tests" that can help you determine certain divisibility properties of numbers without going through lengthy calculations. The following are some simple tests that may be familiar to you.

Number	Divisibility Test
2	The units digit is 0, 2, 4, 6, or 8.
5	The units digit is 0 or 5.
10	The units digit is 0.
100	The units and tens digits are **both** 0.

One way to solve the problem is to list in order all the numbers from 1 to 300 that are divisible by 5 and then remove those listed numbers that do not contain the digit 5. A more effective way is to use the divisibility test for 5 in the table and to consider each case separately.

The units digit is 5. All such numbers will satisfy the conditions of the problem. We know that every set of ten consecutive numbers contains exactly one number whose units digit is 5. Since three hundred page numbers contain thirty sets of ten consecutive numbers, there are thirty different page numbers whose ones' digit is 5.

The units digit is 0. Such numbers will satisfy the conditions of the problem only if they have the digit 5 in the tens place. There are only three of these: 50, 150 and 250.

Answer: **There are thirty-three page numbers from 1 to 300 that contain the digit 5 and that are also divisible by 5.**

★ Problems ★

1. The pages of a certain book are numbered consecutively from 1 to 500. How many page numbers meet each of the following sets of conditions?
   a. The page numbers contain the digit 5 and are also divisible by 5.
   b. The page numbers contain the digit 5 and are not divisible by 5.
   c. The page numbers do not contain the digit 5 but are divisible by 5.

2. All whole numbers can be classified as either odd or even. If the number is divisible by 2 it is EVEN; if the number is not divisible by 2 it is ODD. Suppose that in each of the following sets the numbers are added. Is the sum even or odd?
   a. two even numbers
   b. two odd numbers
   c. one even number and one odd number
   d. three even numbers
   e. three odd numbers
   f. ninety-nine odd numbers and one even number
   g. thirteen even numbers and twenty odd numbers

3. Suppose that the numbers in each of the sets of numbers described in problem 2 are multiplied and not added. Is the product even or odd?

4. In the following tables for addition and multiplication, *E* represents any even number and *O* represents any odd number. Complete each table.

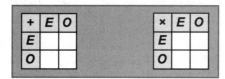

5. For each of the following books, how many page numbers contain the digit 2, but are not divisible by 2? (Assume that the pages of each book are numbered consecutively from 1 to the given number of pages).
   a. 100 pages
   b. 200 pages
   c. 300 pages

6. State a rule for divisibility by each of the following numbers.
   a. 1000
   b. 10,000
   c. 10^n, where n is any whole-number exponent.
   (*Hint:* Notice that $10 = 10^1$, $100 = 10^2$, $1000 = 10^3$, $10,000 = 10^4$, and so on).

7. How many factors does each of the following numbers have?
   a. 1000   b. 10,000   c. 10^n

(Solutions are on pages 166-167.)

3.2 Divisibility Principle For Sums And Differences
The "Week" Link

Does a period of 329 days form a whole number of 7-day weeks?

Notice that this problem does not require you to find *how many* 7-day weeks there may be. Rather, you are only asked whether 329 days forms a *whole number* of 7-day weeks. Therefore, you need only to determine if 329 is divisible by 7.

Obviously, you could solve the problem by performing the division $7\overline{)329}$ to find if the remainder is zero. However, let's use this problem as an opportunity to explore a basic principle of divisibility.

The number 329 can be written as $280 + 49$. We know that 280 and 49 are each divisible by 7: $280 = 7 \times 40$ and $49 = 7 \times 7$. The distributive property of multiplication over division now helps us make this observation.

$$\begin{aligned} 329 &= 280 + 49 \\ &= 7 \times 40 + 7 \times 7 \\ &= 7 \times (40 + 7) \\ 329 &= 7 \times 47 \end{aligned}$$

Since 329 can be written as 7×47, 329 is divisible by 7.

Answer: **A period of 329 days does form a whole number of 7-day weeks.**

The observations that we made in solving this problem are an example of applying a general rule that we shall call the DIVISIBILITY PRINCIPLE FOR SUMS AND DIFFERENCES.

> **For whole numbers *a*, *b*, and *d*, if *a* and *b* are each divisible by *d*, then the sum and the difference of *a* and *b* are each divisible by *d*.**

The following is a related principle:

> **For whole numbers *a*, *b*, and *d*, if *a* is divisible by *d* but *b* is not, then neither the sum nor the difference of *a* and *b* is divisible by *d*.**

★ Problems ★

1. Determine if each of the following sums and differences is divisible by 7.
   a. $56 + 21$ b. $42 + 65$ c. $210 - 49$ d. $770 - 540$

2. Does each of the following periods of days form a whole number of 7-day weeks? Show how to use the divisibility principle for sums and differences to determine the answer without dividing.
   a. 98 days   b. 154 days   c. 133 days   d. 693 days

3. Use the divisibility principle for sums and differences to determine if each of the following numbers is divisible by 11.
   a. 253   b. 784   c. 6589   d. 8777

4. Suppose that a person was born in 1945. Will the number of the year of that person's 62ⁿᵈ birthday be divisible by 5? Explain.

5. Neither 40 nor 32 is divisible by 9. However, the sum $40 + 32 = 72$ is divisible by 9. Does this contradict the divisibility principle for sums and differences?

6. Explain how the divisibility principle for sums and differences is the basis for the divisibility test for 5 as discussed on page 65.

7. How can you determine if a whole number is divisible by 25 without dividing?

8. How can you determine if a whole number is divisible by 125 without dividing?

(Solutions are on pages 167-168.)

3.3 Divisibility by Powers of 2
The Packaging Problem

A toy distributor has to package 19,836,472 marbles in boxes that will each contain 8 marbles. Will any marbles be left over?

We could of course divide 19,836,472 by 8 to see if there is a remainder. However, let's examine a different way to answer the question.

A fact that is useful in this situation is that 1000 is divisible by 8 ($1000 \div 8 = 125$). Let's rewrite the number of marbles as the following sum: $19,836,472 = 19,836,000 + 472$.

The left addend is a multiple of 1000, and so it is divisible by 8. The right addend is also divisible by 8, since $472 \div 8 = 59$. Then according to the divisibility principle for sums, 19,836,472 is divisible by 8.

Answer: **When packaged in boxes of 8, no marbles will be left over.**

Suppose that the toy distributor wants to package the 19,836,472 marbles in boxes that each contain *16* marbles. Will any marbles be left over?

In this case, the fact that is useful to us is that 10,000 is divisible by 16 (that is, $10,000 \div 16 = 625$). Let's rewrite the number of marbles as a different sum: $19,836,472 = 19,830,000 + 6472$.

The left addend is a multiple of 10,000, and so it is divisible by 16. The right addend, however, is *not* divisible by 16, since $6472 \div 16 = 404$ R8. Therefore, 19,836,472 is *not* divisible by 16.

Answer: **When packaged in boxes of 16, there will be marbles left over. Specifically, the number of marbles that will be left over is 8.**

Look back at the packaging problems. What do 8 and 16 have in common? Did you notice that both are powers of 2? That is, $8 = 2^3$ and $16 = 2^4$. When we tested for divisibility by 8, or 2^3, we needed to test just the number formed by the last 3 digits. When we tested for divisibility by 16, or 2^4, we needed to test just the number formed by the last 4 digits. This suggests the following table of tests for divisibility by powers of 2.

Number	Divisibility Test
$2 = 2^1$	The number formed by the last **1** digit is divisible by 2.
$4 = 2^2$	The number formed by the last **2** digits is divisible by 4.
$8 = 2^3$	The number formed by the last **3** digits is divisible by 8.
$16 = 2^4$	The number formed by the last **4** digits is divisible by 16.

★ **Problems** ★

1. Can each of the following numbers of marbles be packaged in boxes that each contain 16 marbles with none left over?
   a. 841,600   b. 1,403,280   c. 250,036

2. Suppose that marbles are packaged in boxes, that each contain 32 marbles.
   a. Use the pattern from the table above to state a test for divisibility by 32.
   b. Can 100,032 marbles be packaged in boxes that each contain 32 marbles with none left over? 2,306,420 marbles? 8,732,128 marbles?

3. Helsinki, Finland was the site of the Summer Olympic games either in 1952 or in 1954. Can you determine which is the correct year without consulting any reference?

4. After 25 tons of silver ore were processed, 2,197,216 ounces of pure silver were extracted. If the pure silver is then cast into one-pound ingots, will any pure silver be left over?

5. What values of the missing digit (■) will make each of the following numbers divisible by 4? by 8?
   a. 47■6   b. 27,■12   c. 732,■82

6. Replace the missing digit in 1,876,9■2 so that the resulting number is divisible by 16.

7. A four-digit number contains each of the digits 1, 4, 5, and 7, but not necessarily in that order. Can any of the numbers be divisible by 4?

8. Which of the three-digit numbers whose digits are 6, 7, and 8 is divisible by 8?

9. List all four-digit numbers that contain each of the digits 1, 2, 3, and 4, and that are also divisible by 4.

10. The pages of a certain book are numbered consecutively from 1 to 1000. How many page numbers have the digit 2 in the units place and are also divisible by 8?

11. A one hundred-digit number ends in the three-digit number 652. Could this number be divisible by 16? Explain.

(Solutions are on pages 169-170.)

3.4 Divisibility by 3 and 9
The Faded Bill of Sale

Suppose that you see this old bill of sale on display in a museum. You notice that some of the digits of the numbers have faded. Can you tell what the numbers must be?

One way to solve this problem is to use guess and check, testing different digits in the faded spaces until you find a combination of digits that works. However, this is not necessarily the most direct approach. Is there another way?

The problem provides a valuable clue. Since each sheep costs $9, the total cost of all the sheep must be a multiple of 9. How can you know if a number is a multiple of 9? Let's choose some examples to see if there is a pattern.

Multiples of 9	Sum of the Digits
$17 \times 9 = 153$	$1 + 5 + 3 = \boxed{9}$
$64 \times 9 = 576$	$5 + 7 + 6 = \boxed{18}$
$104 \times 9 = 936$	$9 + 3 + 6 = \boxed{18}$
$762 \times 9 = 6858$	$6 + 8 + 5 + 8 = \boxed{27}$
$4328 \times 9 = 38,952$	$3 + 8 + 9 + 5 + 2 = \boxed{27}$

What do each of the sums of the digits have in common? Do you see that each sum is itself a multiple of 9? This suggests the following divisibility test for 9.

> **TEST: A number is divisible by 9 if the sum of its digits is divisible by 9.**

Now let's return to the bill of sale. The total cost of the sheep must be a multiple of 9, and so we are looking for a number, ▮38, that is divisible by 9. We know that $8 + 3 = 11$. The next multiple of 9 greater than 11 is 18. Thus the missing digit ▮ of the total must be $18 - 11 = 7$.

Answer: **The total cost of the sheep is $738, and the number of sheep is $738 \div 9$, or 82.**

If you investigate multiples of 3 in the manner that we investigated multiples of 9, you will find that the sums of their digits are always multiples of 3. This leads us to a similar divisibility test for 3.

> **TEST: A number is divisible by 3 if the sum of its digits is divisible by 3.**

☆ *Problems* ☆

1. Replace the missing digit (■) so that the resulting number is divisible by 9.
   a. 1,456,■28   b. ■,649   c. 6,■54,321

2. For each number in problem 1, replace the missing digit so that the resulting number is divisible by 3.

3. Find all possible values for the missing digits in ■5■ so that the resulting number is divisible by 9.

4. Find all possible values for the missing digits in ■5■ so that the resulting number is divisible by 3.

5. How is the divisibility test for 9 helpful in remembering the multiplication facts from 2×9 through 9×9?

6. Some accountants use the divisibility test for 9 to determine a possible source of error in a ledger. Answer these questions to find how they use it.
   a. Compute these differences.

$51	$685	$40,752	$382,861
− 15	− 658	− 40,572	− 328,861

   b. Is each difference in part **a** divisible by 9?
   c. If a business ledger is "off" by a number that is divisible by 9, what is a possible source of the error?

7. Suppose that one number contains the same digits as another number, but in reverse order. What is true of the difference of the two numbers? (*Hint*: Try some examples, such as 6281 and 1826.)

8. Is it possible to use each of the digits from 1 through 9 exactly once to create a nine-digit prime number? Why or why not?

(Solutions are on pages 170-171.)

3.5 *Divisibility by 11*
Search for a Pattern

These numbers are each divisible by 11:
   99,   792,   4015,   87,263,   380,919,   1,644,192.
What do these numbers have in common?

In looking for something common to all these numbers, you are in fact looking for a divisibility test for 11. Where do you begin? You will probably find that organization is important in solving a problem such as this. Start by considering a number of simple cases, then proceed to more difficult ones and see if a pattern emerges along the way.

Let's begin with the two-digit numbers that are divisible by 11: 11, 22, 33, 44, ... , 99. They're easy to recognize, of course, because the two digits are the same. This leads to the observation that the sum of the digits for each number varies, but the *difference* of the digits is always 0.

Can we relate this observation in any way to three-digit numbers? Let's look at these numbers, which are all divisible by 11.

> 121   319   627   792

Again, the sum of the digits for each number varies. A difference of the digits for each number also seems to have no meaning, since each number has three digits. Before you read on, though, try considering *both* addition and subtraction. Did you observe that when you *add* the digits in the units and hundreds places and then *subtract* the digit in the tens place, the result is either 0 or 11 for each number?

② 1 **2** 1	⑫ 3 **1** 9	⑬ 6 **2** 7	⑨ 7 **9** 2
2 − 2 = 0	12 − 1 = 11	13 − 2 = 11	9 − 9 = 0

Let's go on to look at some four-digit numbers that are divisible by 11.

> 1034   3916   4015   5060

Can you see how to apply the same pattern of sums and differences to these numbers? As before, begin by adding the digits in the units and hundreds places. Next add the digits in the tens and thousands places. Subtract one sum from the other. Once again, the difference is either 0 or 11.

④ 1 0 3 4 ④	⑮ 3 9 1 6 ④	⑤ 4 0 1 5 ⑤	⓪ 5 0 6 0 ⑪
4 − 4 = 0	15 − 4 = 11	5 − 5 = 0	11 − 0 = 11

Can you extend the pattern to the larger numbers on the next page? Each number is divisible by 11.

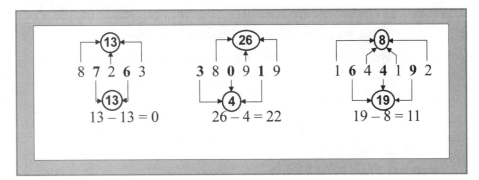

This time the differences between sums are 0, 22, and 11. Do you see that each of these differences is divisible by 11?

Let's introduce some vocabulary that will help us describe this pattern of sums and differences. We shall call the units place an **ODD PLACE** and the tens place an **EVEN PLACE**. The places to the left of the tens place are then alternately called *odd place*, *even place*, *odd place*, *even place*, and so on, as shown at the right in the diagram. We can now use this vocabulary to state the following divisibility test for 11.

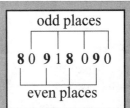

> **TEST: A number is divisible by 11 if the difference between the *sum* of the odd-place digits and the *sum* of the even-place digits is divisible by 11.**

Is 80,918,090 divisible by 11? Notice above that the sum of its odd-place digits is $0 + 1 + 0 + 0 = 1$. The sum of its even-place digits is $8 + 9 + 8 + 9 = 34$. The difference of these sums is $34 - 1 = 33$, which is divisible by 11.

Answer: **The number 80,918,090 is divisible by 11.**

★ *Problems* ★

1. Use the divisibility test to determine if each number is divisible by 11.
   a. 1826   b. 7259   c. 82,907   d. 1,724,943

2. Replace ▇, the missing digit, so that the resulting number is divisible by 11.
   a. 93▇   b. 3,7▇9   c. 39,▇21   d. ▇0,819

3. Replace the missing digits in ▇5▇ so that the resulting number is divisible by 11. How many different answers can you find?

4. A four-digit number contains the digits 1, 4, 7, and 9, but not in that order. Arrange these digits so that the resulting number is divisible by 11. In how many ways can this be done?

5. Find the sum of all four-digit numbers such that each contains the digits 1, 2, 3, and 4, and that are also divisible by 11.

6. The number 1,234,567 is not divisible by 11, but you can change the order of the digits to form numbers that are divisible by 11. Find one such number.

7. There are 1500 students in the freshman class of Central State College. In the autumn they play intramural football with 11 freshmen on each team. If each freshman can play on just one team, what is the greatest number of freshmen that can play?

(Solutions are on pages 172-173.)

3.6 Combined Divisibility
Cheaper by the Dozen

Farmer Brown's hens produced 9762 eggs today. Can these eggs be packed in cartons that each contain exactly one dozen eggs with none left over?

Since there are 12 eggs in a dozen, one way to solve this problem is to perform the division $9762 \div 12$ to see if there is a remainder. However, let's use this problem to see how divisibility tests might be used.

Notice that $12 = 3 \times 4$. To test 9762 for divisibility by 12, we need to test for divisibility *both* by 3 *and* by 4.

9762 is divisible by 3, since the sum of its digits $(9 + 7 + 6 + 2 = 24)$ is a multiple of 3.

9762 is *not* divisible by 4, since the number formed by its last two digits (62) is not divisible by 4.

Therefore, 9762 is *not* divisible by 12.

Answer: **The 9762 eggs cannot be packed in cartons containing exactly one dozen eggs with none left over.**

★ Problems ★

1. Can each of the following numbers of eggs be packed in cartons that each contain exactly one dozen eggs with none left over?
    a. 5824   b. 7416   c. 12,054   d. 428,676

2. Can Farmer Brown's 9762 eggs be packed in cartons that each contain exactly one half dozen eggs with none left over?

3. Is each of the following numbers divisible by 18?
    a. 972   b. 8946   c. 9081   d. 15,018

4. Describe a divisibility test for 15.

5. For each of the following, find all pairs of replacements for the missing digits ▌ so that the resulting number meets the given condition.
    a. ▌23▌ is divisible by 45.
    b. ▌31▌ is divisible by 72.
    c. ▌47▌ is divisible by 36.
    d. ▌47▌ is divisible by 55.

6. List all the three-digit numbers that are divisible by 99.

(Solutions are on page 173.)

3.7 Divisibility by 7, 11, and 13
License Plate Lookout

When traveling with her family, Helen enjoys looking at the license plates of passing cars to see if she can identify any special properties of the numbers on them. When she saw this license plate she said, "That number is divisible by 7 and by 13, but it's not divisible by 11." How can you determine this without dividing?

It would seem that Helen knows one special test that determines divisibility by all three numbers. To discover this test, let's consider the fact that $7 \times 11 \times 13 = 1001$. Do you see that, since 1001 is divisible by 7, 11, and 13, any multiple of 1001 is also divisible by 7, 11, and 13? Many multiples of 1001, such as 5005, 27,027, and 863,863, are easy to recognize and therefore are easy to test for divisibility by 7, 11, and 13.

How was Helen able to apply this test to the license plate number above? She may have recognized that $7 \times 13 = 91$ and that $497,406 = 497,497 - 91$, then used this special divisibility test in combination with the divisibility principle for sums and differences.

Answer: **497,497 and 91 are each divisible by 7 and by 13, so 497,406 is divisible by 7 and by 13.**
(497,497 is divisible by 11, but 91 is not divisible by 11, so 497,406 is not divisible by 11.)

Notice that the divisibility test for 11 discussed on pages 71-73 also applies to divisibility tests of 1001 and multiples of 1001.

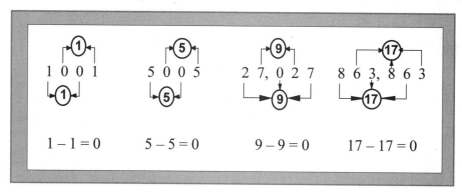

★ Problems ★

1. Use the special divisibility test to determine if each of the following numbers is divisible by 7, by 11, and by 13.

    a. 180,124 b. 621,595 c. 236,346

    d. 430,445 e. 583,660 f. 900,869

    g. 98,126 h. 63,078 i. 52,143

2. The number of the year 2002 has four different prime factors. What are they?

3. What is the least number that has six different prime factors?

4. The special test for divisibility by 7, 11, and 13 can be extended to numbers with more than six digits by using this procedure.

    a. Starting at the right, place the digits in groups of three.

    b. Working from the right, alternately subtract and add the numbers formed by the groups of three digits.

    c. Test the final result for divisibility by 7, 11, or 13.

    Use the above procedure to test each of the following numbers for divisibility by 7, 11, and 13.

    a. 270,060,340 b. 600,515,134 c. 29,482,531

5. The budget figure $125,811,738 has been allocated for thirteen different departments. Can the departments receive equal amounts?

(Solutions are on pages 173-175.)

For a further discussion of the divisiblity tests for 3, 9, and 11,
see Appendix 5 on pages 257-263.

4. Fractions

4.1 Unit Fractions
Ancient Arithmetic

The Rhind Papyrus is an ancient document containing evidence that fractions were in use as early as four thousand years ago in the Egyptian system of numeration. However, the Egyptians seemed to work primarily with the UNIT FRACTION, which is a fraction with a numerator of 1 and a denominator that is any counting number. It is believed that they tried to avoid computational difficulties by representing all fractions except $\frac{2}{3}$ as the *sum* of unit fractions. The Papyrus begins with a table that shows how to write fractions of the form $\frac{2}{n}$ as the sum of distinct unit fractions for all odd values of n from 5 to 101. Here are a few of the sums.

$$\frac{2}{5} = \frac{1}{3} + \frac{1}{15} \qquad \frac{2}{7} = \frac{1}{4} + \frac{1}{28} \qquad \frac{2}{11} = \frac{1}{6} + \frac{1}{66}$$

There are many interesting theories to explain how the Egyptians obtained these sums. One of the theories is based on a pattern among the denominators. What is this pattern? How might the pattern be used to write $\frac{2}{13}$ as the sum of two distinct unit fractions?

As you study the given sums, one element of the pattern may seem fairly obvious. Did you observe that the denominator of the second unit fraction is the product of the denominator of the given fraction and the denominator of the first unit fraction?

$$5 \times 3 = 15 \qquad 7 \times 4 = 28 \qquad 11 \times 6 = 66$$

The problem that remains is how to find the denominator of the first unit fraction. Study the equations below the first paragraph. Do you see that the denominator of the first unit fraction is equal to one-half of the sum of the denominator of the given fraction and 1?

$$\frac{1}{2} \times (\mathbf{5} + 1) = \mathbf{3} \qquad \frac{1}{2} \times (\mathbf{7} + 1) = \mathbf{4} \qquad \frac{1}{2} \times (\mathbf{11} + 1) = \mathbf{6}$$

For $\frac{2}{13}$, the denominator of the first unit fraction is $\frac{1}{2} \times (\mathbf{13} + 1) = 7$. This means that the denominator of the second unit fraction is $13 \times 7 = 91$.

Answer: $\frac{2}{13} = \frac{1}{7} + \frac{1}{91}$

The Egyptians' accomplishments with unit fractions lead us to a related question: can a unit fraction itself be written as the sum of two other unit fractions? Let's investigate by trying to find such sums for $\frac{1}{2}$, $\frac{1}{3}$, and $\frac{1}{5}$.

To begin with, every unit fraction can be written as the sum of two *equal* unit fractions, like this.

$$\frac{1}{2} = \frac{1}{4} + \frac{1}{4} \qquad\qquad \frac{1}{3} = \frac{1}{6} + \frac{1}{6} \qquad\qquad \frac{1}{5} = \frac{1}{10} + \frac{1}{10}$$

Can you describe these results in general terms? Use a variable such as n to represent the denominator of the original unit fraction. Is this your conclusion?

$$\blacklozenge \quad \frac{1}{n} = \frac{1}{2n} + \frac{1}{2n}$$

However, this is not the only type of sum that is possible. An unusual property of any unit fraction is that it also can be written as the sum of two *distinct* unit fractions. Look at these examples.

$$\frac{1}{2} = \frac{1}{3} + \frac{1}{6} \qquad\qquad \frac{1}{3} = \frac{1}{4} + \frac{1}{12} \qquad\qquad \frac{1}{5} = \frac{1}{6} + \frac{1}{30}$$

Can you detect a pattern among these equalities? Once again, try to describe it before reading ahead, using the variable n to represent the denominator of the original unit fraction. Did you get this result?

$$\blacklozenge \quad \frac{1}{n} = \frac{1}{n+1} + \frac{1}{n(n+1)}$$

This fact may be referred to as the **UNIT FRACTION PRINCIPLE.**

It can be shown that the Egyptian Method and the Unit Fraction Principle are equivalent.

★ *Problems* ★

1. Use the Egyptian Method discussed for $\frac{2}{n}$ to write each of the following fractions as the sum of two distinct unit fractions. Check your results.
   a. $\frac{2}{3}$ b. $\frac{2}{9}$ c. $\frac{2}{15}$ d. $\frac{2}{25}$

2. Use the unit fraction principle to write each of the following unit fractions as the sum of two distinct unit fractions. Check your results.
   a. $\frac{1}{4}$ b. $\frac{1}{7}$ c. $\frac{1}{10}$ d. $\frac{1}{11}$

3. Write $\frac{1}{3}$ as the indicated sum of *four* distinct unit fractions.

4. Show two ways to write $\frac{1}{2}$ as the indicated sum of three distinct unit fractions.

5. **CONSECUTIVE UNIT FRACTIONS** are unit fractions whose denominators are consecutive numbers, such as $\frac{1}{3}$, $\frac{1}{4}$, $\frac{1}{5}$, and $\frac{1}{6}$. An immediate consequence of the unit fraction principle is the following principle for the *difference* of two consecutive unit fractions.

$$\frac{1}{n} - \frac{1}{n+1} = \frac{1}{n(n+1)}$$

Use this fact to compute each of the following differences.

    a. $\frac{1}{2} - \frac{1}{3}$ b. $\frac{1}{4} - \frac{1}{5}$ c. $\frac{1}{7} - \frac{1}{8}$ d. $\frac{1}{9} - \frac{1}{10}$

6. Write each of $\frac{1}{12}$ and $\frac{1}{42}$ as the difference of two consecutive unit fractions.

7. Write the following sum as a simple fraction in lowest terms.

    a. $\frac{1}{1\times2} + \frac{1}{2\times3} + \frac{1}{3\times4} + \cdots + \frac{1}{9\times10}$ b. $\frac{1}{1\times3} + \frac{1}{3\times5} + \frac{1}{5\times7} + \cdots + \frac{1}{9\times11}$

    Hint: Express each fraction as the difference of two unit fractions.

8. When the denominator of a unit fraction is a composite number, it is possible to write that unit fraction as the indicated sum of two distinct unit fractions in many different ways. If we choose a and b to represent any factor pair for the composite number, the following statements can be shown to be true.

$$\blacklozenge \quad \frac{1}{ab} = \frac{1}{a(a+b)} + \frac{1}{b(a+b)}$$

$$\blacklozenge \quad \frac{1}{ab} = \frac{1}{a(b+1)} + \frac{1}{ab(b+1)}$$

$$\blacklozenge \quad \frac{1}{ab} = \frac{1}{b(a+1)} + \frac{1}{ab(a+1)}$$

Write each of the following unit fractions as the indicated sum of two unit fractions in each of the five ways shown above.

    a. $\frac{1}{6}$ b. $\frac{1}{10}$ c. $\frac{1}{4}$

9. Use Guess and Check to write each of the following fractions as the indicated sum of two distinct unit fractions.

    a. $\frac{3}{4}$ b. $\frac{5}{6}$ c. $\frac{3}{5}$ d. $\frac{2}{7}$

10. ***For The Adventurous:***

    Suppose the unit fraction $\frac{1}{12} = \frac{1}{12+a} + \frac{1}{12+b}$ where a and b are natural numbers.

    i. Use the given equations to find the product of a and b.

    ii. If a is less than or equal to b, list the values that a and b can have in the form (a,b).

    iii. Use the listed values of a and b to replace a and b in the given equation. How many different equations can be obtained?

(Solutions are on pages 176-179.)

4.2 Complex Fractions
Heart Arithmetic

Suppose that there is a different kind of arithmetic in which the expression $a \heartsuit b$ has the same meaning as the expression $\frac{a}{b}$ in our arithmetic. What is the value of $\frac{2}{3} \heartsuit \frac{4}{7}$ written as a simple fraction in lowest terms?

To begin with, let's rewrite $\frac{2}{3} \heartsuit \frac{4}{7}$ using the meaning given in the problem.

$$\frac{2}{3} \heartsuit \frac{4}{7} = \frac{\frac{2}{3}}{\frac{4}{7}}$$

Obviously, the result is not a simple fraction. In fact, a fraction such as this in which either the numerator or denominator itself contains a fraction is called a COMPLEX FRACTION. Can we find a simple fraction value for a complex fraction?

Recall that the value of any fraction is not changed if you multiply *both* its numerator and denominator by the same nonzero number. For this complex fraction, let's see what happens when we multiply the numerator and denominator by the reciprocal of the fraction in the denominator.

$$\frac{\frac{2}{3}}{\frac{4}{7}} = \frac{\frac{2}{3} \times \frac{7}{4}}{\frac{4}{7} \times \frac{7}{4}} = \frac{\frac{14}{12}}{1} = \frac{14}{12} = \frac{7}{6}$$

If you wish, you could choose a technique that involves multiplying both the numerator and denominator of the complex fraction by the LCM of the two denominators, 3 and 7, or by 21. Notice that the result is the same.

$$\frac{\frac{2}{3}}{\frac{4}{7}} = \frac{\frac{2}{3} \times 21}{\frac{4}{7} \times 21} = \frac{14}{12} = \frac{7}{6}$$

***Answer*: As a simple fraction in lowest terms, the value of $\frac{2}{3} \heartsuit \frac{4}{7} = \frac{7}{6}$.**

★ *Problems* ★

1. Suppose that $a \heartsuit b$ is defined as $\frac{a}{b}$. What is the value of each of the following written as a simple fraction in lowest terms?

    a. $\frac{3}{4} \heartsuit \frac{4}{5}$ b. $\frac{5}{6} \heartsuit \frac{3}{8}$ c. $1\frac{1}{3} \heartsuit 2\frac{1}{4}$ d. $\frac{1}{2} \heartsuit (\frac{1}{3} \heartsuit \frac{1}{4})$

2. Suppose that $a \blacklozenge b$ is defined as $\frac{b}{a}$. What is the value of each of the expressions in problem 1 in lowest terms if each $\heartsuit$ is changed to $\blacklozenge$?

3. What is the value of each of the following complex fractions written as a simple fraction in lowest terms?

    a. $\dfrac{1}{\frac{1}{2}}$ b. $\dfrac{1}{\frac{3}{5}}$ c. $\dfrac{1}{2\frac{1}{4}}$ d. $\dfrac{1}{3.7}$

4   The reciprocal of 3 is $\frac{1}{3}$. What is the reciprocal of $\frac{1}{3}$?

5. What is the reciprocal of the reciprocal of $\frac{3}{8}$?

6. What is the value of each of the following complex fractions written as a simple fraction in lowest terms?

    a. $\dfrac{\frac{2}{5} + \frac{1}{2}}{3}$ b. $\dfrac{3}{4 + \frac{1}{5}}$ c. $\dfrac{\frac{3}{4} + \frac{1}{3}}{\frac{1}{2} + \frac{4}{5}}$ d. $\dfrac{2 - \frac{1}{2}}{2 + \frac{1}{2}}$

7. If $a = \frac{1}{2}$ and $b = \frac{1}{3}$, what is the value of each of the following expressions written as a simple fraction in lowest terms?

   a. $\dfrac{a+b}{a-b}$ b. $\dfrac{a+b}{3}$ c. $\dfrac{a-b}{4}$

8. If $a \boxplus b$ is defined as $\dfrac{a+b}{2}$, what is the value of $\frac{1}{3} \boxplus (\frac{1}{5} \boxplus \frac{1}{7})$ written as a simple fraction in lowest terms?

(Solutions are on pages 179-180.)

4.3 Extended Finite Fractions
Repeat Performance

What is the value of the expression at the right?

$$\cfrac{1}{2+\cfrac{1}{2+\cfrac{1}{2}}}$$

This expression is an example of a special type of complex fraction that is called an **EXTENDED FINITE FRACTION**. It is possible to write its value as a simple fraction. How can this be done?

Examine the expression to see if any *part* of it can be simplified. Did you observe that $2 + \frac{1}{2}$ at the bottom is equal to $2\frac{1}{2}$, or $\frac{5}{2}$? You can use this fact to rewrite the expression in a simpler form.

$$\cfrac{1}{2+\cfrac{1}{\boxed{2+\frac{1}{2}}}} = \cfrac{1}{2+\cfrac{1}{\boxed{\frac{5}{2}}}}$$

Once again, look for any part of the expression that can be simplified. Did you notice this reciprocal at the bottom?

$$\cfrac{1}{\frac{5}{2}} = \frac{2}{5}$$

You can now rewrite the expression again.

$$\cfrac{1}{2+\cfrac{\boxed{1}}{\boxed{\frac{5}{2}}}} = \cfrac{1}{2+\boxed{\frac{2}{5}}}$$

Finally, repeat the process of performing the indicated addition and evaluating the resulting reciprocal.

$$\cfrac{1}{2+\frac{2}{5}} = \cfrac{1}{2\frac{2}{5}} = \cfrac{1}{\frac{12}{5}} = \frac{5}{12}$$

> *Answer:* **Written as a simple fraction in lowest terms, the value of the given expression is $\frac{5}{12}$.**

★ **Problems** ★

1. Write each of the following expressions as a simple fraction in lowest terms.

a. $\dfrac{1}{3+\dfrac{1}{3+\frac{1}{3}}}$ b. $\dfrac{1}{1+\dfrac{1}{1+\dfrac{1}{1+\frac{1}{3}}}}$ c. $2+\dfrac{1}{1+\dfrac{1}{2}}$ d. $1+\dfrac{1}{1+\dfrac{1}{2+\frac{1}{3}}}$

2. It is possible to write any simple fraction as a extended finite fraction by simply reversing the process we discussed in this section. Here is an example.

$$\frac{5}{17}=\frac{1}{\dfrac{17}{5}}=\frac{1}{3+\dfrac{2}{5}}=\frac{1}{3+\dfrac{1}{\frac{5}{2}}}=\frac{1}{3+\dfrac{1}{2+\frac{1}{2}}}$$

Write each of these simple fractions as an extended fraction. (*Hint*: An extended finite fraction terminates when a unit fraction occurs in one of the denominators.)

a. $\frac{3}{7}$ b. $\frac{13}{30}$ c. $\frac{8}{13}$ d. $\frac{14}{3}$

(*Solutions are on pages 180-181.*)

4.4 Fractional Parts
What's My Number?

If $\frac{2}{3}$ of my number is 18, what's my number?

Many methods can be used to solve problems that involve fractional parts of whole numbers. One strategy that may be especially helpful for young children is drawing a diagram. Therefore, let's see how to approach this problem using a figure such as a rectangle to represent the unknown number.

Since the fraction in the problem is *two-thirds,* separate the rectangle into three congruent parts. Each part represents one-third of the number.

Now place the given information on the diagram, and add any conclusions you can draw from this information.

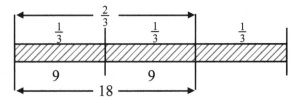

Fractional parts:

Numerical value of parts:

Since two congruent parts of the rectangle represent a total value of 18, do you see that each of these parts should be labeled with a value of 9? This means that the third congruent part must also have a value of 9, and therefore the value represented by the entire rectangle is $3 \times 9 = 27$.

***Answer*: If $\frac{2}{3}$ of a number is 18, the number must be 27.**

☆ Problems ☆

1. What's my number?
   a. $\frac{3}{5}$ of my number is 21.
   b. $\frac{2}{7}$ of my number is 14.
   c. The product of $1\frac{1}{2}$ and my number is 12.
   d. If 56 is added to $\frac{1}{4}$ of my number, the result is the double of my number.
   e. If 6 is added to $2\frac{1}{2}$ times my number, the result is the triple of my number.
   f. If my number is multiplied by 4, the result is the same as adding 15 to $3\frac{1}{4}$ times my number.

2. Dave spent $\frac{2}{5}$ of his money and then had $12 left. How much money did Dave originally have?

3. Anne spent $\frac{1}{3}$ of her money and then lost $\frac{1}{2}$ of what she had left. She then had only 10¢. How much money did Anne originally have?

4. Insert two fractions between $\frac{1}{6}$ and $\frac{1}{5}$ so that the four fractions are in arithmetic sequence. (Recall that arithmetic sequences were discussed in Section 1.1 on pages 38-41.)

5. Insert three fractions between $\frac{1}{3}$ and $\frac{1}{2}$ so that the five fractions are in arithmetic sequence.

6. There is an old story that a certain farmer died, leaving 17 cows. According to the terms of the will, the farmer's eldest child was to receive $\frac{1}{2}$ of the cows, the second child was to receive $\frac{1}{3}$ of the cows, and the youngest child was to receive $\frac{1}{9}$ of the cows. The children were puzzled about how to carry out the terms of their father's will, since none of these fractional parts of 17 cows was a whole number. Finally, a generous neighbor offered to lend a cow to the children. They then had 18 cows; $\frac{1}{2}$ of 18 cows was 9 cows, $\frac{1}{3}$ of 18 cows was 6 cows, and $\frac{1}{9}$ of 18 cows was 2 cows. The total, $9 + 6 + 2$, was the original 17 cows. The 18th cow remained for the children to return to the neighbor with their thanks. How was this possible?

(Solutions are on pages 181-182.)

Note that each of the problems in this section can also be solved by using algebra.

5. Geometry and Measurement

5.1 Squares and Rectangles
The Checkerboard Problem

How many squares are on a checkerboard?

Many people count just the small squares and answer 64. Others remember that the entire board is one large square and answer 65. In fact, there are more than 200 distinct squares! Where are all these other squares? How do we count them?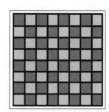

One way to solve a problem that may seem complicated is to consider one or more problems that are related, but simpler. Let's begin by imagining that there are simpler checkerboards and counting the squares on them.

The figures below show a series of simpler checkerboards. Each board is a square, and each, of the small boxes within the boards is also a square. Notice that we name the boards according to the lengths of their sides: a 1 by 1 board measures 1 square along each side, a 2 by 2 board measures 2 squares along each side, and so on.

1 by 1	2 by 2	3 by 3	4 by 4

Clearly, there is only one square in the first figure. How many squares are in the second figure? No, not just four. We'll have to remember to count the large square. There are five squares in all.

Finding the number of squares on a 3 by 3 checkerboard may be more difficult. How many different *sizes* of squares are there? Do you see that there are three sizes: 1 by 1, 2 by 2, and 3 by 3? Now let's count the number of each of the different-sized squares and use a table to record the results.

SQUARES ON A 3 BY 3 CHECKERBOARD	
Size of Square	Number of Squares
1 by 1	9
2 by 2	4
3 by 3	1
Total	**14**

Some people may experience difficulty in counting the 2 by 2 squares. It may help to visualize these squares if we mask the board as shown below. In the classroom, this can be done very effectively by using translucent colored screens on an overhead projector.

Finding the number of squares on a 4 by 4 checkerboard is only slightly more complicated.

SQUARES ON A 4 BY 4 CHECKERBOARD	
Size of Square	**Number of Squares**
1 by 1	16
2 by 2	9
3 by 3	4
4 by 4	1
Total	**30**

To visualize the nine 2 by 2 squares, we can again use a masking technique. You may find it helpful to focus your attention on two adjacent rows at a time, as shown below.

Similarly, to find the four 3 by 3 squares it may help you to look at *three* adjacent rows at a time.

Now let's consider a 5 by 5 checkerboard, How many squares are on it? You could draw a picture and begin to count again, but this process could become time-consuming. When you reach a point such as this, it is sometimes helpful to organize and examine the facts you already know. Let's make a single table of all the data collected so far.

NUMBER OF SQUARES ON A CHECKERBOARD				
	Type of Checkerboard			
Size of Square	**1 by 1**	**2 by 2**	**3 by 3**	**4 by 4**
1 by 1	1	4	9	16
2 by 2		1	4	9
3 by 3			1	4
4 by 4				1
Totals	**1**	**5**	**14**	**30**

Within the structure of the table, a pattern begins to emerge. Do you see that certain numbers repeat along the diagonals of the table? Furthermore, observe that each of these numbers is a perfect-square number: $1 = 1^2$, $4 = 2^2$, $9 = 3^2$, and $16 = 4^2$. This suggests a second way to display the data, as shown in the table below. Notice that we were able to extend the pattern to learn without counting that there are 55 squares on a 5 by 5 checkerboard.

NUMBER OF SQUARES ON A CHECKERBOARD					
	Type of Checkerboard				
Size of Square	**1 by 1**	**2 by 2**	**3 by 3**	**4 by 4**	**5 by 5**
1 by 1	1^2	2^2	3^2	4^2	5^2
2 by 2		1^2	2^2	3^2	4^2
3 by 3			1^2	2^2	3^2
4 by 4				1^2	2^2
5 by 5					1^2
Totals	**1**	**5**	**14**	**30**	**55**

You can now use this pattern to solve the original checkerboard problem. A standard checkerboard is an 8 by 8 board. If the pattern in the table were extended, what would be the entries in the "8 by 8" column? Do you agree that the entries will be the squares of each of the whole numbers from 8 down to 1?

$$8^2 + 7^2 + 6^2 + 5^2 + 4^2 + 3^2 + 2^2 + 1^2 = 204$$

***Answer:* There are 204 squares on an 8 by 8 checkerboard.**

★ *Problems* ★

1. Suppose that you have a 6 by 6 checkerboard. How many squares of each of the following sizes are on it?
   a. 1 by 1   b. 2 by 2   c. 3 by 3   d. 4 by 4   e. 5 by 5   f. 6 by 6

2. What is the total number of squares on each of these checkerboards?
   a. 6 by 6   b. 7 by 7   c. 9 by 9   d. 10 by 10

3. Each small box is a square in the following diagrams. What is the total number of squares in each figure?
   a.   b.   c.   d.

4. Each small box is a square. What is the total number of *rectangles* in each figure? (A square is a type of rectangle.) Can you find a pattern?
   a. ☐   b. ☐☐   c. ☐☐☐

   d. ☐☐☐☐   e. ☐☐☐☐☐   f. ☐☐☐☐☐☐

5. What is the total number of rectangles in each figure?
   a.   b.   c.   d.

(Solutions are on page 183.)

5.2 *Triangles*
The Triangle Tangle

How many triangles are in this picture?

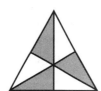

After our discussion of the checkerboard problem in Section 5.1, you may immediately realize that the answer is not simply 6 or 7. The triangle tangle is similar to the checkerboard problem in many ways. However, the arrangement of the triangles suggests that a different method of counting may be appropriate to this situation.

One counting device is that of using a different letter of the alphabet to identify each of the distinct parts formed by the lines of the figure. One way to do this is shown in the figure on the next page, in which the parts have been lettered alphabetically. As we shall see, this system is helpful in organizing information and avoiding duplications.

Clearly, each of the six parts we have identified by a letter is itself a triangle. Let's begin by calling these triangles 1-part triangles and listing them by letter: *a, b, c, d, e,* and *f.*

Using this device, other triangles in the figure may be described as 2-part triangles. Can you identify them? There are three, as shown below. We will name these triangles by combining the letters of the two parts that form them: *fa, bc,* and *de.*

How many 3-part triangles are there? Can you name them? There are six: *abc, bcd, cde, def, efa,* and *fab.*

 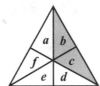

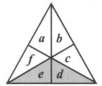 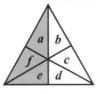

Can you see that there are no 4-part or 5-part triangles? However, the listing is not yet complete. Remember that the entire figure is a triangle, so that there is one 6-part triangle: *abcdef.*

Notice that in all the listings the letters for the parts have been named in a clockwise order. This practice makes it easier to compare listings and to reduce the occurrence of repetitions.

Let's summarize by organizing all the data into one table.

TRIANGLE TANGLE	
Type of Triangle	**Number of Triangles**
1-part	6
2-part	3
3-part	6
6-part	1
TOTAL	16

***Answer:* Altogether, there are 16 triangles in the picture on page 87.**

★ **Problems** ★

1. What is the total number of triangles in each figure? List them.

a.   b.   c.   d.

2. What is the total number of triangles in each figure? Can you find a pattern?

a.  b.  c.

d.  e.   f.

3. How do your answers to problem 2 above compare with your answers to problem 4 on page 87?

4. What is the total number of triangles in each figure?

a. △ b. △ c. △ d. △

(Solutions are on pages 184-185.)

5.3 Circles
Pieces of Pie

Can you cut a pie into seven pieces with just three straight cuts?

People frequently think that this problem is impossible. Do you? If you restrict yourself to the conventional way of cutting a pie, then it is indeed impossible. The most you can get is six pieces, as shown at the right.

Sometimes we hinder our own problem solving efforts by making false assumptions. In this case, you may have incorrectly assumed that the pieces of pie must be equal in size. Notice that this is *not* a condition of the problem. Removing this unnecessary restriction opens a new line of thinking to us.

Let's look at the problem again. One way to cut the pie is to make three cuts independent of each other, with no cut intersecting any other. There are many ways to place these cuts, but as these placements show, they produce only four pieces of pie.

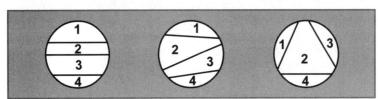

Therefore, if we are to get seven pieces of pie, the cuts cannot be independent. Let's see what happens if we place the cuts so that two of them intersect each other.

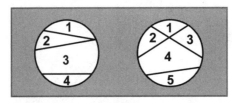

Notice that the cuts may intersect either at the edge of the pie or inside the pie. When the cuts intersect inside, more pieces are formed. When only two cuts intersect, though, the greatest number of pieces you can get is five. Thus it would seem that all three cuts must intersect each other if we are to get seven pieces.

Answer: **When the three cuts intersect in pairs at different points *inside* the pie, there are seven pieces of pie. The figure at the right shows one possible placement of the three cuts.**

★ *Problems* ★

1. What is the greatest number of pieces of pie you can get with the following number of straight cuts?
   a. one   b. two   c. four   d. five

2. Complete the table using your answers to problem 1.

Number of Straight Cuts	Greatest Number of Pieces of Pie
0	1
1	?
2	?
3	7
4	?
5	?

3. Use the completed table from problem 2 to answer the following questions.
   a. Subtract each number in the right-hand column from the number just below it. If your answers are correct, there is a pattern. What is it?
   b. What is the greatest number of pieces of pie you can get if you make eight straight cuts? Use the pattern to find the answer.

4. What is the greatest number of pieces of pie you can get if you make three straight cuts in a pie that is shaped like a *rectangle?*

5. When two circles intersect, they may do so in either one or two points. If they intersect in only one point they form two regions. If they intersect in two points they form three regions.

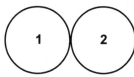 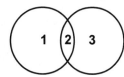

   a. What is the greatest number of regions formed when three circles intersect in a common region?
   b. Complete the table.

Number of Intersecting Circles	Greatest Number of Regions Formed
1	1
2	3
3	?
4	?
5	?

   c. What is the greatest number of non-overlapping regions formed when eight circles intersect?

6. Certain types of cheese are packaged in large "wheels" such as the one shown at the right. Show how to cut a wheel of cheese into eight *equal* pieces with just three straight cuts.

7. On page 90, the diagram accompanying the answer shows three cuts producing the seven pieces of pie. Those three cuts cross each other in three points of intersection. What is the greatest number of points of intersections you can get with the following number of straight cuts?
   a. 1   b. 2   c. 4   d. 5   e. 6   f. 8

8. On page 90, the diagram accompanying the answer shows three cuts producing the seven pieces of pie. Those three cuts partition each other into nine smaller segments. What is the greatest number of smaller segments you can get with the following number of straight cuts?
   a. 1   b. 2   c. 4   d. 5   e. 6   f. 8

(Solutions are on pages 185-186.)

5.4 *Perimeter*
The Missing Dimension

> To prepare an estimate for some work on a city lot, a builder asked the client for the dimensions of the lot.
>
> "I can't remember," said the client. "It's shaped like a rectangle, and I know that they needed ninety meters of fencing to enclose it. Oh, yes! The crew putting up the fence remarked that the lot is exactly twice as long as it is wide."
>
> "Thank you," said the builder. "That's all the information I need."
>
> How did the builder know the dimensions? Can you find the length and width of the lot?

In solving a problem like this, it is important to identify the information that is essential. The core problem can in fact be stated in a *simpler* way.

> The perimeter of a rectangle is ninety meters.
> The length is twice the width.
> Find the dimensions of the rectangle.

There are many ways to solve this problem. For example, you may use the guess and check method, somewhat like this.

The length is twice the width. Try a width of 10 m and a length of 20 m.

$$\text{Perimeter} = 10 + 20 + 10 + 20$$
$$= 60 \text{ m}$$

The first guess is too small. Try doubling the dimensions.

$$\text{Perimeter} = 20 + 40 + 20 + 40$$
$$= 120 \text{ m}$$

The second guess is too large, but now we know that the width is between 10 m and 20 m and that the length is between 20 m and 40 m. Try 15 and 30.

$$\text{Perimeter} = 15 + 30 + 15 + 30$$
$$= 90 \text{ m}$$

It works!

Answer: The width of the lot is 15 m and the length is 30 m.

Another approach to this problem involves organizing a few trial values into a table and using the table to determine a pattern. Let's begin again with a width of 10 m and a length of 20 m and see what happens as the width is *gradually* increased.

Width	10	11	12	...	?
Length	20	22	24	...	?
Perimeter	60	66	72	...	90

Do you see that, each time the width is increased by 1, the length is increased by 2 and the perimeter is increased by 6? To arrive at a perimeter of 90, you would continue the pattern by making five increases of 6 over 60, the first perimeter in the table. This means that you would also have to increase the width five times by 1 and increase the length five times by 2. This leads to a width of $10 + 5 \times 1 = 15$ and a length of $20 + 5 \times 2 = 30$.

The use of Guess and Check or a table puts this type of problem within the grasp of even very young children. There is another method of solution that involves the use of some simple algebra.

*Choose **w** to denote the width in meters. The length is twice the width, so 2**w** is the length. Now you can write and solve an equation.*

$$w + 2w + w + 2w = 90$$

$$6w = 90$$

$$\frac{6w}{6} = \frac{90}{6}$$

$$w = 15$$

Since w = 15, 2w = 30. The width is 15 m and the length is 30 m.

We have discussed three ways to approach the solution of this problem. As you read on, you may notice that some methods help to solve a problem more efficiently than others. It is important to realize, though, that the method appropriate for you is the one that you best understand and that leads you successfully to the solution.

★ **Problems** ★

1. The perimeter of a rectangular plot of land is 42 meters. What are the dimensions of the plot given each of the following conditions?
   a. The length is twice the width.
   b. The length is three meters more than the width.
   c. The length is three meters less than twice the width.
   d. The width is one-fifth of the length.

2. Assume that the length and width of a rectangle are restricted to whole-number measures.
   a. How many rectangles of different shape have a perimeter of 10? 12? 14? 16? 24?
   b. State a rule for finding the number of rectangles of different shape that have a given perimeter.
   c. Is it possible for the perimeter to have an odd-number measure? Why or why not?

3. Assume that the sides of a *triangle* are restricted to whole-number measures. How many different triangles are there that have a perimeter of 10?

4. Each of the small boxes in these figures is a square. All the squares are the same size. If the perimeter of the figure at the right is 30, what is the perimeter of each figure below?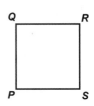

   a.   b.   c.   d.

5. *PQRS* is a square. Imagine that it can be folded.
   a. *P* is folded up onto *Q*. Then *Q* is folded onto *R*. If the perimeter of *PQRS* is 1, what is the perimeter of the new figure?
   b. *Q* is folded onto *R* to form a figure with a perimeter of 24. What is the perimeter of *PQRS*?
   c. *Q* is folded onto the midpoint of side *QR*. The perimeter of the smaller of the two figures formed is 15 cm. What is the perimeter of *PQRS*?

(*Solutions are on pages 187-190.*)

5.5 Circumference
"Circular" Reasoning

Suppose that you just completed a nonstop bicycle trip of 5.5 km. You know that each wheel of your bicycle has a radius of 35 cm. About how many times did each wheel turn during this trip?

Often a problem may seem complex, yet you discover that there is a relatively simple problem at its core. In this instance, the key question is: how far does each wheel travel in just one turn? Let's draw a picture of the progress of a wheel through one turn to see how you might determine this distance by observing the path of a fixed point on the circumference of the wheel.

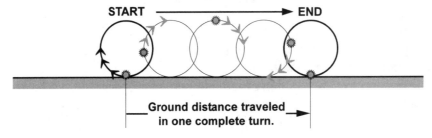

START ———————————→ END

Ground distance traveled in one complete turn.

The starting position of the wheel in this picture is at the left, and here the point of the wheel that is touching the ground has been marked. The wheel is then drawn turning toward the right. When the marked point again touches the ground, you can see that the wheel has traveled a distance equal to its perimeter.

The special name for the perimeter of a circle is the CIRCUMFERENCE. Recall that the formula used to calculate circumference is $c = 2\pi r$ where the value of π is reasonably close to $3\frac{1}{7}$ or 3.14, and r is the length of the radius of the circle. To find the circumference of a wheel of your bicycle, substitute $\frac{22}{7}$ for π and 35 for r. (We chose $\frac{22}{7}$ because the radius is divisible by 7.) Then $c \approx 2 \times \frac{22}{7} \times 35$, which is 220. Therefore, each wheel travels approximately 220 cm in just one turn.

To find how many times each wheel turned in the entire trip of 5.5 km, you now need only to calculate how many 220-cm lengths there are in 5.5 km. Before you proceed, note that one measure is named in centimeters and the other is named in kilometers. The numbers involved should be rewritten so that each of them names the same type of unit. There are usually different ways to do this. In this problem, one way is to rename the 5.5 km as 550,000 cm. To find the number of 220-cm lengths in 550,000 cm, perform the division $220\overline{)550,000}$. The quotient is 2500.

Answer: **Each wheel of your bicycle turned approximately 2500 times.**

★ *Problems* ★

1. Suppose that each wheel of your car has an approximate radius of 42 cm.
   a. Approximately how far does each wheel travel in just one turn?
   b. Approximately how many turns does each wheel make in a nonstop 5.5-km trip?

2. One wheel of a tractor turns 240 times in a one-mile trip. What is its approximate radius?

3. A racetrack is in the shape of a 70-yd by 100-yd rectangle with a semicircle attached to each of the 70-yd sides. What is the approximate distance around the track?

4. Gears *A*, *B*, and *C* rotate on fixed axes, and they form the gear train shown at the right. Gear *A* has 40 teeth, Gear *B* has 20 teeth, and Gear *C* has 30 teeth.
   a. If Gear *A* turns in a clockwise direction, in which direction does Gear *B* turn?
   b. If Gear *A* turns in a clockwise direction, in which direction does Gear *C* turn?
   c. If Gear *A* makes 3 complete turns, how many complete turns does Gear *B* make?
   d. If Gear *A* makes 3 complete turns, how many complete turns does Gear *C* make?

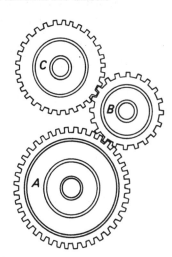

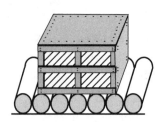

5. The width of this shaded ring at the right is equal to the length of the radius of the inner circle. What is the ratio of the circumference of the inner circle to the circumference of the outer circle?

6. The hour hand of a certain clock is 4 in. long and the minute hand is 6 in. long. How far does the tip of each hand travel in a 24-hour period?

7. The figure at the right shows a crate being moved along the ground by rolling it on cylinders. If the circumference of each cylinder is 75 cm, how far does the crate move for each complete turn of the cylinders?

(*Solutions are on pages 190-192.*)

5.6 Area of Rectangles and Squares
Garden Variety

Suppose that you bought a carton of 36 one-foot sections of decorative garden fencing to enclose a rectangular flower garden. What is the largest garden you can enclose with the fencing that you bought?

Before attempting to solve this problem, you may again find it helpful to identify the essential information and to use it to state a simpler problem. To do this, you need to understand that the fencing represents the PERIMETER of a rectangle and that the size of your garden is associated with the AREA of that rectangle.

The perimeter of a rectangle is 36 feet.
The lengths of the sides are integers, assuming no section is broken.
Find the greatest area that the rectangle can have.

Recall that the formula for the area of a rectangle is *Area = length × width*, or *A = l × w*. The diagram below helps us realize that the sum of a single length and width is half the perimeter (called the SEMIPERIMETER), or 18. Furthermore, the length and width are restricted to whole-number measures because the fencing is made in one-foot sections. Therefore, you only need to consider pairs of natural numbers whose sum is 18.

$$l + l + w + w = 36$$
$$l + w = 18$$

Since the number of possible lengths and widths is limited, an effective strategy to use is organized listing. Let's make a table of the possible lengths, widths, and corresponding areas.

Length	17	16	15	14	13	12	11	10	9
Width	1	2	3	4	5	6	7	8	9
Area	17	32	45	56	65	72	77	80	81

In general, for a given perimeter, the shape that encloses the largest area is a square. This can be proven by mathematics more advanced than the scope of this book.

Answer: **The largest rectangular garden you can make has the shape of a square whose sides each measure 9 ft. Its area is 81 sq. ft.**

(*Note that a square is a special rectangle.*)

☆ **Problems** ☆

1. A certain brand of garden fencing is sold in cartons of 24 one-foot sections.
   a. What is the area of the largest rectangular garden you can enclose if you buy one carton of the fencing? two cartons? three cartons?
   b. State a rule for finding the area of the largest rectangular garden you can enclose with a given number of cartons of this fencing.
   c. What is the least number of cartons of this fencing that you need to buy if you want to enclose a rectangular garden of exactly 32 sq ft? 128 sq ft?

2. The surface of a swimming pool is rectangular in shape and measures 12 m by 20 m. A concrete walk 2 m wide is to be built around the surface of the pool. What will be the surface area of the walk?

3. Find the area of the floor in each floor plan. All angles are right angles.

   a.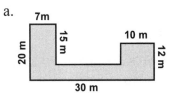

   b.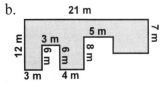

4. How many square feet of plywood will be needed to build an open-top bin if it is to be 3 ft wide, 5 ft long, and 2 ft high?

5. *PQRS* is a square. Imagine that it can be folded.
   a. *P* is folded onto *Q*. Then *Q* is folded onto *R*. If the area of *PQRS* is 1, what is the area of the new figure?
   b. *P* is folded onto the midpoint of side *PQ*. If the area of *PQRS* is 16, what is the area of the new figure?
   c. *Q* is folded onto *R*. If the perimeter of the new figure is 24, what is the area of *PQRS*?

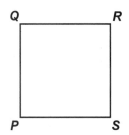

6. Concrete walks, 3 ft wide, are constructed diagonally across a square lawn as shown at the right. What is the total lawn area that remains, as represented by the shaded region?

—12 ft→

7. *ABCD* is a square with sides that measure 2 units in length. *E, F, G,* and *H* are the midpoints of the sides. What is the area of *EFGH?*

8. The area and perimeter of a square are numerically equal. What is the length of a side of the square?

9. If you double the measure of each side of a square, do you double the area of the square, also?

10. The figure at the right shows a square separated into the seven pieces of an ancient puzzle called the *tangram.* If the area of the entire square is one square unit, what is the area of each of the seven tangram pieces?

    (Solutions are on pages 192-194.)

5.7 Area of Circles
Tin Pan Tally

To make a baking pan, a tinsmith is planning to cut the largest possible circular disk from a square sheet of tin that measures 30 cm on each side. What will be the approximate area of the leftover scraps of tin?

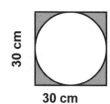

30 cm

30 cm

This is an example of a problem whose solution has a number of smaller problems embedded within it. In this case, it may help you to identify these problems if you begin by drawing a picture such as the one at the right. Looking at the picture, can you see that these are the questions that need to be answered?

- What is the area of the entire sheet of tin?
- What is the area of the circular disk?
- What is the area of the leftover scraps of tin?

Let's answer these questions one by one.

What is the area of the entire sheet of tin? Apply the area formula for a square.

Area of Square = side × side

= 30 cm × 30 cm = 900 sq cm

What is the area of the circular disk? From the diagram on page 98, you can see that the diameter of the largest disk possible has the same length as a side of the square sheet of tin. This means that the diameter of the circle measures 30 cm and its radius measures 15 cm. To approximate the area of the circular disk, remember that you can approximate the area of a circle by using the approximate value of 3.14 or $3\frac{1}{7}$ for π in the formula.

Area of Circle = $\pi \times r^2$

$\approx 3.14 \times (15 \text{ cm})^2$

$\approx 3.14 \times 225 \text{ sq cm} \approx 706.5 \text{ sq cm}$

What is the area of the leftover scraps of tin? Use subtraction to parallel the physical process of cutting the circular disk from the square sheet of tin.

Area of Scraps = Area of Square − Area of Circle

$\approx 900 \text{ sq cm} - 706.5 \text{ sq cm}$

$\approx 193.5 \text{ sq cm}$

Answer: **There will be approximately 193.5 sq cm of tin left over.**

★ *Problems* ★

1. The figure at the right shows a plan for cutting a piece of tin shaped like part of a circle from a square sheet of tin that measures 30 cm on each side. What will be the approximate area of the leftover scrap of tin?

2. A certain rectangular sheet of tin measures 4 ft by 8 ft.
    a. Suppose that a tinsmith cuts eight circular disks from the sheet as shown in the figure at the right. What will be the approximate sum of the areas of the leftover scraps of tin?
    b. What is the greatest possible number of circular disks that could be cut from this sheet if each disk must have a 1-ft diameter? 2-ft radius? 6-in. diameter? 8-in. radius?
    c. For each size of circular disk in part **b**, what would be the approximate area of the leftover scraps of tin after the greatest possible number of circular disks was cut?

3. Suppose that you have a square piece of paper. You draw the largest possible circle, cut it out, and discard the leftover scraps of paper. Inside the circle you draw the largest possible square, cut it out, and discard the leftover scraps of paper. How much of the original square have you discarded in all?

4. A Norman window is shaped like a rectangle that is surmounted by a semicircle. What is the approximate area in square centimeters of a Norman window with the dimensions shown at the right?

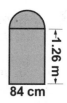

1.26 m

84 cm

5. The figure at the right is formed by two circles with a common center. The diameter of the inner circle is 10 units, and the width of the shaded ring is also 10 units. What is the approximate area of the shaded ring?

6 The inner boundary of a racetrack is formed by two opposite sides of a 400-yd square joined by two semicircles, as shown in the figure at the right. What is the approximate area of the shaded region?

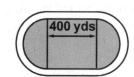

400 yds

7. In the figure at the right, segment AB is the diameter of the large circle. Points X and Y are the centers of the small circles. What is the ratio of the area of the shaded region to the area of the large circle?

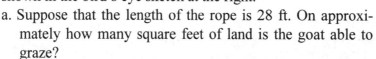

A   X   Y   B

8. A square barn measures 42 ft on each side. A goat is tethered outside by a rope that is attached to one corner of the barn, as shown in the bird's eye sketch at the right.
   a. Suppose that the length of the rope is 28 ft. On approximately how many square feet of land is the goat able to graze?
   b. Suppose that the rope is made twice as long as in part a. On approximately how many square feet of land is the goat now able to graze?

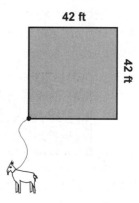

42 ft

42 ft

9. A goat is tethered to the outside corner of a barn as in problem 8, but this barn is rectangular in shape and measures 28 ft by 21 ft. If the length of the rope is 35 ft, on approximately how many square feet of land is this goat able to graze?

   (Solutions are on pages 195-198.)

5.8 *Geometric Patterns*
Tromino Theory

Just about everyone knows what a domino shape looks like. It's basically a plane figure formed by two congruent squares that share a common side. As you can see at the right, there are many ways that a domino can be positioned, but the basic pattern remains the same. There is only one *type* of domino.

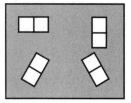

When *three* congruent squares share common sides, the resulting figure is called a *tromino*. How many different types of tromino are there?

A problem that involves the manipulation of shapes is often best approached by some simple experimenting. In this case, a good way for you to find all the trominoes may be to physically move three squares on a flat surface. Use pattern blocks if they're handy, or simply cut the squares out of paper.

As you manipulate the squares, you will probably realize that there are literally dozens of ways to arrange them. However, you will notice that most of the arrangements do not fulfill the conditions of our problem. In patterns like these, for example, the squares do not share common sides; they only share single points or *parts* of their sides.

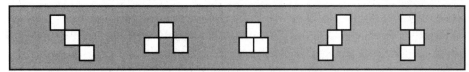

There is an arrangement that is obviously a tromino. When the three squares are joined together end-to-end, we see a tromino pattern that is very similar to the familiar domino. Again, there are many ways that this tromino can be positioned, but they do not change the shape of the tromino.

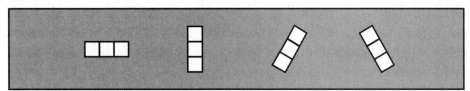

Can you find a second type of tromino? Did you discover that the only other way to fulfill the requirements is to arrange the squares into an L-shape? Your pattern may be positioned in many ways, but these are all the same L-shaped tromino in different positions.

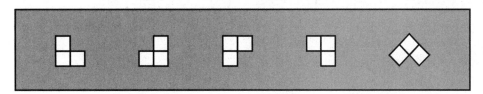

Answer: **There are only two types of tromino: the end-to-end shape and the L-shape.**

☆ **Problems** ☆

1. A *tetromino* is formed by *four* congruent squares that share common sides.
   a. How many different types of tetromino are there? Sketch them.
   b. Which tetromino has the least perimeter?

2. Suppose that the squares in our dominoes, trominoes, and tetrominoes are replaced by congruent equilateral triangles. How many different types of each are there? Sketch them.
   a. triangle-dominoes
   b. triangle-trominoes
   c. triangle-tetrominoes

3. In the trapezoid below, each of the three short sides has the same length, and the longest side is exactly twice as long as a short side. How many different trapezoid-dominoes can you make using this figure? Sketch them.

4. A *pentomino* is formed by five congruent squares that share common sides.
   a. There are twelve different types of pentomino. Sketch them.
   b. Which of the pentomino patterns could be folded to make a box with an open top?
   c. Draw the twelve pentominoes on graph paper and cut them out. Using the pentominoes like pieces of a jigsaw puzzle, assemble them into a 6 by 10 rectangle.

5. Suppose that each of the 9 small squares of a 3 by 3 tic-tac-toe grid is congruent to each of the individual squares in a set of dominoes. Can the grid be covered completely by placing a whole number of dominoes on it with no overlapping?

6. Suppose that each of the 64 small squares of an 8 by 8 checkerboard is congruent to each of the individual squares of a set of dominoes. Two squares are removed from diagonally opposite corners of the checkerboard. Can the remaining board be covered completely by placing a whole number of dominoes on it with no overlapping?

(Solutions are on pages 198-199.)

> *For a listing of common geometric formulas,*
> *see Appendix 1 on pages 225-226.*

6. Trains, Books, Clocks, and Things

6.1 Motion Problems
Trains of Thought

Suppose two trains leave from the same station at the same time, but move in opposite directions. One train averages 56 mph and the other averages 64 mph. (1) How far apart will the trains be at the end of three hours? (2) How much time will it take for the trains to be 600 mi apart?

A problem such as this is called a MOTION PROBLEM because it concerns the behavior of one or more moving objects. In solving a motion problem you generally need to consider three items: the *rate* at which each object is moving, the *time* interval during which each object moves, and the *distance* that each object moves. The relationship among these three items is summarized by this formula.

$$\text{Distance} = \text{rate} \times \text{time}$$
$$d = r \times t$$

For the given problem, let's start by considering a simpler problem; how far apart will the trains be at the end of just one hour? To answer this question you may find it helpful to draw a diagram of the situation, somewhat like this one.

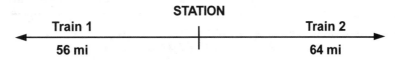

STATION

Train 1   Train 2

56 mi   64 mi

Can you see that at the end of one hour the distance between the backs of the trains will be $56 + 64 = 120$ mi? Therefore, the two trains separate at the rate of 120 mi per hour.

Answer: **(1) At the end of three hours, the trains will be $3 \times 120 = 360$ miles apart.**
(2) For the trains to be 600 mi apart, the amount of time needed will be $600 \div 120 = 5$ h.

Suppose that the two trains described in our problem start from the same station at the same time and move in the *same* direction along parallel tracks. How far apart will the fronts of the trains be at the end of three hours? How much time will it take for the fronts of the trains to be 80 mi apart?

As before, let's approach this problem by considering how far apart the trains will be at the end of one hour. A diagram may again prove to be helpful.

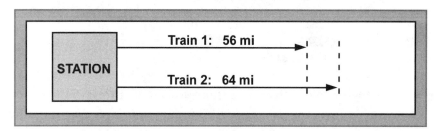

This time, do you see that the distance between the fronts of the trains at the end of one hour will be $64 - 56 = 8$ mi? Although the trains are moving in the same direction, the fronts are separating at the rate of 8 mi each hour.

Answer: **At the end of three hours, the distance between the fronts of the trains will be $3 \times 8 = 24$ mi.**

For the fronts of the two trains to be 80 mi apart, the amount of time needed will be $80 \div 8 = 10$ h.

These train problems are examples of two basic PRINCIPLES OF MOTION.

> When two objects move from the same point at the same time, but in opposite directions, they separate from each other at a rate equal to the *sum* of their two individual rates.
>
> When two objects move from the same point at the same time and in the same direction, they separate from each other at a rate equal to the *difference* of their two individual rates.

★ Problems ★

1. Two trains leave from the same station at the same time, moving in opposite directions. One train averages 95 km/h and the other averages 105 km/h.
   a. How far apart will the trains be at the end of $2\frac{1}{2}$ h?
   b. How much time will it take for the trains to be 350 km apart?

2. Two trains leave from the same station at 10:00 A.M. and move in the same direction along parallel tracks. One train averages 72 km/h and the other averages 108 km/h.
   a. How far apart will the trains be at 1:05 P.M. of the same day?
   b. At what time will the trains be 270 km apart?

3. Riding their bicycles, Helen and Kenji leave from two different places at the same time and ride directly toward each other. Helen rides at 6 mph and Kenji rides at 8 mph. If they meet in $\frac{1}{2}$ hr, how far apart were they when they started?

4. A man left his home and drove along a certain road at 48 km/h. One hour later his son left the same home and drove along the same road in the same direction at 72 km/h. How many hours does the son need to overtake his father?

5. Lisa can row a boat at the rate of 3 mph in still water. However, the river in which she is rowing has a current that flows at the rate of 1 mph. Lisa rows 8 mi downstream, then turns and rows back upstream to her starting point. How much time does her entire trip take?

6. A passenger train and a freight train leave at the same time from stations that are 270 km apart. The trains are traveling toward each other, and the rate of the passenger train is twice the rate of the freight train. If the trains pass each other in three hours, what is the rate of each train?

7. A train that is 1 km long is traveling at 30 km/h. If the train enters a tunnel that is 1 km long, how much time will it take the train to clear the tunnel?

8. A passenger train traveling at 40 mph passes a freight train traveling in the opposite direction at 20 mph. Leo, riding on the passenger train, notes that the freight train passes him in 15 seconds. What is the length of the freight train?

9. Two passenger trains traveling in opposite directions meet and pass each other. Each train is $\frac{1}{12}$ mi long and is traveling at 50 mph. How many seconds after the front parts of the trains meet will their rear parts pass each other?

10. Two trains leave at the same time from stations that are 60 km apart. The trains travel towards each other, one at 55 km/h and the other at 65 km/h. At the same time, a bee flying at a constant rate of 80 km/h starts at the front of one train, flies to the front of the other train, immediately turns and flies back to the front of the first train, and so on. When the two trains meet, what is the total distance that the bee will have flown?

(Solutions are on pages 200-201.)

6.2 Book Problems
A Pressing Problem

Suppose that a printer is using an old-style printing press and needs one piece of type for each digit in the page numbers of a book. How many pieces of type will the printer need to number pages from 1 through 250?

One way to solve this problem is to consider the structure of the counting numbers assigned to the pages of the book. Here is how you might proceed.

How many one-digit page numbers are there? There are 9, of course, since the first pages would be assigned counting numbers 1 through 9. For these, 9 pieces of type will be necessary.

How many two-digit page numbers are there? These consist of the 90 two-digit counting numbers from 10 through 99. The printer will need $90 \times 2 = 180$ pieces of type for these pages.

How many three-digit page numbers are there? The page numbers to be considered begin at 100 and go through 250. Notice that there are 151 pages in this set. Therefore, $151 \times 3 = 453$ pieces of type will be needed for these pages.

> **Answer**: **For page numbers 1 through 250, the printer will need $9 + 180 + 453 = 642$ pieces of type.**

Now let's consider an extension of this problem.

> **Using one piece of type for each digit, how many 2s will the printer need in printing page numbers from 1 through 250?**

You may find it helpful to once again focus on the structure of the counting numbers. This time, though, we'll consider the numbers place-by-place.

How many times will the digit 2 appear in the ones place? This occurs once in every group of 10 consecutive counting numbers. For page numbers 1 through 250 there are 25 such groups, so 2 appears in the ones place 25 times.

$$2, \quad 12, \quad 22, \quad 32, \quad 42, \quad \dots, \quad 242$$

How many times will the digit 2 appear in the tens place? This happens 10 times in every group of 100 consecutive counting numbers. For pages numbered 1 through 250, this is 30 times.

$$20, \quad 21, \quad 22, \quad 23, \quad 24, \quad \dots, \quad 29$$
$$120, \quad 121, \quad 122, \quad 123, \quad 124, \quad \dots, \quad 129$$
$$220, \quad 221, \quad 222, \quad 223, \quad 224, \quad \dots, \quad 229$$

How many times will the digit 2 appear in the hundreds place? This occurs in each of the last 51 numbers.

$$200, \quad 201, \quad 202, \quad 203, \quad 204, \quad \dots, \quad 250$$

Answer: **The total number of 2s that the printer will need is $25 + 30 + 51 = 106$.**

★ Problems ★

1. Suppose that a printer is using an old-style printing press and needs one piece of type for each digit in the page numbers of a book. A certain book contains pages numbered from 1 to 375.
   a. What is the total number of pieces of type that the printer will need to print these page numbers?
   b. How many 3s will the printer need?
   c. How many 4s will the printer need?
   d. How many 8s will the printer need?

2. Suppose that a printer uses a total of 402 pieces of type in numbering the pages of a certain book. If the first page number is 1, how many numbered pages does this book contain?

3. A book is opened, and the product of the two facing page numbers that appear is 1190. What are the two page numbers?

4. One section of a certain book contains six pages. The sum of all the page numbers in this section is 513. What are the page numbers?

(*Solutions are on pages 201-203.*)

6.3 **Work Problems**
On the Job

Working alone, Dan can do a certain job in three hours and Stan can do the same job in two hours. At these rates, how long would it take Dan and Stan to do this job working together?

Problems such as the one above are often referred to as WORK PROBLEMS. Since work problems can be associated with fractional parts, let's approach this problem by drawing a diagram, which was the strategy that we applied to fractional parts problems in Section 4.4. In this case, we choose a rectangle to represent the entire job and draw two rectangles — one for Dan and one for Stan.

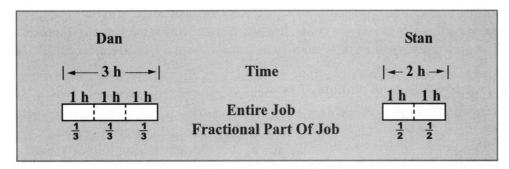

When we use the diagram to interpret the given information, we observe that Dan can do $\frac{1}{3}$ of the job in one hour and Stan can do $\frac{1}{2}$ of the job in one hour. If they work together they can do $\frac{1}{3} + \frac{1}{2}$ of the job in one hour.

We now know how long it would take Dan and Stan together to do $\frac{5}{6}$ of the job. We still need to determine how long it would take them to do the *entire* job. At this point, let's draw a new diagram that represents their *combined* work.

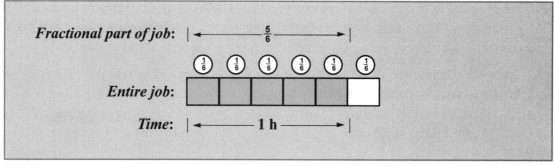

As you can see from the diagram, since $\frac{5}{6}$ of the job requires one hour, $\frac{1}{6}$ of the job requires $\frac{1}{5}$ of one hour or twelve minutes. Therefore, the additional $\frac{1}{6}$ of the job requires an additional twelve minutes.

Answer: **Dan and Stan together can do the job in one hour and twelve minutes, which is equivalent to seventy-two minutes.**

For a different job, Dan is able to work at the same rate as Stan. Together they can complete this job in six days. Suppose that they are joined by Fran, who can also work at the same rate. How long would it take Dan, Stan, and Fran together to do this job?

Notice that each of the individuals involved in this problem works at the same rate. Although we could again use a diagram to solve the problem, let's see how a different strategy might be used.

Consider a simpler question: how long would it take any one of these people working *alone* to do this job? Since we know that two people working together require six days, it follows that one person working alone would need twice as much time, or twelve days.

Now consider another question: how much of the job can any one of these people working alone do in just one day? Since one person can do the job in twelve days, that person alone can do *one-twelfth* of the job in one day. Therefore, three people working together can do *three-twelfths* of the job in one day. This is equal to one-fourth of the job. If one-fourth of the job is done each day, it will take four days to complete the job.

Answer: **Dan, Stan, and Fran together can do the job in four days.**

☆ *Problems* ☆

1. Working alone, an adult requires three hours to do a certain job. A child working alone requires seven hours to do the same job. How long will it take the adult and child working together to do this job?

2. An old-model machine can stamp 1000 parts in four hours. A new-model machine can stamp 1000 parts in just two hours. How long will it take one old-model and one new-model machine to stamp 1000 parts working together?

3. Laura needs three days to do a certain job, Eric needs four days to do the same job, and Connie also needs four days to do the job. How long will it take Laura, Eric, and Connie working together to do this job?

4. It takes three minutes to fill a tub to the top and four minutes to drain the full tub. If the faucet and drain are both open, how long will it take to fill the tub?

5. It takes nine days for eight workers to pave a stretch of road. If each worker works at the same rate as each of the others, how long will it take twelve workers to pave the same stretch of road?

6. A group of six scouts purchases rations sufficient for a 15-day camping trip. If three more scouts join the group but no additional rations are purchased, how many days will the rations last?

7. Four duplicating machines together require six minutes to make a certain number of copies. Each machine has the same capability. If one of the machines becomes inoperative, how long will it take the remaining machines to make the same number of copies?

8. A company payroll is prepared by two computers in $13\frac{1}{3}$ min. Working alone, the faster of the two computers can prepare the payroll in 20 min. How much time does the slower computer alone require to prepare the payroll?

(Solutions are on pages 203-204.)

6.4 Clock Problems
As Time Goes By

A certain clock gains one minute of time every hour. If the clock shows the correct time now, in how many hours will it next show the correct time again without regard to a.m. or p.m.?

This type of clock problem concerns ELAPSED TIME, which is the amount of time that passes between two events. Elapsed time problems sometimes seem complicated, but they often can be solved by reasoning with familiar facts about time.

Here is one way to regard this problem. We know that a clock keeping time properly *always* shows the correct time. Therefore, let's consider an extreme: what about a clock that has stopped and is not keeping time at all? This clock, of course, shows the correct time only once in every twelve-hour interval.

The clock in our problem must then gain the *equivalent* of twelve hours before it once again shows the correct time. How many hours will this take? Twelve hours contain $12 \times 60 = 720$ min. Since the clock gains one minute in one hour, it will gain 720 min in 720 h.

Answer: **The clock will again show the correct time in 720 hours, or in 30 days.**

A different type of clock problem involves the positions of the hands of a clock in relation to each other. Here is an example.

How many times during the day do the hands of a clock coincide? (Assume that the clock is keeping time properly.)

Recall that the minute hand is moving faster than the hour hand, and each time the minute hand passes over the hour hand they will *coincide*. How frequently does this happen?

If you have a watch or clock available, you may wish to experiment. Does it seem that the hour hand passes the minute hand once each hour? Be careful. Note that this is true for every hour *except* the eleventh hour. At 11 o'clock the hour hand points to 11 and the minute hand points to 12. Now the minute hand tries to overtake the hour hand but does not accomplish that until both hands point to 12.

Answer: **The hour hand and the minute hand of a clock coincide 11 times in each twelve-hour interval, or 22 times in each 24-hour day.**

★ *Problems* ★

1. Suppose that a clock shows the correct time now. Under each of the following conditions, when will it show the correct time again?
   a. It gains three minutes every hour.
   b. It loses two minutes every hour.
   c. It gains two seconds every three hours.

2. At which *hours* do the hands of a clock form an angle that measures 60° ?

3. How many times each day do both hands satisfy each of the following conditions?
   a. Both hands lie directly opposite each other.
   b. Both hands are perpendicular to each other.

4. Larry's clock has sixty marks that identify the sixty minutes of the hour. At a certain time Larry noticed that the hour hand pointed exactly to one of these marks while the minute hand pointed exactly to the mark beside it. What time was it?

5. One afternoon Maria observed that the time that had elapsed since noon was equal to half the time that remained until midnight. What time was it?

6. A certain digital clock constantly displays the digits for the hour and the minute. During how many minutes of the day is there at least one 2 in the display of this clock? (Assume that the clock is keeping time properly.)

7. A certain clock loses six minutes every hour. One day this clock is set to the correct time at 10:30 A.M. What will be the correct time when the clock first shows 12:00 on that same day?

(Solutions are on pages 204-205.)

6.5 Related Problems
Handshakes

Five people are introduced to each other, and each person shakes hands with each of the others exactly once. How many handshakes are exchanged altogether among the five people?

Where should you begin a problem like this? Try considering the simplest handshake problem of all: how many handshakes are exchanged when only two people are introduced? The answer, of course, is just one. Let's represent the people by A and B and use this notation to represent their handshake.

$$A, B$$

Suppose now that A and B are joined by a third person, C. Persons A and B already exchanged a handshake with each other, so only two new handshakes are necessary: A must shake hands with C and B must shake hands with C. A total of three handshakes have been exchanged. Let's make an organized list of these handshakes. We'll also make a table to record the totals, using n to represent the number of people and h to represent the number of handshakes.

new handshakes

$$A, B \quad \begin{array}{|c|} \hline A, C \\ B, C \\ \hline \end{array}$$

n	h
2	1
3	3

$\rangle$ +2

What happens if a fourth person, D, joins the group? Do you see that three new handshakes are necessary? Pause to list and record them all according to the scheme established above. Did you arrive at this list of six?

new handshakes

$$A, B \quad A, C \quad \begin{array}{|c|} \hline A, D \\ B, C \quad B, D \\ C, D \\ \hline \end{array}$$

n	h
2	1
3	3
4	6

$\rangle$ +2

$\rangle$ +3

Do you see that a pattern is emerging in the listing and in the table? How many handshakes will be added to the total if a fifth person joins this group? Each of the four people already in the group will have to shake hands with the new person, and so four handshakes will be added to the previous total of six. If we represent the fifth person by E, all ten handshakes can be listed as follows.

new
handshakes

A, B	A, C	A, D	A, E
	B, C	B, D	B, E
		C, D	C, E
			D, E

n	h
2	1
3	3
4	6
5	10

$>$ +2
$>$ +3
$>$ +4

Answer: **When five people are introduced to each other, a total of ten handshakes are exchanged in all.**

Students may enjoy solving this problem by acting out the procedure that we have just discussed.

One interesting aspect of the handshake problem is the variety of ways that it can be approached. For example, another way to make an organized list of all the handshakes is to make a tree diagram that focuses on the handshakes from the viewpoint of each of the five individuals.

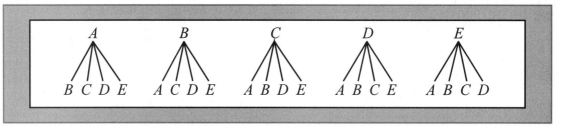

Using this method of listing, it would seem that there is a total of $5 \times 4 = 20$ handshakes. However, notice that each handshake has been counted twice: a handshake between *B* and *A* is the same as a handshake between *A* and *B;* a handshake between *C* and *A* is the same as a handshake between *A* and *C*; and so on. Since each handshake is listed two times, the number of distinct handshakes is $20 \div 2 = 10$, which is the same as our previous conclusion.

Now consider a different problem: how many segments can be drawn connecting five points, no three of which lie on the same line?

Let's make a diagram showing five points that meet the conditions of the problem. We'll label the points *A*, *B*, *C*, *D*, and *E*. As shown below, you can then draw all the segments by connecting each pair of points.

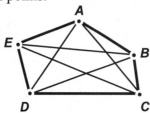

How many segments are there? Do you see that there are ten in all? To verify this, we can make an organized list.

$$\overline{AB} \quad \overline{AC} \quad \overline{AD} \quad \overline{AE}$$
$$\overline{BC} \quad \overline{BD} \quad \overline{BE}$$
$$\overline{CD} \quad \overline{CE}$$
$$\overline{DE}$$

We can also use the reasoning we employed with the tree diagram of the handshakes.

There are 5 points, and each one of the points is connected to the other 4 points. Thus there appear to be $5 \times 4 = 20$ segments. However, in this set of 20 segments, each segment has been counted twice. For example, $\overline{AB}$ and $\overline{BA}$ are the same segment, $\overline{AC}$ and $\overline{CA}$ are the same segment, and so on. Therefore, there are $20 \div 2 = 10$ distinct segments.

> **Answer: Given five points, no three of which lie on the same line, ten segments can be drawn connecting them.**

Looking back, does the list of ten segments seem familiar? It appears to be almost a duplicate of the list of handshakes exchanged by five people. Instead of handshakes that "connect" people, this problem involves segments that connect points. In each problem the total is the same: ten "connections." Though the two problems may seem very different, they are related because they are both instances of the same mathematical model.

★ Problems ★

1. Six people are introduced to each other, and each person shakes hands with each of the others exactly once. How many handshakes are exchanged altogether?

2. Using A, B, C, D, E, and F to represent six people, draw a tree diagram to verify your answer to problem 1.

3. Complete the following table.

Number of People	2	3	4	5	6	7	8
Number of Handshakes	1	?	?	10	?	?	?

4. In the completed table for problem 3, the entries in the "Number of Handshakes" column should form a familiar number pattern. Extend this pattern to determine the number of handshakes that would be exchanged by ten people.

5. Each person in a certain group of people shakes hands with each of the others exactly once, and 120 handshakes are exchanged altogether. How many people are in this group?

6. Twenty chess players hold a tournament in which each player plays just one game with each of the other players. How many games are played altogether?

7. How many segments can be drawn connecting each of the following numbers of points, if no three of the points lie on the same straight line?

a. 6   b. 7   c. 8   d. 10

8. How many different segments can be named in this figure, using the labeled points as endpoints? List the segments. As on page 113, count $\overline{AB}$ and $\overline{BA}$ as the same segment.

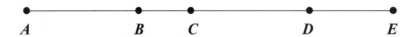

9. The figure below shows a ten-sided polygon, which is called a DECAGON. How many diagonals can be drawn in it?

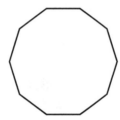

10. How many different rectangles are there in each figure? (all angles are right angles.)

a. ▢   b. ▢▢

c. ▢▢▢   d. ▢▢▢▢

e. ▢▢▢▢▢   f. ▢▢▢▢▢▢

11. Each of the small boxes in the following figures is a square. How many different rectangles are there in each figure? (Remember that a square is a type of rectangle.)

a.   b.   c.   d.

12. How many different rectangles are on a standard 8 by 8 checkerboard?

(Solutions are on pages 206-208.)

7. Logic

7.1 Cryptarithms
Aha!

In the addition shown at the right, *A* and *H* represent two different digits. What are the values of *A* and *H*?

```
    A
    A
  + A
   HA
```

A problem such as the one given here is called a CRYPTARITHM. This is the special name given to a puzzle in which all or several digits of an arithmetic exercise have been replaced by some type of placeholder. In this case, the placeholders are letters of the alphabet. The challenge is to discover the missing digits represented by the letters. How do you solve a cryptarithm? Perhaps the most common method is to use properties of numbers that are familiar to you and apply logical reasoning. Here is how you might regard the cryptarithm above.

The sum $A + A + A$ has A as its ones digit. Then A must be either 0 or 5.

The sum $A + A + A$ is also a two-digit number. This eliminates the possibility that $A = 0$, since $0 + 0 + 0 = 0$. This sum could then be written as 00, but this form violates the condition that each letter of *HA* represents a different digit. Therefore, A must be 5.

Since we have found the value of A, we can substitute that value into the cryptarithm to discover the value of H.

Answer: $A = 5$ and $H = 1$.

```
    5
    5
  + 5
   15
```

In solving the cryptarithm above, we remarked that different letters must represent different digits. It is equally important to note that these letters must each represent only one digit throughout the problem.

Furthermore, if we represent a four-digit number by *PQRS*, then the *lead-digit P* cannot be zero. Otherwise, *PQRS* would actually represent a three-digit number. The lead-digit of any number of two or more digits is never zero.

Other cryptarithms use blank boxes as placeholders for missing digits. Whereas letters of the alphabet may each represent only one digit, it is possible for blank boxes to represent many different digits. Can you reconstruct this multiplication?

3 ▨	*first factor*
× ▨ 2	*second factor*
▨ 4	*first partial product*
1 4 ▨	*second partial product*
▨ ▨ ▨ 4	*product*

Once again, let's use our knowledge of some simple number properties and follow a process of logical reasoning.

The missing digit in the first factor must be multiplied by 2 to produce a 4 in the first partial product. There are only two digits for which this is possible: 2 and 7.

The missing digit in the second factor must multiply the first factor 3▪ to produce the second partial product 14▪. The missing digit in the second factor must be 4.

4 × 32 = 128 and 4 × 37 = 148. Therefore, the missing digit in the first factor must be 7.

Since we have found the missing digits in both factors, we can now multiply to find the missing digits in the partial products and in the product.

Answer:

```
        3 7
    ×   4 2
    ─────────
        7 4
    1 4 8
    ─────────
    1 5 5 4
```

Each part of the multiplication cryptarithm that we just discussed was labeled only for the purpose of facilitating our discussion. As you work through other cryptarithms on your own, you will probably find this step unnecessary.

Note that, in some sources, you may find cryptarithms referred to as *alphametics* or *mathematical cryptograms*.

★ Problems ★

1. In each of the following cryptarithms, each letter represents a different digit. What is the value of each letter?

a.
```
      I
  +  M
  ─────
   M E
```

b.
```
  S O N G
+ B I R D
─────────
S I N G S
```

c.
```
    A T
  +  A
  ─────
  T E E
```

d.
```
  S E N D
+ M O R E
─────────
M O N E Y
```

e.
```
    A B
  ×    C
  ─────
  A A A
```

f.
```
    A B C
  ×      C
  ───────
    D B C
```

g.
```
  A B C D
  ×      4
  ───────
  D C B A
```

h.
```
  A B C D E F
  ×          3
  ───────────
  B C D E F A
```

i.
```
    A B
  × C D
  ------
  C B C
  A B
  ------
  B E C
```

j.
```
    G O
  × T O
  ------
  T G O
  G O
  ------
  F R O
```

k.
```
      N I P
  ×     I N
  --------
  A N O N
  N I P
  --------
  C O R N
```

l.
```
      S Z T N
  ×     F Q N
  ----------
  X H T X Q
  S Z T N
  H F Q U F
  ----------
  H X U E Z F Q
```

m.
```
            I T
  W E ) S E W
        S O
       ----
        E W
        W E
       ----
          S
```

n.
```
              O N
  B E T ) T H A T
          T E N
         -----
          B E T
          B E T
```

o.
```
                D B C
  A B C ) B D E A C
          A B C
         -------
          F A A
          E G C
         -------
          D D E C
          D D E C
```

p. *(H E)² = H E E*   q. *(E E)² = E Y E*   r. $\sqrt{M A D A M} = M A M$

2. Reconstruct each of the following multiplications and divisions.

a.
```
      ■ 8
   ×  ■ ■
   ------
    3 ■ ■
  ■ 1 2
  --------
  ■ ■ ■ 0
```

b.
```
      ■ 1 ■
   ×  3 ■ 2
   --------
      ■ 3 ■
    3 2 ■
  ■ 2 5
  ----------
  1 8 ■ 3 0
```

c.
```
       ■ ■ 5
   ×   1 4 6
   --------
     4 ■ ■ 0
   ■ ■ 0 0
  ■ ■ ■
  --------------
  ■ ■ ■ ■ 8 ■ ■
```

d.
```
            ■ ■ ■ ■ ■
  4 ■ ) ■ ■ ■ ■ ■ ■ ■
        ■ 0
       ----
        ■ ■ ■
        ■ 3 ■
       ----
          ■ ■
          ■ 5
```

e.
```
          9 ■ ■
  3 ■ ) ■ 4 ■ 9
        ■ 1 ■
       ----
         ■ ■ ■
         ■ 1 ■
        ----
          2 ■ 5
          ■ ■ ■
```

f.
```
             ■ ■ 8 ■ ■
  ■ ■ ) ■ ■ ■ ■ ■ ■ ■
        ■ ■ ■
       ----
         ■ ■
         ■ ■
        ----
          ■ ■ ■
          ■ ■ ■
```

3. Some cryptarithms use both letters of the alphabet and blank boxes as placeholders. Reconstruct each of the following multiplications. What is the value of each letter?

a.
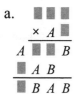
```
       ■ ■ ■
    ×    A ■
    --------
  A ■ ■ B
  ■ A B
  --------
  ■ B A B
```

b.
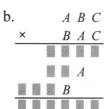
```
        A B C
   ×    B A C
   --------
   ■ ■ ■ ■
   ■ ■ A
   ■ ■ ■ B
   ----------
   ■ ■ ■ ■ ■ ■
```

c.
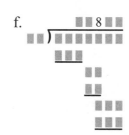
```
         ■ A A ■
   ×     ■ ■ ■
   ----------
   ■ ■ A ■
   ■ ■ ■ A
   A ■ ■ A
   ------------
   ■ ■ ■ ■ ■ ■ ■
```

4. You will find that some cryptarithms have more than one solution. In the cryptarithm at the right, different letters represent different digits. Find two different solutions.

$$\begin{array}{r} S\,E\,V\,E\,N \\ -\ N\,I\,N\,E \\ \hline E\,I\,G\,H\,T \end{array}$$

5. Find a four-digit number such that if 14 is placed at its right, the resulting number is two times as great as the number formed if 14 is placed at its left.

(Solutions are on pages 209-210.)

7.2 Certainty Problems
Sure Thing!

Suppose you know that there are ten black and ten navy blue socks in your drawer. The room is dark and you cannot turn on a light. What is the smallest number of socks that you must take out of your drawer to be certain that you have a pair of the same color?

The solution of a problem such as this is related to the likelihood that something will happen. Mathematically, this is referred to as the PROBABILITY THAT AN EVENT WILL OCCUR. Although you may be familiar with some techniques that are fairly advanced, you can solve this problem using some simple strategies that are within the grasp of even young children. Here is one method that you might use.

Let's use the letter B to represent a black sock and the letter N to represent a navy blue sock. You know that you have to take at least two socks out of your drawer, so start by considering *how many ways* you could do this. We can list all the possibilities in the following way.

$$B, B \qquad B, N \qquad N, B \qquad N, N$$

Here "B, N" means that B was the first selection and N was the second selection. In probability problems the order in which events occur may make a difference. In this case "B, N" and "N, B" are listed as two distinct possibilities. Notice that the two other possibilities, "B, B" and "N, N" do contain a matched pair. However, only one of these four possibilities can actually happen, so taking only two socks out of your drawer is not sufficient to be certain that you'll get a pair of the same color.

How many ways could you take three socks out of your drawer? Again, let's make an organized list.

$$\begin{array}{llll} B, B, B & B, B, N & B, N, B & N, B, B \\ B, N, N & N, B, N & N, N, B & N, N, N \end{array}$$

This time there are eight possibilities, and each possibility contains a matched pair of either black or navy blue socks.

> ***Answer:*** **If there are only two colors, to be certain that you have a pair of the same color, you must take three socks out of your drawer.**

Suppose that in the same situation you need to be certain that you have a pair of *navy blue* socks. What is the smallest number of socks that you must take out of your drawer?

In this case, you could again make listings of what might happen if you take various numbers of socks out of your drawer. However, this process would probably be unnecessarily time-consuming. You may find it a more direct approach to reason through the problem somewhat like this.

Consider the "worst" that could happen: you could take ten socks out of your drawer and all ten might be black. However, at least you would know that there were no more black socks in your drawer. If you then take two *more* socks out of your drawer, you know that you must have a pair of navy blue socks.

Answer: **To be certain that you have a pair of navy blue socks, you must take twelve socks out of your drawer.**

★ *Problems* ★

1. Suppose you know that there are ten black, ten navy blue, and ten green socks in your drawer. The room is dark and you cannot turn on a light. What is the smallest number of socks that you must take out of your drawer to be certain that you meet each of the following conditions?
    a. You have a pair of the same color.
    b. You have a pair of black socks.
    c. You have one pair of each color.

2. Suppose you know that there are eight black and ten navy blue socks in your drawer. The room is dark and you cannot turn on a light. What is the smallest number of socks that you must take out of your drawer to be certain that you meet each of the following conditions?
    a. You have a pair of the same color.
    b. You have a pair of black socks.
    c. You have a pair of navy blue socks.
    d. You have one pair of each color.

3. A complete set of checkers usually consists of twelve black checkers and twelve red checkers. Suppose that a complete set of checkers is placed in a bag. Without looking, how many checkers must you select from the bag to be certain that you have four checkers of the same color?

4. A box contains buttons of five different colors and there are ten buttons of each color. Each button is the same size as the others. If you are blindfolded, how many buttons must you select from this box to be certain that you have four buttons of the same color?

5. A standard deck of 52 playing cards is placed face-down on a table. How many cards must you draw from the deck to be certain that you have a pair of the same value?

6. What is the smallest number of people that must be gathered together to be certain that at least two people of the group were born in the same month?

7. A certain school has an enrollment of 400 students. Must there be at least two students in this school whose birthdays fall on the same day of the year? Why or why not?

8. What is the smallest enrollment that a school must have to be certain that there are three students enrolled whose birthdays fall on the same day of the year? For this problem, consider only nonleap years.

9. How many people must be gathered together to be certain that each of the following sets of conditions is met?
a. Two of the people have the same first-name initial.
b. Three of the people have the same last-name initial.
c. Two of the people have the same first-name initial and the same last-name initial.

10. Some biologists claim that the greatest number of hairs that can be on a person's head is one million. Suppose that there are one million bald people in New York City. Show that, if these biologists are correct, there must be at least two people in New York City who have the same number of hairs on their heads.

(Solutions are on pages 211-212.)

7.3 *Venn Diagram Problems*
School Daze

> **There are 400 students enrolled at Castleton School. Of these students, 85 study French and 50 study Spanish. If 120 students study either French or Spanish, how many students study both French *and* Spanish?**

This is an example of a type of problem that can be solved by representing the situation with a VENN DIAGRAM. In this special kind of diagram, circles are usually used to represent sets of people, animals, or objects that possess certain characteristics. The positioning of the circles in relation to one another represents relationships among these sets. The diagram can then be used to help solve the problem. These diagrams were named after John Venn (1834-1923), an English mathematician who was among the first to use them extensively.

Let's solve our problem using the Venn diagram at the right. Here circle *F* represents those students who study French and circle *S* represents those students who study Spanish. (Note that the size of each circle is not necessarily related to the number of students in the group it represents.) The rectangle drawn around the circles represents the entire enrollment of Castleton School.

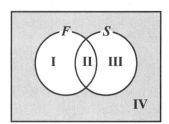

The circles separate the interior of the rectangle into four distinct regions, and these are labeled I, II, III, and IV. Region IV represents those students at Castleton School who study neither French nor Spanish, so for the purposes of this problem we will not be concerned with this region. Region I represents students who study French but not Spanish, while region III represents students who study Spanish but not French. It follows that region II represents those students who study both French and Spanish, and it is the value of this region that we must find.

We can now label our Venn diagram with the data given in the problem: there are 85 students in circle F and 50 students in circle S. What about regions I, II, and III? If we introduce the variable n to represent the number of students in region II, do you see that we can represent the number of students in region I as $85 - n$ and in region III as $50 - n$?

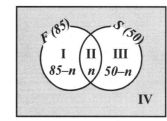

There is one other fact that we have not yet used, namely that the total number of students who study either French or Spanish is 120. In the diagram, this is the same as the total of students in regions I, II, and III. Let the number of students in each region also be represented by I, II, and III. We can then write a simple equation.

$$\begin{aligned} \mathrm{I} \quad + \mathrm{II} + \quad \mathrm{III} \quad &= 120 \\ (85 - n) + \quad n \ \ + (50 - n) &= 120 \\ 135 - n &= 120 \\ n &= 15 \end{aligned}$$

Answer: **There are 15 students who study both French and Spanish.**

Note that the fact that Castleton School has an enrollment of 400 is irrelevant.

Sometimes you need to consider relationships among three or more groups. For example, suppose that we also had information about the group of students who study German at Castleton School. You could picture the relationships among the three groups of students — those who study French, Spanish, and German — with a Venn diagram such as the one shown.

This time the circles separate the interior of the rectangle into eight distinct regions. The meaning of each of these regions is described in the table on the next page. An entry of "Yes" under any language indicates that the students assigned to that region *do* study the language; an entry of "No" indicates that the students assigned to that region do *not* study the language.

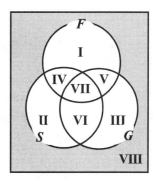

Region	French	Spanish	German
I	Yes	No	No
II	No	Yes	No
III	No	No	Yes
IV	Yes	Yes	No
V	Yes	No	Yes
VI	No	Yes	Yes
VII	Yes	Yes	Yes
VIII	No	No	No

★ Problems ★

1. There are 30 students in Mrs. Murale's homeroom.

   a. All the students study either French or Spanish. If 21 study French and 14 study Spanish, how many students study both French and Spanish?

   b. All the students study mathematics. The number of students who passed the first math test this year is 24; the number who passed the second math test is 27. If 23 students passed both math tests, how many students *failed* both?

   c. Of the students in the homeroom, 9 do not study either chemistry or physics, but 14 study chemistry. How many students study physics but not chemistry?

   d. Of the students in the homeroom, 14 are boys. There are 13 students who play a musical instrument, and 6 of these are boys. How many girls in the homeroom do *not* play a musical instrument?

2. The following information was obtained in a survey of 120 students.

   > 66 students study English.
   > 42 students study history.
   > 38 students study math.
   > 19 students study English and history.
   > 18 students study English and math.
   > 16 students study history and math.
   > 8 students study English, history, and math.

   a. How many students study math but neither English nor history?
   b. How many students study English and math but not history?
   c. How many students study none of the three subjects?

3. The members of an English class were assigned books *A*, *B*, and *C* to read during one semester. A poll of the class after two months showed that each student had read at least one of the books. It also showed this additional information.

    > 10 students had read all three books.
    > 15 students had read books *A* and *B*.
    > 17 students had read books *A* and *C*.
    > 13 students had read books *B* and *C*.
    > 28 students had read book *A*.
    > 21 students had read book *B*.
    > 24 students had read book *C*.

    How many students were in the class?

4. The following information was obtained by studying the orders of the people who dined in a certain restaurant one evening.

    > 50 people ordered salad.
    > 40 people ordered soup.
    > 65 people ordered dessert.
    > 20 people ordered soup and dessert.
    > 15 people ordered salad and soup.
    > 30 people ordered salad and dessert.
    > 8 people ordered salad, soup, and dessert.
    > 12 people ordered no salad, no soup, and no dessert.

    a. How many people ordered salad and dessert but not soup?
    b. How many people ordered salad but not dessert?
    c. How many people ordered only soup?
    d. How many people were there in all?

5. Thirty people took a trip to Europe to visit France, England, or Spain. Of this group, 16 visited France, 16 visited England, 11 visited Spain, 5 visited France and Spain, 5 visited only Spain, 8 visited only England, and 3 visited all three countries. How many visited only France?

6. A psychologist ran 50 mice through a maze experiment and reported the following data: 25 mice were male; 25 were previously-trained; 20 turned left at the first point where there was a choice; 10 were previously-trained males; 4 males turned left; 15 previously-trained mice turned left; and 3 previously-trained males turned left. How many female mice who were not previously-trained did *not* turn left?

    (Solutions are on pages 212-216.)

7.4 Whodunits
Who's on First?

Finley, Garber, and Harris are a banker, a computer programmer, and a secretary, but not necessarily in that order. Finley is neither the banker nor the secretary. Harris is not the secretary. What is the occupation of each?

A WHODUNIT is a puzzle that involves a group of people or objects and one or more sets of characteristics associated with the people or objects. Each characteristic can be matched one-to-one with each person or object. The problem is to determine this one-to-one matching.

One way to sort through all the information you are given in this whodunit is to make a chart like the one below. Here the letters *F*, *G*, and *H* represent, respectively, Finley, Garber, and Harris of our problem. The letters *B*, *CP*, and *S* represent their occupations: banker, computer programmer, and secretary, respectively.

Occupations

	B	CP	S
F			
G			
H			

Names

Reread the problem to search for clues. Can you determine that any person is *not* associated with a certain occupation? If so, mark an ✕ on the chart in the appropriate block.

Finley is neither the banker nor the secretary.

	B	CP	S
F	✕		✕
G			
H			

Harris is not the secretary.

	B	CP	S
F	✕		✕
G			
H			✕

Now look at each row and column of the chart. Does any row or column have only one possible association remaining? If so, mark a ✓ in those blocks.

	B	CP	S
F	✕	✓	✕
G			✓
H			✕

Any row or column of the chart can contain only one ✓, so use ✗s to fill out any rows or columns that now have ✓s.

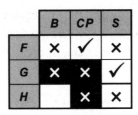

Recalling that each row and each column must contain one and only one ✓, mark any remaining blocks.

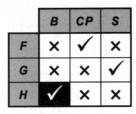

> *Answer:* **Finley is the computer programmer, Garber is the secretary, and Harris is the banker.**

The problem that we have just discussed involved matching a single set of characteristics to a group of people. How do you proceed if you are given *two* sets of characteristics? Let's consider the same problem, but with some additional information.

> **Finley, Garber, and Harris are a banker, a computer programmer, and a secretary, but not necessarily in that order. *Their first names are Alex, Bob, and Cynthia.* Finley is neither the banker nor the secretary. Harris is not the secretary, *and Alex is not the banker. Cynthia is older than both Garber and Harris.* What is the complete name and occupation of each?**

It is possible to solve this problem by using an expanded form of the chart that we used to solve our original whodunit. As shown on the next page, this chart permits you not only to compare the people with their occupations, but also to compare the people with their first names and to compare their first names with their occupations.

		Occupations			First Names		
		B	**CP**	**S**	**A**	**B**	**C**
Last Names	**F**						
	G						
	H						
First Names	**A**						
	B						
	C						

A, *B*, and *C* represent the names Alex, Bob, and Cynthia.

The procedure to use with this type of chart is essentially the same as before. Probably the most significant difference is that it is often possible to mark a ✔ or ✗ in one section of this chart by linking information from the other two sections. Here is an example.

As a result of our previous discussion, we are already able to complete the "Last Names/ Occupations" section of this chart. Note that we have already deduced that Harris is the banker. One of the *new* clues is that Alex is *not* the banker. Therefore, we also know that Alex's last name is not Harris, and we can mark the chart in two locations.

		Occupations			First Names		
		B	**CP**	**S**	**A**	**B**	**C**
Last Names	**F**	✗	✔	✗			
	G	✗	✗	✔			
	H	✔	✗	✗	✗		
First Names	**A**	✗					
	B						
	C						

Alex is not the banker.

Alex's last name is not Harris.

Now it's your turn. Complete the chart and solve this whodunit.

Answer:

		Occupations			*First Names*		
		B	CP	S	A	B	C
Last Names	F	✗	✓	✗	✗	✗	✓
	G	✗	✗	✓	✓	✗	✗
	H	✓	✗	✗	✗	✓	✗
First Names	A	✗	✗	✓			
	B	✓	✗	✗			
	C	✗	✓	✗			

Alex Garber is the secretary, Bob Harris is the banker, and Cynthia Finley is the computer programmer.

Charts such as the ones that we have used in this section are an effective strategy to use for solving many whodunits. However, it is important to note that you may not find such charts necessary or even appropriate to solving *all* whodunits that you encounter. There may be times when you feel other reasoning processes are more appropriate.

☆ Problems ☆

1. Art, Bill, and Dave play first base, second base, and third base on their school's baseball team, but not necessarily in that order. Art and the third baseman took Dave to the movies yesterday. Art does not play first base. Who's on first?
2. Kate, Linda, and Maya each ate something different for supper yesterday. One ate steak, one ate fish, and one ate chicken. Maya did not have fish or chicken, and Linda did not have fish. What did each person eat for supper?
3. Doctors Pierce, Otis, and Simmons specialize in pediatrics, orthopedics, and surgery. Simmons' specialty is not orthopedics. None of the last names of the doctors begins with the same letter as that doctor's specialty. What is the specialty of each doctor?
4. The last names of Helen, Irving, and Jacqueline are Abrams, Barrow, and Clancy, but not necessarily in that order. Clancy is Jacqueline's uncle. Helen's last name is not Barrow. What are each person's first and last names?

5. Each of Ina, Jill, Louis, and Miguel has a different favorite color among red, blue, green, and orange. No person's name contains the same number of letters as his or her favorite color. Louis and the boy who likes blue live in different parts of town. Red is the favorite color of one of the girls. What is each person's favorite color?

6. A certain family has four pets: a rabbit, a turtle, a dog, and a cat. Two pets are male and two are female. The nicknames of the pets are Star, Mike, Butch, and Pete. The rabbit and the cat recently gave birth. The rabbit is younger than Pete but older than Mike, who is a mother. Pete is older than the dog. Star likes to have his back rubbed. What is the nickname of each pet?

7. Ivanov, Jacobowski, Lebedev, and Malinkov are an architect, a composer, a dancer, and a singer. Ivanov and her husband invited the composer and his wife to dinner. The dancer said that he enjoyed playing chess with Lebedev. The singer complimented Malinkov on her excellent recipe for cabbage soup. What is the occupation and gender of each person?

8. The last names of Charles, Dolores, Edward, and Felice are Gold, Hendricks, Insull and Jackson, but not necessarily in that order. Insull is Jackson's grandmother but is not related to Charles. Dolores is an infant and is not related to either Felice or Hendricks. What is the first and last name of each person?

9. Charlotte, Deborah, and Ethan are students at Bayview Elementary School. Their last names are Jones, Knutsen, and Lattimer. Their ages are 10, 11, and 12. Charlotte is younger than both Deborah and Knutsen. Lattimer is older than Knutsen. What are the first name, last name, and age of each student?

10. For a project, Nancy, Oliver, and Peter used a saw, a hammer, and a wrench. Each used just one of the tools. Their last names are Ellis, Farelli, and Gross.

    Oliver's last name is not Ellis.
    Gross and the boy who used the hammer live in the same neighborhood.
    Farelli likes to go fishing with her father.
    Nancy did not use the saw.
    What is the first and last name of each student, and what tool did each use?

11. Smith, Robinson, and Jones are a conductor, a porter, and an engineer on a certain train. Also aboard the train are three passengers with the same last names: Mr. Smith, Mr. Robinson, and Mr. Jones.

    Mr. Robinson lives in Detroit.
    The porter lives exactly halfway between Chicago and Detroit.
    Mr. Jones earns exactly $50,000 per year.
    The porter's nearest neighbor, who is one of the three passengers, earns exactly
        three times as much as the porter.
    Smith usually beats the conductor at tennis.
    The passenger whose last name is the same as the porter's lives in Chicago.
    Who is the engineer?

12. Alice, Betty, and Carolyn went on vacation. One went to Algeria, one went to Bali, and one went to China. Only one of the following four statements is true.

    i.   Carolyn went to Algeria.

    ii.   Carolyn did not go to Bali.

    iii.   Alice did not go to Bali.

    iv.   Alice did not go to China.

Where did each go on vacation?

(Solutions are on pages 216-220.)

Solutions to
Parts A and B

Part D

Solutions to Part A

    1.   **What is Problem Solving?**

    2.   **Looking Back (Section 2.4)**

Solutions to Part B

    1.   **Drawing a Picture or Diagram**

    2.   **Making an Organized List**

    3.   **Making a Table**

    4.   **Solving a Simpler Related Problem**

    5.   **Finding a Pattern**

    6.   **Guessing and Checking**

    7.   **Experimenting**

    8.   **Acting Out The Problem**

    9.   **Working Backwards**

    10. **Writing an Equation**

    11. **Changing Your Point of View**

    12. **Miscellanea**

SOLUTIONS TO PART A PROBLEMS

*If an answer and solution are given together, the answer itself is **boldfaced**, as in number 4 below.*

1. What is Problem Solving?
Page 2

1. 6

2. 60 cents; $0.60

3. Greatest value: set of quarters (25¢). Least value: set of nickels (15¢)

4. **12.** The following twelve amounts in cents can be made using 1 or more coins: 5, 10, 15, 20, 25, 30, 35, 40, 45, 50, 55, and 60.

5. **23.** Let N, D, and Q represent the words *nickels*, *dimes*, and *quarters*. The number preceding N, D, and Q represents the number of coins used in each combination.

1N,	2N,	3N,	1D,	2D,	1Q

1N + 1D,	1N + 2D,	1N + 1Q	1D + 1Q
2N + 1D,	2N + 2D,	2N + 1Q	2D + 1Q
3N + 1D,	3N + 2D,	3N + 1Q	

1N + 1D + 1Q,	1N + 2D + 1Q
2N + 1D + 1Q,	2N + 2D + 1Q
3N + 1D + 1Q,	3N + 2D + 1Q

    Therefore, twenty-one different combinations can be made using 3N, 2D, and 1Q.

6. **13.** The table at the right shows 13 different ways of having a total of 60 cents using nickels, dimes, and quarters.

Quarters	Dimes	Nickels
2	1	0
2	0	2
1	3	1
1	2	3
1	1	5
1	0	7
0	6	0
0	5	2
0	4	4
0	3	6
0	2	8
0	1	10
0	0	12

2.4 Looking Back
Pages 5-6

1. **6.** Just the central cube of each of the six faces has red paint on one face. Six one-cm cubes have red paint on just one face.

2. **12.** Just the middle cube of each of the 12 edges has red paint on two faces. 12 one-cm cubes have red paint on just two faces.

3. **8.** Just the corner cubes have red paint on three faces. Eight one-cm cubes have red paint on just three faces.

4. No.

5. **8.** If the cubes in the six outer faces of the four-cm cube were removed, only a two-cm cube would remain with no red paint on any face. Eight one-cm cubes of a four-cm cube have no red paint on any face.

6. **27.** If the cubes in the six outer faces of the five-cm cube were removed, only a three-cm cube would remain with no red paint on any face. 27 one-cm cubes of a five-cm cube have no red paint on any face.

A 5-cm cube: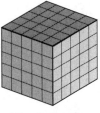

The full cube

Its unpainted interior

7.

Size of Painted Cubes	No. of 1-cm Interior Unpainted Cubes
3-cm cube	1-cm cube, or **1** = 1^3 1-cm cubes
4-cm cube	2-cm cube, or **8** = 2^3 1-cm cubes
5-cm cube	3-cm cube, or **27** = 3^3 1-cm cubes

Pattern: If the exterior of a c-unit cube is painted, the interior unpainted cubes form a $(c-2)$-unit cube. Therefore, the number of unpainted unit cubes is $(c-2)^3 = (c-2) \times (c-2) \times (c-2)$. Other patterns may be found.

SOLUTIONS TO PART B PROBLEMS

*If an answer and solution are given together, the answer itself is **boldfaced**, as in number 1 below.*

1. Drawing a Picture or Diagram
Pages 14-15

1. **4.**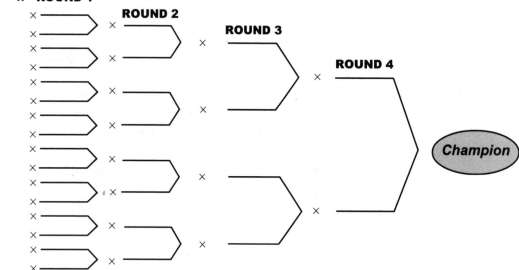

The championship team will have to play four tournament games.

2.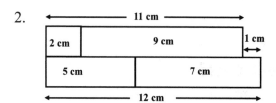

3. **20.** To obtain 4 pieces, the lumberjack needs to make only 3 cuts. Since 3 cuts take 12 minutes, each cut takes 12 ÷ 3 = 4 minutes.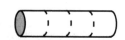

To obtain 6 pieces, the lumberjack will have to make 5 cuts. Since each cut takes 4 minutes, 5 cuts will take 5 × 4 = 20 minutes.

4. (1) Fill the 9-ℓ container with water. Then empty as much of this water as possible into the 5-ℓ container, leaving 4 liters in the 9-ℓ container.

   (2) Fill the 3-ℓ container from the 5-ℓ container, leaving 2 liters in the 5-ℓ container.

   (3) Empty the 3 liters of water in the 3-ℓ container into the 9-ℓ container for a total of $3+4=7$ liters.

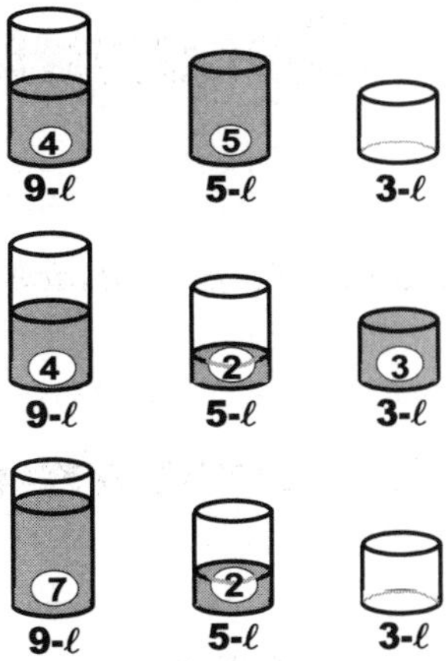

5. **9.** The least number of tacks you need is 9, as shown at the right.

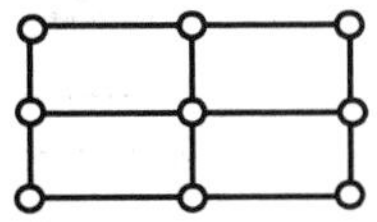

6. **4.** Refer to the layout of the tournament. For easy reference, competitors are numbered from 1 through 9.

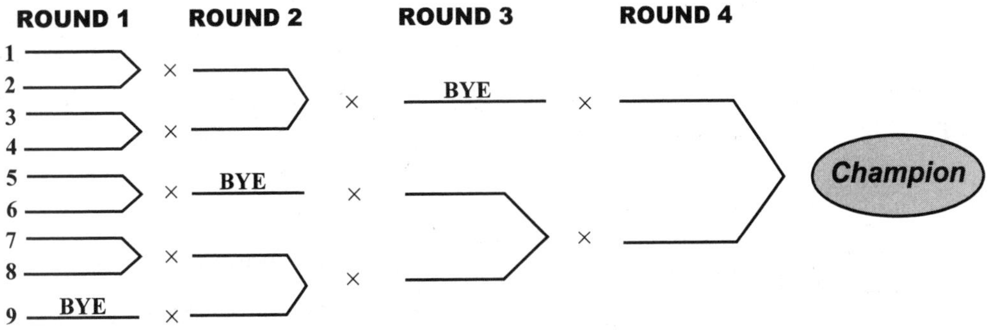

Either player #7 or #8 would be the champion in this case. If any other player was the champion, that player would have played just 3 games. The maximum that a champion would have to play is 4 games.

2. Making an Organized List

Pages 16-17

1. **7.**

3 Darts Hit Bull's Eye	2 Darts Hit Bull's Eye	1 Dart Hits Bull's Eye	0 Darts Hit Bull's Eye
7+7+7 = 21	7+7+5 = 19	7+5+5 = 17	5+5+5 = 15
	7+7+3 = 17	7+5+3 = 15	5+5+3 = 13
		7+3+3 = 13	5+3+3 = 11
			3+3+3 = 9

Seven different point totals are possible: 21, 19, 17, 15, 13, 11, and 9.

2. 9.

4 Darts Hit Bull's Eye	3 Darts Hit Bull's Eye	2 Darts Hit Bull's Eye	1 Dart Hits Bull's Eye	0 Darts Hit Bull's Eye
7+7+7+7 = 28	7+7+7+5 = 26	7+7+5+5 = 24	7+5+5+5 = 22	5+5+5+5 = 20
	7+7+7+3 = 24	7+7+5+3 = 22	7+5+5+3 = 20	5+5+5+3 = 18
		7+7+3+3 = 20	7+5+3+3 = 18	5+5+3+3 = 16
			7+3+3+3 = 16	5+3+3+3 = 14
				3+3+3+3 = 12

Nine different point totals are possible: 28, 26, 24, 22, 20, 18, 16, 14, 12.

3. 27.

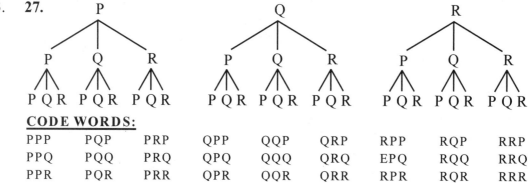

CODE WORDS:

PPP	PQP	PRP	QPP	QQP	QRP	RPP	RQP	RRP
PPQ	PQQ	PRQ	QPQ	QQQ	QRQ	EPQ	RQQ	RRQ
PPR	PQR	PRR	QPR	QQR	QRR	RPR	RQR	RRR

Twenty-seven different code "words" are possible if repetitions of a letter are permitted.

4. 12.

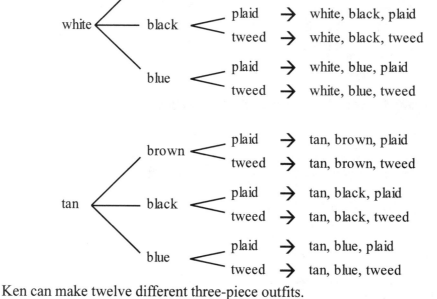

Ken can make twelve different three-piece outfits.

5. **28.** 0,0
0,1   1,1
0,2   1,2   2,2
0,3   1,3   2,3   3,3
0,4   1,4   2,4   3,4   4,4
0,5   1,5   2,5   3,5   4,5   5,5
0,6   1,6   2,6   3,6   4,6   5,6   6,6

There are twenty-eight dominoes in a complete set.

6. **55.** 0,0
0,1 1,1
0,2 1,2 2,2
0,3 1,3 2,3 3,3
0,4 1,4 2,4 3,4 4,4
0,5 1,5 2,5 3,5 4,5 5,5
<u>0,6 1,6 2,6 3,6 4,6 5,6 6,6</u>
0,7 1,7 2,7 3,7 4,7 5,7 6,7 7,7
0,8 1,8 2,8 3,8 4,8 5,8 6,8 7,8 8,8
0,9 1,9 2,9 3,9 4,9 5,9 6,9 7,9 8,9 9,9

Observe that the first seven rows of this list are identical with the seven rows in problem 5. Therefore, to find the number of entries in this list we need only add the number of pairs that appear in the last three rows to the sum of the list in problem 5. The sum of the entries in this list is $28 + 8 + 9 + 10 = 55$.

3.   *Making a Table*
Pages 18-19

1. $\frac{3}{36}$ **or** $\frac{1}{12}$.

First Cube						
+	0	1	2	3	4	5
0	0	1	2	3	4	5
1	1	2	3	4	5	6
2	2	3	4	5	6	7
3	3	4	5	6	7	**8**
4	4	5	6	7	**8**	9
5	5	6	7	**8**	9	10

(Second Cube labels the rows.)

The probability of rolling a sum of 8 is the ratio of the number of entries of 8 in the table to the total number of entries in the table. If each of two cubes has its faces numbered from 0 through 5, the probability of rolling a sum of 8 is $\frac{3}{36}$ or $\frac{1}{12}$.

2. a.

First Pyramid				
+	**1**	**2**	**3**	**4**
1	2	3	4	**5**
2	3	4	**5**	6
3	4	**5**	6	7
4	**5**	6	7	8

(Second Pyramid labels the left column: 1, 2, 3, 4)

b. $\frac{4}{16}$ or $\frac{1}{4}$. The table at the left shows that just four of the 16 sums are 5. The probability that the two pyramids have a sum of 5 is $\frac{4}{16}$ or $\frac{1}{4}$.

3. **13.**

Number of stools	0	1	2	3	. . .	**?**
Number of chairs	30	29	28	27	. . .	**?**
Number of legs	120	119	118	117	. . .	**103**

Each time one chair is "exchanged" for one stool, there is one less leg in the total of legs. To reduce the first number of legs, 120, to 103, 17 of the 30 chairs must be "exchanged" for stools. The carpenter made 30 – 17 = 13 chairs and 17 stools. Checking, 13 chairs have 52 legs and 17 stools have 51 legs; there is a total of 103 legs.

4. **19.**

Number of Dimes	1	1	1	1	1	1	1	1	1	1	0	0	0	0	0	0	0	0	0
Number of Nickels	1	1	1	1	1	0	0	0	0	0	1	1	1	1	1	0	0	0	0
Number of Pennies	4	3	2	1	0	4	3	2	1	0	4	3	2	1	0	4	3	2	1
Total Value, in ¢	19	18	17	16	15	14	13	12	11	10	9	8	7	6	5	4	3	2	1

It is possible to make nineteen different amounts.

5. **10.**

Number of Quarters	2	1	1	1	0	0	0	0	0	0
Number of Dimes	0	2	1	0	5	4	3	2	1	0
Number of Nickels	0	1	3	5	0	2	4	6	8	10

There are ten different ways that a driver can pay the toll.

6. **9 quarters and 21 dimes.**

Quarters	0	1	2	3	4	...	**?**
Dimes	30	29	28	27	26	...	**?**
Total value	$3.00	$3.15	$3.30	$3.45	$3.60	...	**$4.35**

Each time one dime is "exchanged" for one quarter, the total value increases by 15¢. To increase the first total of $3.00 to $4.35, 9 of the 30 dimes must be "exchanged" for quarters, since 135¢ ÷ 15¢ = 9. Therefore, 9 quarters and 21 dimes are in the collection.

4. Solving a Simpler Related Problem
Pages 20-21

1. (9) **24.** 15 numbers have 9 in the units place (9, 19, 29, 39, ... , 99, 109, ... , 149).
   $10 - 1 = 9$ other numbers have 9 in the tens place (90, 91, 92, 93, ... , 98). Notice that 99 is not counted in the tens category because it was counted before.
   $15 + 9 = 24$ house numbers contain at least one digit 9.

   (4) **33.** 15 numbers have 4 in the units place (4, 14, 24, 34, 44, ... 124, 134, 144).
   $20 - 2 = 18$ other numbers have 4 in the tens place (40, 41, 42, 43, 45, 46, 47, 48, 49, 140, 141, 142, 143, 145, 146, 147, 148, 149). 44 and 144 are not counted this time.
   $15 + 18 = 33$ house numbers contain at least one digit 4.

   (1) **70.** 15 numbers have 1 in the units place (1, 11, 21, 31, ... , 121, 131, 141).
   $20 - 2 = 18$ other numbers have 1 in the tens place (11 and 111 are not counted).
   $51 - 14 = 37$ other numbers have 1 in the hundreds place (100, 102, ... , 150). 14 of the 51 numbers in this last category have been counted before.
   $15 + 18 + 37 = 70$ house numbers contain at least one digit 1.

2. **3.** After the value 3 is entered, the display shows 6, 12, 3 in that order. The $\Diamond$ key is pressed three times.

3. **11.** The $\Diamond$ key produces a repeating cycle of nine displays: 14, 5, 10, 1, 2, 4, 8, 16, and finally 7. Then 5 appears as the 2nd, 11th, 20th, ... , 83rd, and 92nd displays. The display 5 appears 11 times.

4. The ✪ key produces the sequence 2, 5, 8, 11, 14, 17, and so forth. It increases endlessly by 3 and does not produce a repeating cycle. To find the display after pressing the ✪ key any number of times, multiply that number by 3 and add the product to 2.
   a. $2 + 3 \times 3 = \mathbf{11}$ b. $2 + 5 \times 3 = \mathbf{17}$ c. $2 + 10 \times 3 = \mathbf{32}$ d. $2 + 100 \times 3 = \mathbf{302}$

5. Finding a Pattern
Pages 22-23

1. a. **250,000.** The series $1 + 3 + 5 + ... + 997 + 999$ contains the first 500 odd numbers. Its sum is $500^2 = 250,000$.

   b. **2550.** According to *1a*, the first fifty odd numbers have a sum of $50 \times 50 = 2500$.
   $$1 + 3 + 5 + 7 + 9 + \cdots + 99 = 2500$$
   $$2 + 4 + 6 + 8 + 10 + \cdots + 100 = \quad ?$$
   Each of the first 50 even numbers is 1 more than the odd number above it.
   $$2 + 4 + 6 + 8 + 10 + \cdots + 100 = 2500 + 50 = 2550.$$

2. **1540.**   Series A $1^2 + 2^2 + 3^2 + 4^2 + \cdots + 9^2 + 10^2 = 385$
               Series B $2^2 + 4^2 + 6^2 + 8^2 + \cdots + 18^2 + 20^2 = \ ?$
Evaluate each term:
               Series A $1 + 4 + 9 + 16 + \cdots + 81 + 100 = 385$
               Series B $4 + 16 + 36 + 64 + \cdots + 324 + 400 = \ ?$
Each term of Series B is 4 times the associated term of Series A.
$$4 + 16 + 36 + 64 + \cdots + 324 + 400 = 4(1 + 4 + 9 + 16 + \cdots + 81 + 100)$$
$$= 4 \times 385 = 1540$$
The sum of $2^2 + 4^2 + 6^2 + 8^2 + \cdots + 18^2 + 20^2$ is 1540.

3. **1.** $7 = 7$
      $7 \times 7 = 49$
      $7 \times 7 \times 7 = 343$
      $7 \times 7 \times 7 \times 7 = 2401$
      $7 \times 7 \times 7 \times 7 \times 7 = 16,807$
      $7 \times 7 \times 7 \times 7 \times 7 \times 7 = 117,649$

From the above series of simpler problems, we see that the ones digits of the products repeat in a cycle of four: 7, 9, 3, 1, 7, 9, 3, 1, ... Every fourth product has 1 as its ones digit. When one hundred 7s are multiplied, the ones digit of the product will be 1.

4. **2.** $5 \div 7 = 0$ **R5**
      $5 \times 5 \div 7 = 3$ **R4**
      $5 \times 5 \times 5 \div 7 = 17$ **R6**
      $5 \times 5 \times 5 \times 5 \div 7 = 89$ **R2**
      $5 \times 5 \times 5 \times 5 \times 5 \div 7 = 446$ **R3**
      $5 \times 5 \times 5 \times 5 \times 5 \times 5 \div 7 = 2232$ **R1**
      $5 \times 5 \times 5 \times 5 \times 5 \times 5 \times 5 \div 7 = 11,160$ **R5**
      $5 \times 5 \times 5 \times 5 \times 5 \times 5 \times 5 \times 5 \div 7 = 55,803$ **R4**

From the above series of simpler problems, we see that the remainders repeat in a cycle of six: 5, 4, 6, 2, 3, 1, 5, 4, 6, 2, 3, 1, ... Every sixth quotient has a remainder of 1, and so when the product of ninety-six 5s is divided by 7, the remainder will be 1. When the product of one hundred 5s is divided by 7, the remainder will be the fourth number in the cycle, which is 2. This, of course, assumes the pattern continues.

5. **45.**   The first person to enter shakes hands with no one. The second person shakes hands with 1 person. The third shakes hands with 2 people, and so forth, until the tenth person, who shakes hands with 9 people. Therefore, the total number of handshakes is $1 + 2 + 3 + 4 + \cdots + 9 = 45$.

6. **Thursday.**   Not being a leap year, 1941 contained 365 days. Including January 1, 1942, the total number of days was 366. Dividing 366 by 7 yields 52 weeks *and 2 days*. The 7th, 14th, 21st, ... , 364th days were all Tuesdays. The 366th day was two days later. January 1, 1942 was on a Thursday, two days after the 52nd Tuesday.

7.   a. 987,654,321   b. 27

8.   **E.** Use the facts that each row has 6 entries and that consecutive rows count in opposite directions. Then the difference between any pair of entries two rows apart is always 12. Enter 0 in column C in the first row. Notice that the entries in column C in the odd-numbered rows are 0, 12, 24, 36, and so forth. Since these are the multiples of 12, divide 101 by 12. This produces a remainder of 5. The entry 101 appears in the same column as 5, namely column E.

A	B	C	D	E	F
			1	2	3
9	8	7	6	5	4
10	11	12	13	14	15
21	20	19	18	17	16

... and so on.

6. *Guessing and Checking*
Pages 24-25

D

1.   a.   b.   c.

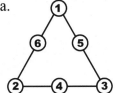   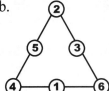   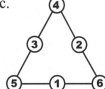

2.   3.

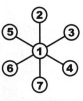

2	7	6
9	5	1
4	3	8

4.   Answer may vary. One possible solution is given for a, b, c, d, and e.

   a. $44 - 44$ b. $\dfrac{4 \times 4}{4 + 4}$ c. $\dfrac{4 + 4 + 4}{4}$ d. $\dfrac{4 + 4}{4} + \sqrt{4}$ e. $4^4 - \dfrac{4}{4}$

5.   Answers may vary. One possible solution is given.
   $1 + 2 + 3 + 4 + 5 + 6 + 7 + 8 \times 9 = 100$

6.

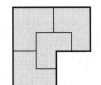

7. Experimenting
Pages 26-27

1.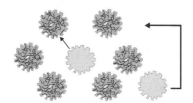

2.

3.

4.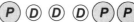

5. Fold forward along the left vertical fold so that section 3 rests on top of section 4 and section 6 rests on top of section 5. Now fold the entire bottom half backward so that section 5 is behind section 4, section 1 is behind section 2, and section 8 is behind section 7. Fold forward along the left vertical fold so that section 3 rests on top of section 2. Finally, fold forward along the remaining vertical fold so that section 7 rests on top of section 6.

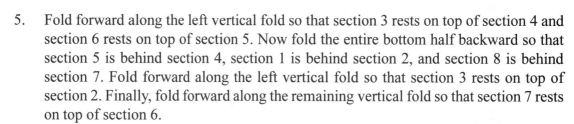

The sections now lie on top of one another so that they are numbered 1 to 8 in order from the back.

8. Acting Out the Problem
Pages 28-29.

1. **$13.** Suppose that you start with $25. After the first trade, you have the stamp and you have $25 − $15 = $10. After the second trade you have $10 + $20 = $30. After the third trade you have the stamp and $30 − $22 = $8. After the final trade you have $8 + $30 = $38. In buying and selling the stamp, you made $38 − $25 = $13.

2. **19.** After each counting, one third of the students who counted stood up. Therefore, after the first counting $\frac{1}{3}$ of 27 = 9 students stood up, leaving 27 − 9 = 18 students seated. After the second counting of 18 students, $\frac{1}{3}$ of 18 = 6 students stood up, leaving 18 − 6 = 12 students seated. After the third counting $\frac{1}{3}$ of 12 = 4 students stood up, leaving 8 students seated. After the third counting, there were 27 − 8 = 19 students standing.

3. Call the slices A, B, and C, and the sides A1 and A2, B1 and B2, and C1 and C2. In the first minute, toast A1 and B1. In the second minute, toast A2 and C1. In the third minute, toast B2 and C2.

4. **3.** There only need to be three ducks in this group to satisfy all of the conditions of the problem.

9. Working Backwards
Pages 29-31

D

1. **$120.** Work backwards from $0, the final amount. Each time that *half* of the remaining money was spent, consider that there was twice as much money previously.
$0 + $20 = $20; $20 × 2 = $40; $40 + $20 = $60; $60 × 2 = $120.
The speaker had $120 to begin with.

2. **20.** Work backwards from 40, the number in the END circle.
40 × 2 = 80; 80 − 20 = 60; 60 ÷ 3 = 20.
The number that belongs in the START circle is 20.

3. **30.** Work backwards from the 17 crayons that the teacher had at the end of the day.
17 + 11 = 28; 28 − 12 = 16; 16 + 14 = 30.
The teacher had 30 crayons at the start of the day.

4. **$7.** Work backwards from $43, the final amount.
$43 − $5 = $38; $38 ÷ 2 = $19; $19 − $5 = $14; $14 ÷ 2 = $7
The speaker first placed $7 in the box.

5. The problem has four stages. Work backwards from the final stage in which each subdivision has 16 reapers. Each time that a subdivision loans the others as many reapers as each had, consider that the others had only half as many reapers as in the previous stage. Note that the total number of reapers in any stage must be 3 × 16 = 48.

	A	*B*	*C*	**SUM**
stage 4	16	16	16	48
stage 3	8	8	32	48
stage 2	4	28	16	48
stage 1	26	14	8	48

To begin with, A had 26 reapers, B had 14 reapers, and C had 8 reapers.

10. Writing an Equation
Pages 31-33

1. Let n represent the unknown number in each case.

   a. $4n = n + 12$
   $4n - n = n + 12 - n$
   $3n = 12$
   $3n \div 3 = 12 \div 3$
   $n = 4$ **The number is 4.**

   b. $5n - 1 = 2n + 11$
   $5n - 1 - 2n = 2n + 11 - 2n$
   $3n - 1 = 11$
   $3n - 1 + 1 = 11 + 1$
   $3n = 12$
   $3n \div 3 = 12 \div 3$
   $n = 4$ **The number is 4.**

   c. $2n = 2 - n$
   $2n + n = 2 - n + n$
   $3n = 2$
   $3n \div 3 = 2 \div 3$
   $n = \frac{2}{3}$ **The number is $\frac{2}{3}$.**

   d. $\frac{1}{3}n + 11 = n - 7$
   $\frac{1}{3}n + 11 - \frac{1}{3}n = n - 7 - \frac{1}{3}n$
   $11 = \frac{2}{3}n - 7$
   $11 + 7 = \frac{2}{3}n - 7 + 7$
   $18 = \frac{2}{3}n$
   $\frac{3}{2} \times 18 = \frac{3}{2} \times \frac{2}{3}n$
   $27 = n$ **The number is 27.**

2. Let p represent the weight of one pear, q represent the weight of one quince, and r represent the weight of one raspberry. Use the information in the problem to write two equations.

   $$3p = q \qquad q = 18r$$

   Since $q = 18r$, we can substitute $18r$ for q in the first equation.

   $$3p = q$$
   $$3p = 18r$$
   $$3p \div 3 = 18r \div 3$$
   $$p = 6r$$

   Six raspberries have the same weight as one pear.

3. If q is used to represent the number of quarters, then $2q$ can be used to represent the number of nickels. Since one quarter has a value of 25 cents, the value in cents of q quarters is $25q$. Since one nickel has a value of 5 cents, the value in cents of $2q$ nickels is $5 \times 2q$, or $10q$. You can now write and solve a simple equation, using 420 as the total value in cents.

   $$25q + 10q = 420$$
   $$35q = 420$$
   $$35q \div 35 = 420 \div 35$$
   $$q = 12 \qquad \textbf{The speaker has 12 quarters.}$$

4. Let S represent Sophia's present age in years. Then $S + 10$ represents her age ten years from now, and 3S represents three times her present age. You can now write and solve a simple equation.

$$S + 10 = 3S$$
$$S + 10 - S = 3S - S$$
$$10 = 2S$$
$$10 \div 2 = 2S \div 2$$
$$5 = S \qquad \textbf{Sophia is 5 years old.}$$

5. Let n represent the first number. Then the three consecutive numbers that follow can be represented by $n + 1$, $n + 2$, and $n + 3$. You can now write and solve a simple equation.

$$n + (n + 1) + (n + 2) = (n + 3) + 12$$
$$3n + 3 = n + 15$$
$$3n + 3 - n = n + 15 - n$$
$$2n + 3 = 15$$
$$2n + 3 - 3 = 15 - 3$$
$$2n = 12$$
$$2n \div 2 = 12 \div 2$$
$$n = 6 \qquad \textbf{The four numbers are 6, 7, 8, and 9.}$$

11. Changing Your Point of View
Pages 33-34

1. It is not possible to solve this problem if you restrict yourself to a single plane surface. Arrange the sticks as the three-dimensional triangular pyramid shown; the four equilateral triangles are the four faces of the pyramid.

2. Since $5 \times 4 = 20$, it is not possible to plant the 10 trees in 5 distinct rows; some of the trees must appear in more than one row. Arrange the trees in the star-shape shown in the bird's-eye view at the right.

3   **55 minutes.**   Consider the situation not from the viewpoint of the commuter, but rather from the viewpoint of her husband. If they arrive home exactly ten minutes earlier than usual, then her husband's round trip was shortened by ten minutes, and his one-way trip was shortened by *five minutes*. This means that the commuter's husband met her at 5:55, five minutes earlier than his usual 6:00 arrival time at the station. Therefore, the commuter was walking for 55 minutes, from 5:00 to 5:55.

4. **302.** Since the tourmament will be a single-elimination tournament, each member will be out of the tournament after just one loss. Since there are 303 members in all, 302 members will each have to lose one game. This means that 302 tournament games will have to be played before a winner is declared.

5. **10 cm.** Segment *PR* is one of two diagonals of rectangle *OPQR*; the other diagonal is segment *OQ*. Segment *OQ* is a radius of the circle and its measure is 10 cm. Since the two diagonals of a rectangle have the same length, the measure of segment *OQ*, 10 cm, is the radius of the circle.

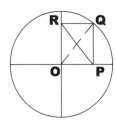

6. If you consider the four pens to be separate, there is no way to solve this problem. Try positioning one or more of the pens within a larger pen. The diagram below then shows one of many possible solutions.

12. Miscellanea
Pages 35-36

1. **62¢.** Combine the given information to obtain the fact that six oranges and six bananas cost 87¢ + 99¢ = $1.86. Then *one* orange and *one* banana cost $\frac{1}{6}$ of $1.86, = 31¢, and *two* oranges and *two* bananas cost 2 × 31¢ = 62¢.

2. Separate the nine coins into three groups containing three coins apiece. Place one group of three coins in each pan of the balance scale. If the pans balance, the counterfeit coin is in the group of coins that is not in either pan. If the pans do *not* balance, the counterfeit coin is in the group of coins in the higher pan because it is lighter. Now use the group of three coins that you know contains the counterfeit coin. Place one of the three coins in each pan of the balance scale. If the pans balance, the counterfeit coin is the coin that is not in either pan. If the pans do *not* balance, the counterfeit coin is in the pan that is higher than the other pan.

3. a. From the first and third views of the cube, the only face that is not *adjacent* to ⊡ is ▣. Therefore, ▣ is *opposite* ⊡.

    b. From the second and third views of the cube, the only face that is not *adjacent* to ⬤ is ⬚. Therefore, ⬚ is *opposite* ⬤.

    c. From the first and second views of the cube, the only face that is not *adjacent* to ⊞ is ⊠. Therefore, ⊠ is *opposite* ⊞.

4. **Only the third person is a nonswimmer.** The only possible answer to the question "Are you a swimmer?" is "Yes." A swimmer would tell the truth about this, while a nonswimmer would lie and also say "Yes." Therefore, the second person has to be telling the truth: the first person is a swimmer, and so is the second person. Since both the first and second persons are swimmers, they both tell the truth. The third person's statement is a lie. The third person is a nonswimmer.

5. ***For the Adventurous***

    Each number cube has 6 faces, so there are $6 \times 6 = 36$ different ways that the two cubes could land when they are rolled on a level surface. Since there needs to be an equal probability that the sum of the uppermost faces is any of the numbers from 1 through 12, then there must be $36 \div 12 = 3$ ways that the cubes could land to form each of the sums.

    There are 8 different ways that a pair of cubes can be numbered with whole numbers that satisfy the conditions of this problem. The first table below shows the eight different ways each pair of cubes can be numbered.

Solution	Cube 1						Cube 2					
#1	1	2	3	4	5	6	0	0	0	6	6	6
#2	0	1	2	3	4	5	1	1	1	7	7	7
#3	1	2	3	7	8	9	0	0	0	3	3	3
#4	0	1	2	6	7	8	1	1	1	4	4	4
#5	1	3	5	7	9	11	0	0	0	1	1	1
#6	0	2	4	6	8	10	1	1	1	2	2	2
#7	1	2	5	6	9	10	0	0	0	2	2	2
#8	0	1	4	5	8	9	1	1	1	3	3	3

Table 1   *Table 2*

    Notice that solutions #2, #4, #6, and #8 are related to solutions #1, #3, #5, and #7, respectively.

    The table on the next page shows how the first solution in *Table 1* produces each of the 12 sums in three ways. Each of the other seven solutions will produce the same result.

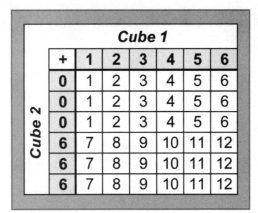

Table 3

Each entry in Table 3 appears exactly 3 of the 36 times. Therefore the probability of picking a particular sum at random, say 10, is 3 out of 36 or 1 out of 12. The same is true for each of the other solutions in the table.

If the condition that the numbers be whole numbers is removed, an infinite number of solutions can be obtained by adding any number n, rational or irrational, to each of the six numbers of cube 1 and by subtracting n from each of the six numbers of cube 2.

Solutions to Part C

Part E

1. **Number Patterns**
2. **Factors and Multiples**
3. **Divisibility**
4. **Fractions**
5. **Geometry and Measurement**
6. **Trains, Books, Clocks and Things**
7. **Logic**

E

SOLUTIONS TO PART C PROBLEMS

*If an answer and solution are given together, the answer itself is **boldfaced**, as in 2c below.*

1. Number Problems

1.1 Addition Patterns
Pages 38-41

1. a. 19   b. 31   c. 226   d. 601

2. a.

number of strokes	1	2	3	4	5
number of parts	3	5	7	9	11

Notice that, each time a new stroke is drawn, the number of parts increases by 2.
   b. 3, 5, 7, 9, 11, …
   c. **Yes.** If n is the order of the term, one way to state a rule is that each term is one greater than twice its order $(2n + 1)$. Another way to state the rule: each given term is the sum of 3, the first term, and a number of 2s that is one less than the order of the given term.
   d. **201.** $2 \times 100 + 1 = 200 + 1 = 201$ *or* $3 + 99 \times 2 = 3 + 198 = 201$.
   Either way, the result is that the symbol is separated into 201 parts.
   e. 82

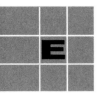

3. a. 23, 27, 31
   b. 11, 12, 13
   c. $4\frac{1}{2}$, 5, $5\frac{1}{2}$
   d. 6.5, 6.8, 7.1

4. a. **199**: $(4 \times 50 - 1,$ or $3 + 49 \times 4)$
   b. **55**: $(1 \times 50 + 5,$ or $6 + 49 \times 1)$
   c. **$26\frac{1}{2}$**: $(\frac{1}{2} \times 50 + 1\frac{1}{2},$ or $2 + 49 \times \frac{1}{2})$
   d. **19.7**: $(0.3 \times 50 + 4.7,$ or $5 + 49 \times 0.3)$

5. **21.** **Method 1:** Each term of the sequence is 3 less than 5 times the order of the term. If we choose n to represent the order of the term, then the term can be represented as $5n - 3$. The given term has a value of 102, so solve the equation $5n - 3 = 102$ to get $n = 21$. Then 102 is the 21st term of this sequence.

<u>**Method 2:**</u> The sequence follows a pattern of adding 5s. Starting at 2, the first term of the sequence, the number of 5s that must be added to arrive at 102 is 20. 102 is the 21st term of the sequence.

6. **5, 12, 19, 26, 33, 40, 47, 54, 61, and 68.** The tenth term of any arithmetic sequence is equal to the first term increased by nine times the constant difference. In this arithmetic sequence, the total of these nine constant differences is $68 - 5 = 63$. Therefore, *each* constant difference is $63 \div 9 = 7$. The first ten terms of the sequence are 5, 12, 19, 26, 33, 40, 47, 54, 61, and 68.

7. **100.**

number of wraparounds	1	2	3	4	5
number of pieces	2	4	6	8	10

When you organize some data as in the table above, you see that the number of pieces is always twice the number of wraparounds. For 50 wraparounds, the number of pieces formed would be $2 \times 50 = 100$.

8. a. **E**   b. **G**
For both parts *a* and *b*, consider each column to represent an arithmetic sequence whose constant difference is 7 and whose first term is either 1, 2, 3, 4, 5, 6, or 7. You can find the correct column for 999 by dividing by 7: $999 \div 7 = 142$ R5. This gives you the information that 999 is the result of adding 142 sevens to 5. Therefore, 5 is the first term of the appropriate sequence for 999. In part *a*, 999 appears under E; in part *b*, 999 appears under G.

9. **Monday.** Tuesdays occur on days 1, 8, 15, and 22.

10. **Friday.** January 1 falls on Friday as does January 8, 15, 22, and 29. January 31 falls on Sunday. Then February 1, 8, and 15 fall on Monday and February 19 falls on Friday.

11. **April 10.** January, February, and March have a total of $31 + 28 + 31 = 90$ days.

12. Show that 3n + 1 equals 4 + 3(n – 1):
$4 + 3(n - 1) = 4 + 3n - 3 = 3n + 1$

1.2 *Multiplication Patterns*
Page 42-44

1. a.

Day	1	2	3	4	5
Pay (in ¢)	5	15	45	135	405

b. 5, 15, 45, 135, 405, …

   c. **Yes.** One way to state the rule is that each term is the product of 5 multiplied by a power of 3, where the power of 3 is one less than the order of the term.

   d. **$984.15.** $5 \times 3^9 = 5 \times 19{,}683 = 98{,}415¢ = \$984.15$

2.   a. 486, 1458, 4374

    b. 9375; 46,875; 234,375

    c. $\frac{64}{729}, \frac{128}{2187}, \frac{256}{6561}$

    d. 0.05, 0.005, 0.0005

3.   a. 2×3^{19}

    b. 3×5^{19}

    c. $\frac{2}{3} \times \left(\frac{2}{3}\right)^{19}$, or $\left(\frac{2}{3}\right)^{20}$

    d. $5000 \times (0.1)^{19}$, or $5000 \times \left(\frac{1}{10}\right)^{19}$

4.   **8th.** The sequence follows a pattern of multiplying the first term, 4, by a number of 3s. Consider that $8748 \div 4 = 2187$, and $2187 = 3^7$. The number of 3s being multiplied is one less than the order of the given term. 8748 is the eighth term of this sequence.

5.   **2, 10, 50, 250, and 1250.** The fifth term of any geometric sequence is equal to the first term multiplied by the constant quotient four times. In this geometric sequence, the product of these four constant quotients is $1250 \div 2 = 625$. Since $625 = 5^4$, the constant quotient is 5. The first five terms of the sequence are 2, 10, 50, 250, and 1250.

6.   **1048.576 in.**

number of tears	1	2	3	4	5
number of pieces	2	4	8	16	32

When you organize some data as in the table for problem 7 on the previous page, you see that the number of pieces is always a power of 2. Specifically, the number of pieces is equal to 2 raised to an exponent that equals the number of tears: 1 tear yields $2 = 2^1$ pieces; 2 tears yield $4 = 2^2$ pieces; 3 tears yield $8 = 2^3$ pieces, and so on. Therefore, 20 tears would yield $2^{20} = 1{,}048{,}576$ pieces. Since each piece is 0.001 in. thick, the height of the final pile is $1{,}048{,}576 \times 0.001 = 1048.576$ in., which is approximately 87 ft or 29 yd.

7.   **2 hr. 57 min.** If each amoeba reproduces itself in three minutes, then every three minutes the volume is doubled. Working backwards, if the jar was filled in three hours, then it was half full only three minutes before. It took two hours and fifty-seven minutes for the jar to become half-full.

1.3 More Addition Patterns
Pages 44-46

1.   a. 78   b. 120   c. 171   d. 210

2.

layer	1	2	3	4	5
number of grapefruits	1	4	9	16	25

When you organize some data as in the table above, you see that the number of grapefruits in each layer is the square of the number of the layer.

　a. $12^2 = 144$　　b. $15^2 = 225$　　c. $50^2 = 2500$　　d. $100^2 = 10,000$

3.　a. **27, 35, 44.**　　$2 \xrightarrow{+3} 5 \xrightarrow{+4} 9 \xrightarrow{+5} 14 \xrightarrow{+6} 20 \xrightarrow{+7} 27 \xrightarrow{+8} 35 \xrightarrow{+9} 44$

　　b. **37, 50, 65.**　　$2 \xrightarrow{+3} 5 \xrightarrow{+5} 10 \xrightarrow{+7} 17 \xrightarrow{+9} 26 \xrightarrow{+11} 37 \xrightarrow{+13} 50 \xrightarrow{+15} 65$

　　c. **43, 57, 73.**　　$3 \xrightarrow{+4} 7 \xrightarrow{+6} 13 \xrightarrow{+8} 21 \xrightarrow{+10} 31 \xrightarrow{+12} 43 \xrightarrow{+14} 57 \xrightarrow{+16} 73$

　　d. **67, 92, 121.**　　$2 \xrightarrow{+5} 7 \xrightarrow{+9} 16 \xrightarrow{+13} 29 \xrightarrow{+17} 46 \xrightarrow{+21} 67 \xrightarrow{+25} 92 \xrightarrow{+29} 121$

4.　a. Each term is one greater than the square of its order:　　$(n^2 + 1)$
　　b. Each term is one less than the square of its order:　　$(n^2 - 1)$
　　c. Each term is twice the square of its order:　　$(2n^2)$
　　d. Each term is the sum of the order and its square:　　$(n^2 + n)$

5.　a. $12^2 + 1　= 144 + 1　= 145$
　　b. $12^2 - 1　= 144 - 1　= 143$
　　c. $2 \times 12^2　= 2 \times 144　= 288$
　　d. $12^2 + 12　= 144 + 12　= 156$

6.　a. **35, 51, 70, 92, 117, and 145.**
　　　$1 \xrightarrow{+4} 5 \xrightarrow{+7} 12 \xrightarrow{+10} 22 \xrightarrow{+13} 35 \xrightarrow{+16} 51 \xrightarrow{+19} 70 \xrightarrow{+22} 92 \xrightarrow{+25} 117 \xrightarrow{+28} 145$

　　b. **45, 66, 91, 120, 153, and 190.**
　　　$1 \xrightarrow{+5} 6 \xrightarrow{+9} 15 \xrightarrow{+13} 28 \xrightarrow{+17} 45 \xrightarrow{+21} 66 \xrightarrow{+25} 91 \xrightarrow{+29} 120 \xrightarrow{+33} 153 \xrightarrow{+37} 190$

　　c. **30, 42, 56, 72, 90, and 110.**
　　　$2 \xrightarrow{+4} 6 \xrightarrow{+6} 12 \xrightarrow{+8} 20 \xrightarrow{+10} 30 \xrightarrow{+12} 42 \xrightarrow{+14} 56 \xrightarrow{+16} 72 \xrightarrow{+18} 90 \xrightarrow{+20} 110$

1.4　Unusual Patterns
Pages 46-49

1.　a. **12, 42.** The numbers are multiples of 3 with the order of their digits reversed.
　　b. **96, 1.** The numbers are formed by adding 4 to the previous number, and then reversing the order of the digits in this sum.
　　c. **89, 145.** The numbers are formed by adding the squares of the digits of the previous number.

d. **14,11.** One pattern could be: subtract 3, add 4; subtract 3, add 6; subtract 3, add 8, subtract 3, add 10; and so on.

2. a. **E.** Each letter is the first letter of the name of a counting number, in order: One, Two, Three, Four, Five, Six, Seven.
    b. **5 and its mirror image:** ᴙ
       Each symbol is a numeral for a counting number and its mirror image over a vertical line at its left: **ᴙ, ꙅ2, ꗱ3, ᴤ4**

3. a. Beginning with the third term of the sequence, each term is the sum of the two preceding terms.
    b. **21, 34, 55.** $8 + 13 = 21$, $13 + 21 = 34$, $21 + 34 = 55$.
    c.

Order of Middle Term	Consecutive Terms	Square of Middle Term	Product of Outer Terms
2nd	1, 1, 2	$1^2 = 1$	$1 \times 2 = 2$
3rd	1, 2, 3	$2^2 = 4$	$1 \times 3 = 3$
4th	2, 3, 5	$3^2 = 9$	$2 \times 5 = 10$
5th	3, 5, 8	$5^2 = 25$	$3 \times 8 = 24$
6th	5, 8, 13	$8^2 = 64$	$5 \times 13 = 65$

When you organize the sets of consecutive terms as in the table above, you see that the product of the outer terms is one greater or one less than the square of the middle term. If the *order* of the middle term is even, then the product of the outer terms is one *greater* than the square of the middle term; otherwise, the product of the outer terms is one *less*.

d.

Order of First Term	Consecutive Terms	Product of Middle Terms	Product of Outer Terms
1st	1, 1, 2, 3	2	3
2nd	1, 2, 3, 5	6	5
3rd	2, 3, 5, 8	15	16
4th	3, 5, 8, 13	40	39

When you organize some data as in the table in part 3c, you see that the products differ by one. If the order of the first of the consecutive terms is odd, then the product of the outer terms is one *greater* than the product of the middle terms. If it is even, the outer product is one *less* than the product of the middle terms. Another way to generalize: the product of the inner terms is one smaller than the product of the outer terms for odd-numbered lines; the reverse is true for even-numbered lines.

4. $\frac{34}{55}$.

leaf	2	3	4	5	6	7	8	9
distance from previous leaf	$\frac{1}{2}$	$\frac{2}{3}$	$\frac{3}{5}$	$\frac{5}{8}$	$\frac{8}{13}$	$\frac{13}{21}$	$\frac{21}{34}$	$\frac{34}{55}$

The numerators and denominators of the fractions follow the progression of the Fibonacci sequence. The 9th leaf will sprout $\frac{34}{55}$ of the way around the stalk from the 8th leaf.

5. Draw a diagram following a portion of the male bee's ancestry, then record the data in a table.

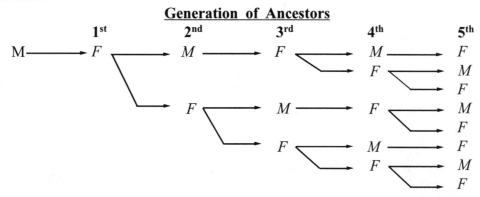

Generation of Ancestors

generation of ancestors	1	2	3	4	5	6	7	8	9	10
number of ancestors	1	2	3	5	8	13	21	34	55	89

The ancestry of the male bee follows the Fibonacci sequence of numbers.

Answer: **The male bee has two 2nd generation ancestors, three 3rd generation ancestors, five 4th generation ancestors, eight 5th generation ancestors, and eighty-nine 10th generation ancestors.**

6 a. Each interior entry of the array is the sum of the two closest entries above it.
   b. The numbers in the 8th row are 1, 7, 21, 35, 35, 21, 7, 1
   c. 1, 1, 1; 7, 8, 9; 21, 28, 36; 35, 56, 84

7. a. The number of different routes to each position is shown on this grid. The number of routes from Pascal's house to each location is shown in parentheses.

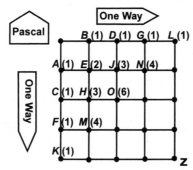

b. **70.** Note that, when viewed diagonally, the numbers on the grid at the right are the numbers of the Pascal triangle. Continue the pattern across the grid, as shown below. There are 70 different routes to location Z.

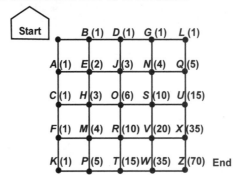

8. a. Proceeding clockwise, the number in each link is the sum of the numbers in the two preceding links, providing that the sum is less than 10. If the sum is 10 or greater, the number in the new link is just the ones digit of the sum.

   b. Proceeding clockwise from the *2, 2, 4* sequence at the top of the bracelet, the numbers in the twenty links are as follows, including 2, 2, 4:

   Answer: **2, 2, 4, 6, 0, 6, 6, 2, 8, 0, 8, 8, 6, 4, 0, 4, 4, 8, 2, 0**

   c. Proceeding clockwise from the *1, 1, 2* sequence that is given, the numbers in the sixty links are as follows:

   1, 1, 2, 3, 5, 8, 3, 1, 4, 5, 9, 4, 3, 7, 0,
   7, 7, 4, 1, 5, 6, 1, 7, 8, 5, 3, 8, 1, 9, 0,
   9, 9, 8, 7, 5, 2, 7, 9, 6, 5, 1, 6, 7, 3, 0,
   3, 3, 6, 9, 5, 4, 9, 3, 2, 5, 7, 2, 9, 1, 0

   If you proceed beyond the sixtieth number, the sequence of numbers will begin repeating at the *1, 1, 2* sequence with which you started.

1.5 Patterns and Sums
Pages 49-51

1. a. **55.** There are 5 pairs of numbers that each have the sum 11. The total is $5 \times 11 = 55$.

   b. **1275.** There are 25 pairs of numbers that each have the sum 51. The total is $25 \times 51 = 1275$.

   c. **2850.** $1 + 2 + 3 + \ldots + 38 + \ldots + 73 + 74 + 75$

   There are 37 pairs of numbers that each have the sum 76, but there is also the number 38 that cannot be paired with another number. The sum of all the numbers is $37 \times 76 + 38 = 2812 + 38 = 2850$.

d. **75.** There are 5 pairs of numbers that each have the sum 15. The total is $5 \times 15 = 75$.

e. **4085.** There are 43 pairs of numbers that each have the sum 95. The total is $43 \times 95 = 4085$.

f. **1435.** This problem is similar to problem 1c on page 156. In this case, there are 20 pairs of numbers that each have the sum 70, but there is also the number 35 that cannot be paired with another number. Therefore, the sum of all the numbers is $20 \times 70 + 35 = 1400 + 35 = 1435$.

2. **$667.95.** $1¢ + 2¢ + 3¢ + \ldots + 183¢ + \ldots + 363¢ + 364¢ + 365¢ = 182 \times 366¢ + 183¢ = 66{,}795¢$ or \$667.95

3. **820.** The numbers of pins in the 40 rows is the sum of the first 40 counting numbers. The total number of pins in the arrangement is $20 \times 41 = 820$.

4. The sum of all the numbers on the clock face is $1 + 2 + 3 + \ldots + 10 + 11 + 12 = 6 \times 13 = 78$. If the two lines that you draw do not intersect, they will separate the clock face into 3 regions. Therefore, the sum of the numbers in each region would have to be $78 \div 3 = 26$. The placement of lines shown will give you the desired result because $1+12 = 2+11 = 3+10 = 4+9 = 5+8 = 6+7 = 13$, and $2 \times 13 = 26$.

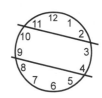

Note that, if you tried to draw two lines so that they intersected within the clock face, the lines would separate the clock face into 4 regions. But $78 \div 4 = 19.5$, so it would be impossible for the sum of the numbers in each of the 4 regions to be the same.

5. Answers may vary. One possible answer is given here.
   a. 1, 2, 3 $(1 + 2 + 3 = 6)$
   b. 1, 2, 3, 4, 5, 6, 7, 8, 9, 10, 11, 12 $(1 + 2 + 3 + \cdots + 10 + 11 + 12 = 78)$
   c. 0, 1, 2, 3, 4, 5, 6, 7, 8 $(1 + 2 + 3 + \cdots + 6 + 7 + 8 = 36)$
   d. 0, 1, 2, 3, 4, 5, 6, 7, 20 $(0 + 1 + 2 + 3 + 4 + 5 + 6 + 7 + 20 = 48)$

6. a. **2500.** The numbers can be paired so that there are 25 pairs of numbers, each having the sum 100. The sum of all 25 pairs is $25 \times 100 = 2500$.
   b. **1225.** The numbers can be paired so that there are 12 pairs of numbers, each having the sum 98. There is also the number 49, which cannot be paired with another different number. The sum of all the numbers is $12 \times 98 + 49 = 1176 + 49 = 1225$.
   c. **2850.** The numbers can be paired so that there are 19 pairs of numbers, each having the sum 150. The sum of all 19 pairs is $19 \times 150 = 2850$.
   d. **1650.** The numbers can be paired so that there are 16 pairs of numbers, each having the sum 100. The number 50 cannot be paired with a different number. The sum of all the numbers is $16 \times 100 + 50 = 1650$.

7. **400.**

number of rings	1	2	3	4	5	...	20
number of guests	1	3	5	7	9	...	39
total number of guests	1	4	9	16	25	...	?

Compare the total number of guests with the total number of rings. Observe that the total number of guests is the square of the corresponding number of rings. The total number of guests is 20^2 or 400.

8. There are many possible answers.
    Case 1: Place 1 in the center circle; 4 arrangements of the other numbers are possible.

one diagonal	other diagonal
2, 3, 8, 9	4, 5, 6, 7
2, 4, 7, 9	3, 5, 6, 8
2, 5, 6, 9	3, 4, 7, 8
2, 5, 7, 8	3, 4, 6, 9

    Case 2: Place 3 in the center circle; 3 arrangements of the other numbers are possible.

one diagonal	other diagonal
1, 4, 7, 9	2, 5, 6, 8
1, 5, 6, 9	2, 4, 7, 8
1, 5, 7, 8	2, 4, 6, 9

    Case 3: Place 5 in the center circle; 4 arrangements of the other numbers are possible.

one diagonal	other diagonal
1, 2, 8, 9	3, 4, 6, 7
1, 3, 7, 9	2, 4, 6, 8
1, 4, 6, 9	2, 3, 7, 8
1, 4, 7, 8	2, 3, 6, 9

    Case 4: Place 7 in the center circle; 3 arrangements of the other numbers are possible.

one diagonal	other diagonal
1, 3, 6, 9	2, 4, 5, 8
1, 4, 6, 8	2, 3, 5, 9
1, 4, 5, 9	2, 3, 6, 8

    Case 5: Place 9 in the center circle; 4 arrangements of the other numbers are possible.

one diagonal	other diagonal
1, 2, 7, 8	3, 4, 5, 6
1, 3, 6, 8	2, 4, 5, 7
1, 4, 5, 8	2, 3, 6, 7
1, 4, 6, 7	2, 3, 5, 8

Note that an even number cannot be placed in the center circle, since that would leave five odd numbers to be distributed along the diagonals. No matter how you did this, one diagonal would have to have an odd sum while the other diagonal would have an even sum.

9. **255.**

Day	Number of People Told	Total	
1. Sunday	1	1	$(1 = 2^1 - 1)$
2. Monday	2	$1 + 2 = 3$	$(3 = 2^2 - 1)$
3. Tuesday	3	$1 + 2 + 4 = 7$	$(7 = 2^3 - 1)$
4. Wednesday	8	$1 + 2 + 4 + 8 = 15$	$(15 = 2^4 - 1)$
5. Thursday	16	$1 + 2 + 4 + 8 + 16 + = 31$	$(31 = 2^5 - 1)$

If we assign the counting numbers to the days as shown in the table above, on day n the total number of people who know the secret is $2^n - 1$. The following Sunday would be day 8 of this progression, and so the total number of people who would know the secret by the end of that day would be $2^8 - 1 = 256 - 1 = 255$.

2. Factors and Multiples

2.1 Factors
Pages 52-54

1. 1, 2, 3, 6, 9, 18

2. 1, 2, 3, 4, 6, 9, 12, 18, 36
    $1 \times 36, 2 \times 18, 3 \times 12, 4 \times 9$
    6 has to be paired with itself

3. 1×90, 2×45, 3×30, 5×18, 6×15, 9×10

4. 1, 4, 9, 16, 25, 36, 49, 64, 81, 100

5. 225, 256, 289, or 15^2, 16^2, 17^2

6. **31.** The largest square number less than 1000 is $961 = 31^2$. Then each of the following square numbers is less than 1000: $1^2, 2^2, 3^2, 4^2, 5^2, \dots , 31^2$.

7. $11^2 = 121 < 132 < 12^2 = 144$. Therefore, 132 lies between 11^2 and 12^2.

8. $2045 = 45^2$

9. **10.** $2000 < 2045 = 45^2; 2916 = 54^2 < 3000$
    Square numbers between 2000 and 3000 are 45^2, 46^2, 47^2, 48^2, ..., 54^2.
    There are 10 perfect squares between 2000 and 3000.

10. a. **3 Terminal Zeros.** $(700 \times 80 = 56,000)$
     b. **4 Terminal Zeros.** $(80 \times 400 \times 30 = 960,000)$
     c. **5 Terminal Zeros.** $(500 \times 600 = 300,000)$
     d. **6 Terminal Zeros.** $(5 \times 10 \times 100 \times 1000 = 5,000,000)$

11. **3, 3, and 8.** The table at the right lists all the ways that 72 can be expressed as the product of three whole numbers. Include in the table the sum of each combination of whole numbers.

     Since the census worker knew the house number, he or she would know the children's ages in every case *except* if the house number was 14, because there are two combinations of possible ages that have a sum of 14. Therefore, this must be

Numbers	Sum
1, 1, 72	74
1, 2, 36	39
1, 3, 24	28
1, 4, 18	23
1, 6, 12	19
1, 8, 9	18
2, 2, 18	22
2, 3, 12	17
2, 4, 9	15
2, 6, 6	14
3, 3, 8	14
3, 4, 6	13

the source of the census worker's confusion; the ages of the children could be 2, 6, and 6, or 3, 3, and 8. The additional information that there is an *oldest* child eliminates 2, 6, and 6 as possible ages for the children. Therefore, the children's ages are 3, 3, and 8.

2.2 *Factors and Primes*
Pages 54-56

1.

		# Factors			# Factors
a.	$64 = 2^6$	7	e.	$400 = 2^4 \times 5^2$	15
b.	$81 = 3^4$	5	f.	$648 = 2^3 \times 3^4$	20
c.	$125 = 5^3$	4	g.	$875 = 7 \times 5^3$	8
d.	$343 = 7^3$	4	h.	$540 = 2^2 \times 3^3 \times 5$	24

2. 13, 17, 19

3. 23, 29, 31, 37, 41, 43, 47

4. 97

5. (11, 11), (17, 71), (37, 73), (79, 97)

6. **Neither.** $72 = 3^2 \times 2^3$ has 12 factors; $96 = 2^5 \times 3$ has 12 factors also. Neither has more factors.

7. $1 \times 1 \times 24$; $1 \times 2 \times 12$; $1 \times 3 \times 8$; $1 \times 4 \times 6$; $2 \times 2 \times 6$; $2 \times 3 \times 4$

8. **24, 25, and 26.** $20^3 = 8000 < 15,600$; $30^3 = 27,000 > 15,600$.

    Therefore the three consecutive numbers are between 20 and 30. Since 15,600 has two terminal zeros, the product has two factors of 5 and 2 factors of 2 or 1 factor of 4. We conclude that one of the three consecutive numbers is 25 and the only possibilities for the three consecutive numbers are: $23 \times 24 \times 25$, $24 \times 25 \times 26$, and $25 \times 26 \times 27$.

    The third product does not satisfy the condition that the product is divisible by 4. Check the remaining two products: $23 \times 24 \times 25 = 13,800$ and $24 \times 25 \times 26 = 15,600$. The three consecutive numbers are 24, 25, and 26.

9. A terminal zero occurs when a number has a factor of 5 and a factor of 2. In a factorial product, we need to find the terms which have a factor of one or more 5s. From the table on the next page, observe that every other term of a factorial product has a factor of 2 and that the number of 2s as a factor will be greater than the numbers of 5s in a factorial product.

# in factorial form	Terms with 5 as a factor	Total # of 5s	# of terminal zeros
7!	5	1	1
10!	10, 5	2	2
18!	15, 10, 5	3	3
25!	25, 20, 15, 10, 5	6 *(Note: 25 = 5 × 5)*	6

Observation: 25! has six 5s as factors and twenty-two 2s as factors.

10. a. **15.** $5! \div 2^3 = 120 \div 8 = 15$

b. **210.** $7! \div 4! = 5040 \div 24 = 210$

c. **600.** $6! - 5! = 5! \times 6 - 5! \times 1 = 5! \times (6-1) = 120 \times 5 = 600$

11. **32 and 3125.** $100,000 = 10^5 = (2 \times 5)^5 = 2^5 \times 5^5$

$2^5 = 32$ and $5^5 = 3125$. Check: the product of 32 and 3125 is 100,000.

12. Each of the following sixteen numbers is less than 100 and has exactly six factors:

$2^2 \times 3, \quad 2^2 \times 5, \quad 2^2 \times 7, \quad 2^2 \times 11, \quad 2^2 \times 13, \quad 2^2 \times 17, \quad 2^2 \times 19, \quad 2^2 \times 23$

$3^2 \times 2, \quad 3^2 \times 5, \quad 3^2 \times 7, \quad 3^2 \times 11$

$5^2 \times 2, \quad 5^2 \times 3$

$7^2 \times 2$

2^5

Answer: **In standard form, the numbers are: 12, 18, 20, 28, 32, 44, 45, 50, 52, 63, 68, 75, 76, 92, 98, and 99.**

13. a. 6: $3 + 3$

10: $3 + 7$ or $5 + 5$

28: $5 + 23$ or $11 + 17$

b. 7: $2 + 2 + 3$

9: $2 + 2 + 5$ or $3 + 3 + 3$

21: $2 + 2 + 17$; $3 + 5 + 13$; $3 + 7 + 11$; $5 + 5 + 11$; $7 + 7 + 7$

2.3 Greatest Common Factor
Pages 57-60

1. a. GCF(18,30) = 6   b. GCF(84,56) = 28
c. GCF(12,60) = 12   d. GCF(21,10) = 1

2. a. GCF(54,144) = 18   b. GCF(38,95) = 19
c. GCF(629,2257) = 37. Use Euclid's Algorithm (see next page).

$$629\overline{)2257} \qquad 370\overline{)629} \qquad 259\overline{)370} \qquad 111\overline{)259} \qquad 37\overline{)111}$$

$$\begin{array}{c}\underline{1887}\\370\end{array} \quad \begin{array}{c}\underline{370}\\259\end{array} \quad \begin{array}{c}\underline{259}\\111\end{array} \quad \begin{array}{c}\underline{222}\\37\end{array} \quad \begin{array}{c}\underline{111}\\0\end{array}$$

GCF (629,2257) = 37

3.   a. $\frac{3}{4}$. GCF(54,72) = 18. $\dfrac{54}{72} = \dfrac{54 \div 18}{72 \div 18} = \dfrac{3}{4}$

   b. $\frac{7}{23}$. GCF(119,391) = 17. $\dfrac{119}{391} = \dfrac{119 \div 17}{391 \div 17} = \dfrac{7}{23}$

   c. $\frac{7}{13}$. Use Euclid's Algorithm.

$$679\overline{)1261} \qquad 582\overline{)679} \qquad 97\overline{)582} \qquad \text{GCF}(679,1261) = 17.$$

$$\begin{array}{c}\underline{679}\\582\end{array} \qquad \begin{array}{c}\underline{582}\\97\end{array} \qquad \begin{array}{c}\underline{582}\\0\end{array}$$

$$\dfrac{679}{1261} = \dfrac{679 \div 97}{1261 \div 97} = \dfrac{7}{13}$$

   d. $\frac{17}{23}$. Use Euclid's Algorithm.

$$1921\overline{)2599} \qquad 678\overline{)1921} \qquad 565\overline{)678} \qquad 113\overline{)565} \qquad \text{GCF } (1921,2599) = 113.$$

$$\begin{array}{c}\underline{1921}\\678\end{array} \quad \begin{array}{c}\underline{1356}\\565\end{array} \quad \begin{array}{c}\underline{565}\\113\end{array} \quad \begin{array}{c}\underline{679}\\0\end{array}$$

$$\dfrac{1921}{2599} = \dfrac{1921 \div 113}{2599 \div 113} = \dfrac{17}{23}$$

4.   **24.** GCF (48,72,96) = 24. The greatest number of discussion groups is 24.

USA $96 \div 24 = 4$
Canada $72 \div 24 = 3$
Mexico $48 \div 24 = 2$

Answer: **Each discussion group will be attended by 4 USA students, 3 Canadian students, and 2 Mexican students.**

5.   a. 27 and 64 are relatively prime because GCF(27,64) = 1
   b. 112 and 175 are not relatively prime because they have a common factor of 7.
      $112 = 7 \times 16$ and $175 = 7 \times 25$.
   c. 18, 35, 75 are not coprime pairwise because 35 and 75 have a common factor of 5.
   d. 13, 45, 56 are relatively prime pairwise because each of the pairs (13,45), (45,56), and (13,56) is relatively prime pairwise.

6. 4.

Power of 3	3^1	3^2	3^3	3^4	3^5	3^6	3^7	3^8
Value	3	9	27	81	243	729	2187	6561
Remainder	3	4	2	1	3	4	2	1

The remainders repeat in cycles of 4. If the exponent of 3 is a multiple of 4 (3^4, 3^8, 3^{12}, and so on), the remainder is 1. For all other exponents greater than 4, subtract the largest multiple of 4 which is less than the exponent. This leaves either 3^1, 3^2, or 3^3. The corresponding remainders 3, 4, and 2 can be read from the table. The remainder when 3^{10} is divided by 5 is the same as the remainder you get when 3^2 is divided by 5. That remainder is 4.

7. a. 2 tiles by 3 tiles:
    The line crosses 4 tiles.

    4 tiles by 6 tiles:
    The line crosses 8 tiles.

    6 tiles by 9 tiles:
    The line crosses 12 tiles.

    8 tiles by 12 tiles:
    The line crosses 16 tiles.

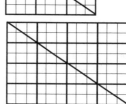

   b. **56.** If the floor measures 24 × 40 tiles, the line will cross 56 tiles.
   c. Add the dimensions of the tiled floor. Subtract the GCF of the two dimensions from their sum. The result is the number of tiles crossed by the diagonal line.
   d. **144.** 54 + 96 = 150 and GCF (54,96) = 6.
      150 − 6 = 144. The diagonal line will cross 144 tiles.

2.4 Least Common Multiple
Pages 60-63

1. a. LCM (6,10) = $2 \times 3 \times 5$ = 30 because 6 = 2×3 and 10 = 2×5
    b. LCM (24,54) = $2^3 \times 3^3$ = 216 because 24 = $2^3 \times 3$ and 54 = 2×3^3
    c. LCM (108,126) = $2^2 \times 3^3 \times 7$ = 756 because 108 = $2^2 \times 3^3$; 126 = $2 \times 3^2 \times 7$
    d. LCM (6,8,15) = $2^3 \times 3 \times 5$ = 120 because 6 = 2×3; 8 = 2^3; 15 = 3×5

2. LCM (4,5,6) = $2^2 \times 3 \times 5$ = 60 because 4 = 2^2; 6 = 2×3; 5 = 5

3. LCM $(6,7,8) = 2^3 \times 3 \times 7 = 168$ because $6 = 2 \times 3$; $8 = 2^3$; $7 = 7$

4. LCM $(9,10,11,12) = 2^2 \times 3^2 \times 5 \times 11 = 1980$ because $9 = 3^2$; $10 = 2 \times 5$; $11 = 11$; and $12 = 2^2 \times 3$

5. $16 \times 20 = 320$ $18 \times 48 = 864$
    GCF $(16,20) = 4$ GCF $(18,48) = 6$
    LCM $(16,20) = 80$ LCM $(18,48) = 144$
    GCF $\times$ LCM $= 320$ GCF $\times$ LCM $= 864$

    a. The product of the two numbers equals the product of their GCF and LCM.
        That is, if A and B are two natural numbers, then $A \times B =$ GCF $(A,B) \times$ LCM (A,B).

    b. To find the LCM of two numbers, divide their product by their GCF.
        That is, LCM $(A,B) = \dfrac{A \times B}{\text{GCF}(A,B)}$.

    c. **180.** The product of 36 and 60 is 2160. 2160 divided by 12 is 180.
        The LCM of 36 and 60 is 180.

6. **61.** The number we seek is 1 more than the LCM of 2, 3, 4, and 5.
    The LCM of 2, 3, 4, and 5 is 60. The smallest number that satisfies the conditions is 61.

7. **59.** If 1 is added to the number we seek, the result is divisible by each of the numbers 2, 3, 4, and 5. The result is divisible by 60. 60 is 1 more than the number we seek. The smallest number that satisfies the conditions is 59.

8. **3 tables of 5 and 8 tables of 8.** If we subtract a multiple of 5 from the 79 (people), that leaves a multiple of 8 ending in 4 such as 24 or 64. Consider both possible solutions.
    Case 1:   3 tables of 5 people leaves $79 - 15 = 64$ people to be seated at 8 tables of 8. This requires a total of 11 tables.
    Case 2:   11 tables of 5 people leaves $79 - 55 = 24$ people to be seated at 3 tables of 8. This requires a total of 14 tables.
    Notice that only Case 1 satisfies the condition that fewer than 12 tables should be used.

9. ***For The Adventurous***
    301. LCM $(2,3,2^2,5,6) = 2^2 \times 3 \times 5 = 60$
    The number must be 1 more than a common multiple of 2, 3, 4, 5, and 6. That is, the number we seek must be 1 more than a multiple of 60. Candidates for this number are: 61, 121, 181, 241, 301, 361, ... The first member of this set that is divisible by 7 is 301. The smallest number which has a remainder of 1 when divided by 2, 3, 4, 5, or 6 and also is exactly divisible by 7 is 301.

3. Divisibility

3.1 Divisibility by 2, 5, 10, 100
Pages 65 – 66

1. a. **56.** There are two cases to consider.

    Case 1: The ones digit is 5. Every set of ten consecutive whole numbers contains one number whose ones digit is 5. Since 500 page numbers contain 50 such sets, there are 50 different page numbers whose ones digit is 5.

    Case 2: The ones digit is 0. These numbers will satisfy the conditions of the problem only if they have a 5 in the tens or hundreds places. There are 6 such numbers: 50, 150, 250, 350, 450, and 500.

    Considering both cases, there are 50 + 6 = 56 page numbers that contain the digit 5 and that are also divisible by 5.

    b. **40.** The digit 5 cannot be in the ones place, since the number would be divisible by 5. The only number with the digit 5 in the hundreds place is 500, and this is divisible by 5. Therefore, consider only those numbers that contain the digit 5 in the tens place. The following page numbers satisfy the conditions of the problem.

    $$51, \quad 52, \quad 53, \quad 54, \quad 56, \quad 57, \quad 58, \quad 59$$
    $$151, \ 152, \ 153, \ 154, \ 156, \ 157, \ 158, \ 159$$
    $$251, \ 252, \ 253, \ 254, \ 256, \ 257, \ 258, \ 259$$
    $$351, \ 352, \ 353, \ 354, \ 356, \ 357, \ 358, \ 359$$
    $$451, \ 452, \ 453, \ 454, \ 456, \ 457, \ 458, \ 459$$

    The 40 page numbers listed above contain the digit 5 but none are divisible by 5.

    c. **44.** Consider only those numbers whose ones digit is 0. The following numbers satisfy the conditions of the problem.

    $$10, \quad 20, \quad 30, \quad 40, \quad 60, \quad 70, \quad 80, \quad 90$$
    $$100, \ 110, \ 120, \ 130, \ 140, \ 160, \ 170, \ 180, \ 190$$
    $$200, \ 210, \ 220, \ 230, \ 240, \ 260, \ 270, \ 280, \ 290$$
    $$300, \ 310, \ 320, \ 330, \ 340, \ 360, \ 370, \ 380, \ 390$$
    $$400, \ 410, \ 420, \ 430, \ 440, \ 460, \ 470, \ 480, \ 490$$

    In the above list, there are 44 numbers, each of which does not contain the digit 5 but each number is divisible by 5.

2. a. even   b. even   c. odd   d. even   e. odd
    f. odd   g. even

3. a. even   b. odd   c. even   d. even   e. odd
   f. even   g. even

4. a.

   b.

×	E	O
E	E	E
O	E	O

5. a. 5:   21, 23, 25, 27, 29
   b. 10:   21, 23, 25, 27, 29, 121, 123, 125, 127, 129
   c. 60:   21, 23, 25, 27, 29   241, 243, 245, 247, 249
           121, 123, 125, 127, 129   251, 253, 255, 257, 259
           201, 203, 205, 207, 209   261, 263, 265, 267, 269
           211, 213, 215, 217, 219   271, 273, 275, 277, 279
           221, 223, 225, 227, 229   281, 283, 285, 287, 289
           231, 233, 235, 237, 239   291, 293, 295, 297, 299

6. a. A number is divisible by 1000 if it has 3 terminal zeros.
   b. A number is divisible by 10,000 if it has 4 terminal zeros.
   c. A number is divisible by 10^n if it has n terminal zeros.

					Number of factors
7. a. 1000	$= 10^3$	$= (2 \times 5)^3$	$= 2^3 \times 5^3$		16
b. 10,000	$= 10^4$	$= (2 \times 5)^4$	$= 2^4 \times 5^4$		25
c. 10^n		$= (2 \times 5)^n$	$= 2^n \times 5^n$		$(n + 1)^2$

3.2 Divisibility Principle for Sums and Differences
Pages 67-68

1. a. **Yes.** $56 + 21 = 7 \times 8 + 7 \times 3$
   b. **No.**   42 is divisible by 7, but 65 is not.
   c. **Yes.** $210 - 49 = 7 \times 30 - 7 \times 7$
   d. **No:**   770 is divisible by 7, but 540 is not.

2. a. **Yes:** $98 = 70 + 28 = 7 \times 10 + 7 \times 4$
   b. **Yes.** $154 = 140 + 14 = 7 \times 20 + 7 \times 2$
   c. **Yes.** $133 = 140 - 7 = 7 \times 20 - 7 \times 1$
   d. **Yes.** $693 = 700 - 7 = 7 \times 100 - 7 \times 1$

3. a. **Yes.** $253 = 220 + 33 = 11 \times 20 + 11 \times 3$
   b. **No.** $784 = 770 + 14$
             $770 = 11 \times 70$, but 14 is not divisible by 11.

  c. **Yes.** $6589 = 6600 - 11 = 11 \times 600 - 11 \times 1$

  d. **No.** $8777 = 8800 - 23$

       $8800 = 11 \times 800$, but 23 is not divisible by 11.

4. **No.** The person will be 62 in the year whose number is $1945 + 62$. 1945 is divisible by 5, but 62 is not divisible by 5. The sum $1945 + 62$ is not divisible by 5.

5. **No.** The divisibility principle for sums and differences states, in effect, that if one of two addends is divisible by a given number, the sum is divisible by the given number only if the second addend is also divisible by the given number. The principle does not address a case in which neither addend is divisible by the given number.

6. Any whole number greater than 10 can be written as the sum of its ones digit and a multiple of 10. Any multiple of 10 is divisible by 5. Therefore, according to the divisibility principle for sums and differences, if the ones digit is divisible by 5, the sum is divisible by 5. The only ones digits that are divisible by 5 are 0 and 5.

  Example: $147 = 140 + 7$

       140 is divisible by 5, but 7 is not divisible by 5.

       Therefore, $140 + 7 = 147$ is not divisible by 5.

7. A number is divisible by 25 if the number formed by its last two digits is divisible by 25. Therefore, a number is divisible by 25 if its last two digits are 00, 25, 50, or 75. This test works because any whole number greater than 100 can be written as the sum of a multiple of 100 and the number formed by its last two digits. Any multiple of 100 is divisible by 25. Therefore, according to the divisibility principle for sums and differences, if the number formed by the last two digits is divisible by 25, the sum is divisible by 25.

  Example: $675 = 600 + 75$

       600 is divisible by 25, and 75 is divisible by 25.

       Therefore $600 + 75 = 675$ is divisible by 25.

8. A number is divisible by 125 if the number formed by its last three digits is divisible by 125. Therefore, a number is divisible by 125 if its last three digits are 000, 125, 250, 375, 500, 625, 750, or 875. This test works because any whole number greater than 1000 can be written as the sum of a multiple of 1000 and the number formed by its last three digits. Any multiple of 1000 is divisible by 125. Therefore, according to the divisibility principle for sums and differences, if the number formed by the last three digits is divisible by 125, the sum is divisible by 125.

  Example: $3425 = 3000 + 425$

       3000 is divisible by 125, but 425 is not divisible by 125.

       Therefore, $3000 + 425 = 3425$ is not divisible by 125.

3.3 Divisibility by Powers of 2
Pages 68-69

1. Test just the last four digits for divisibility by 16 (2^4).
   a. Yes
   b. Yes
   c. No

2. a. Following the pattern for the table, since $32 = 2^5$, a number is divisible by 32 if the number formed by the last 5 digits is divisible by 32.
   b. **Yes.** 1<u>00,032</u> **No.** 2,3<u>06,420</u> **Yes.** 8,7<u>32,128</u>

3. **Yes.** The Summer Olympic games are held every four years in a year whose number is divisible by 4. Since 1952 is divisible by 4, the Olympic games were held in Helsinki in that year.

4. **No.** The relationship between ounces and pounds is 16 oz = 1 lb. Therefore, test just the last four digits of 2,197,216 for divisibility by 16. Since 7216 is divisible by 16, there will be no pure silver left over.

5. For divisibility by 4:
   a. 1, 3, 5, 7, or 9
   b. any replacement
   c. no replacement

   For divisibility by 8:
   a. 3 or 7
   b. 1, 3, 5, 7, or 9
   c. no replacement

6. **1 and 9, only.** To be divisible by 16, the number must also be divisible by 4. Therefore, the candidates for the missing digit are 1, 3, 5, 7, and 9. Of these candidates, only 1 and 9 will make the number divisible by 16.

7. **No.** If the number is to be divisible by 4, the number must be even. Therefore, the digit in the ones' place must be 4. But neither 14, 54, or 74 is divisible by 4. Since the number formed by the last two digits must be divisible by 4, it is impossible for this number to be divisible by 4.

8. **768.** Either 6 or 8 must be in the ones' place. Test the following combinations: 876, 786, 678, 768. Only 768 is divisible by 8.

9. **3412; 4312; 1324; 3124; 1432; 4132.** Of the two-digit numbers that can be formed from 1, 2, 3, and 4, only 12, 24, and 32 are divisible by 4. Therefore, the last two digits of the four-digit number must be 12, 24, or 32. The six numbers that satisfy the conditions of the problem can be listed as above.

10. **25.** <u>Method 1:</u> If the page number is divisible by 8, it is also divisible by 4. Therefore, consider only those page numbers whose last two digits are 12, 32, 52, 72, and 92. The following table contains all two-digit and three-digit numbers which end in the above numbers.

12	**32**	52	**72**	92
112	132	**152**	172	**192**
212	**232**	252	**272**	292
312	332	**352**	372	**392**
412	**432**	452	**472**	492
512	532	**552**	572	**592**
612	**632**	653	**672**	692
712	732	**752**	772	**792**
812	**832**	852	**872**	892
912	932	**952**	972	**992**

The numbers in the above table which are in bold print are divisible by 8. Each column of the above table has five numbers in bold print. There are twenty-five two-digit and three-digit numbers which end in 2 and which are also divisible by 8.

<u>Method 2:</u> The smallest number divisible by 8 and ending in 2 is 32. To obtain the next number satisfying the conditions of the problem we need to add to 32 the smallest multiple of 8 which ends in 0. This preserves divisibility by 8 and a number that ends in 2. That number is 40. There are $1000 \div 40 = 25$ numbers less than 1000, divisible by 8, and ending in 2.

The following sequence shows the structure of the numbers:

$$32$$
$$32 + 1 \times 40$$
$$32 + 2 \times 40$$
$$32 + 3 \times 40$$
$$\vdots$$
$$32 + 24 \times 40.$$

Notice that there are 25 terms in the sequence and that the last term equals 992.

11. **No.** For a 100-digit number to be divisible by 16, it must also be divisible by 8. The 3-digit number formed by the last three digits of the 100-digit number is 652. Since 652 is not divisible by 8, the 100-digit number is not divisible by 16.

3.4 Divisibility by 3 and 9
Pages 70-71

1. a. Sum of the digits = 26 + ▇, so ▇ = 1.
   b. Sum of the digits = 19 + ▇, so ▇ = 8.
   c. Sum of the digits = 21 + ▇, so ▇ = 6.

2. a. ▮ = 1, 4, or 7   b. ▮ = 2, 5, or 8   c. ▮ = 0, 3, 6, or 9

3. The sum of the two replacement digits must be either 4 or 13. There are 11 possible numbers which are each divisible by 9:

    054   153   252   351   450   459   558   657   756   855   954

4. The sum of the replacement digits must be either 1, 4, 7, 10, 13, or 16. There are 33 numbers which are each divisible by 3:

1:	051	150						
4.	054	153	252	351	450			
7:	057	156	255	354	453	552	651	750
10:	159	258	357	456	555	654	753	852	951
13:	459	558	657	756	855	954		
16:	759	858	957					

5. The sum of the digits must be 9. The tens digit of the product is always one less than the number multiplying 9, and the ones digit is simply the difference between 9 and the tens digit.

6. a.

$51	$685	$40,752	$382,861
− 15	− 658	− 40,572	− 328,861
$36	$ 27	$ 180	$ 54,000

    b. Yes

    c. A possible source of error is a reversal of two digits, called a TRANSPOSITION, when a figure is entered into the ledger.

7. *Examples:*

6281	472	94	87,654,321
− 1826	− 274	− 49	− 12,345,678
4455	198	45	75,308,643

    If one number contains the same digits as another, but in reverse order, the difference of the two numbers will be divisible by 9. (In fact, the same is true if one number contains the same digits as another, but in any order.)

8. **No.** No matter how the digits are arranged, the sum $1 + 2 + 3 + \ldots + 7 + 8 + 9$ is equal to 45. No matter how the digits are arranged, the digit-sum will always be 45, a multiple of both 3 and 9. Then the original nine-digit number is divisible by 3 and 9, and it cannot be prime.

3.5 Divisibility by 11
Pages 71-74

1. a. **1826 is divisible by 11.** $8 + 6 = 14$; $1 + 2 = 3$; $14 - 3 = 11$
   b. **7259 is *not* divisible by 11.** $2 + 9 = 11$; $7 + 5 = 12$; $12 - 11 = 1$
   c. **82,907 is divisible by 11.** $8 + 9 + 7 = 24$; $2 + 0 = 2$; $24 - 2 = 22$
   d. **1,724,943 is divisible by 11** $1 + 2 + 9 + 3 = 15$; $7 + 4 + 4 = 15$; $15 - 15 = 0$

2. a. **5.** $(9 + \blacksquare) - 3 = 6 + \blacksquare$. $6 + 5 = 11$, so $\blacksquare = 5$
   b. **2.** $(7 + 9) - (3 + \blacksquare) = 13 - \blacksquare$. $13 - 2 = 11$, so $\blacksquare = 2$
   c. **7.** $(9 + 2) - (3 + \blacksquare + 1) = 7 - \blacksquare$. $7 - 7 = 0$, so $\blacksquare = 7$
   d. $(\blacksquare + 8 + 9) - (0 + 1) = \blacksquare + 16$. $6 + 16 = 22$, so $\blacksquare = 6$

3. **055, 154, 253, 352, 451, and 550; 759, 858, and 957.** The sum of the replacement digits must be either 5 or 16 for the 3-digit number to be divisible by 11. The above 9 numbers satisfy the divisibility requirement:

4. **1749 and 1947, 4719 and 4917, 7194 and 7491, 9174 and 9471.** The digits must be arranged so that 1 and 4 are paired as either odd-place or even-place digits, and 7 and 9 are paired as even-place or odd-place digits. There are 8 different combinations which are each divisible by 11.

5.
   ```
     1243
     1342
     2134
     2431
     3124
     3421
     4213
   + 4312
   ```
   22,220. The digits must be arranged so that 1 and 4 are paired as either odd-place digits or even-place digits, and 2 and 3 are paired as either even-place or odd-place digits. The 8 different combinations are shown at the left. Notice that each of the digits 1, 2, 3, and 4 appears twice in each column. The sum of the digits in each column is 20; the sum of the eight numbers is 22,220.

6. **There are 144 possible answers.** Since the digit-sum is 28, the number will be divisible by 11 only if the sum of the odd-place digits is 14 and the sum of the even-place digits is 14. Then the difference between the two sums will be $14 - 14 = 0$. The digits that will satisfy these conditions are listed in the following table:

odd-place digits	2, 3, 4, 5	1, 3, 4, 6	1, 2, 5, 6	1, 2, 4, 7
even-place digits	1, 6, 7	2, 5, 7	3, 4, 7	3, 5, 6

It is possible to write 144 different numbers using *each* of the above sets of odd-place and even-place digits. Therefore, there are a total of $4 \times 144 = 576$ different numbers that contain the digits 1, 2, 3, 4, 5, 6, and 7 and that are divisible by 11. Some examples are 2,136,475; 5,621,473; and 3,741,265.

7.   **1496.** Try the number 149■. Then $(1 + 9) - (4 + ■) = 6 - ■$. Since $6 - 6 = 0$, ■ $= 6$. The greatest number of students who can play football is 1496.

3.6 Combined Divisibility
Pages 74-75

1.   a. **No.**   5824 is divisible by 4, but not by 3. Therefore, 5824 is not divisible by 12.
     b. **Yes.** 7416 is divisible by 4 and by 3. Therefore, 7416 is divisible by 12.
     c. **No.**   12,054 is divisible by 3 but not by 4. Therefore, 12,054 is not divisible by 12.
     d. **Yes.** 428,676 is divisible by 4 and by 3. Therefore, 428,676 is divisible by 12.

2.   **Yes.** The number 9762 is divisible by both 2 and 3, and therefore by 6. The 9762 eggs can be packed in 6-egg cartons with none left over.

3.   a. **Yes.** 972 is divisible by 2 and by 9. Therefore, 972 is divisible by 18.
     b. **Yes.** 8946 is divisible by 2 and by 9. Therefore, 8946 is divisible by 18.
     c. **No.**   9081 is divisible by 9 but not by 2. Therefore, 9081 is not divisible by 18.
     d. **No.**   15,018 is divisible by 2 but not by 9. Therefore, 15,018 is not divisible by 18.

4.   A number is divisible by 15 if it is divisible both by 3 and by 5. Therefore, a number is divisible by 15 if the sum of its digits is divisible by 3 and its units digit is 0 or 5.

5.   a. **4230** and **8235.**   Each of the numbers is divisible by both 5 and by 9.
     b. **3312.**   The number is divisible by both 8 and by 9.
     c. **5472** and **1476.**   Each of the numbers is divisible by both 4 and 9.
     d. **8470** and **2475.**   Each of the numbers is divisible by both 5 and 11.

6.   **198; 297; 396; 495; 594; 693; 792; 891; 990.**
     Each of the above numbers is divisible by both 9 and 11.

3.7 Divisibility by 7, 11, and 13
Pages 75-76

1.   a. $180,124 = 180,180 - 56$
        $56 = 7 \times 8$
        Therefore, 180,124 is divisible by 7, but not by 11 or 13.

     b. $621,595 = 621,621 - 26$
        $26 = 13 \times 2$
        Therefore, 621,595 is divisible by 13, but not by 7 or 11.

c. $236,346 = 236,236 + 110$
$110 = 11 \times 10$
Therefore, 236,346 is divisible by 11, but not by 7 or 13.

d. $430,445 = 430,430 + 15$
$15 = 3 \times 5$
Therefore, 430,445 is not divisible by 7, 11, or 13.

e. $583,660 = 583,583 + 77$
$77 = 7 \times 11$
Therefore, 583,660 is divisible by 7 and by 11, but not by 13.

f. $900,869 = 900,000 - 31$
31 is prime.
Therefore, 900,869 is not divisible by 7, 11, or 13.

g. $98,126 = 98,098 + 28$
$28 = 7 \times 4$
Therefore, 98,126 is divisible by 7, but not by 11 or 13.

h. $63,078 = 63,063 + 15$
$15 = 3 \times 5$
Therefore, 63,078 is not divisible by 7, 11, or 13.

i. $52,143 = 52,052 + 91$
$91 = 7 \times 13$
Therefore, 52,143 is divisible by 7 and by 13, but not by 11.

2. **$2 \times 7 \times 11 \times 13$.** Since $2002 = 2 \times 1001$ and $1001 = 7 \times 11 \times 13$, $2002 = 2 \times 7 \times 11 \times 13$.

3. **30,030.** The numbers 2, 3, 5, 7, 11, and 13 are the six least prime numbers, so their product is the required number. $2 \times 3 \times 5 = 30$, and $7 \times 11 \times 13 = 1001$, so their combined product is $30 \times 1001 = 30,030$. The least number that has six different prime factors is 30,030.

4. a. $340 - 060 + 270 = 550$
$550 = 11 \times 50$
270,060,340 is divisible by 11, but not by 7 or by 13.

b. $134 - 515 + 600 = 219$
$219 = 3 \times 73$
600,515,314 is not divisible by 7, 11, or 13.

c. $531 - 482 + 29 = 78$
$78 = 13 \times 6$
29,482,531 is divisible by 13, but not by 7 or by 11.

5.   **Yes.**   Apply the divisibility test discussed in problem 4 above.
$738 - 811 + 125 = 52$
$52 = 13 \times 4$
\$125,811,738 is divisible by 13.
The departments can receive equal amounts.

4. Fractions

4.1 Unit Fractions
Pages 77-79

1. a. 1st denominator: $\quad \frac{1}{2}\times(3+1)=\frac{1}{2}\times 4 = 2$

   2nd denominator: $\quad 3 \times 2 = 6$

   $\frac{2}{3}=\frac{1}{2}+\frac{1}{6}$

   b. 1st denominator: $\quad \frac{1}{2}\times(9+1)=\frac{1}{2}\times 10 = 5$

   2nd denominator: $\quad 9 \times 5 = 45$

   $\frac{2}{9}=\frac{1}{5}+\frac{1}{45}$

   c. 1st denominator: $\quad \frac{1}{2}\times(15+1)=\frac{1}{2}\times 16 = 8$

   2nd denominator: $\quad 15 \times 8 = 120$

   $\frac{2}{15}=\frac{1}{8}+\frac{1}{120}$

   d. 1st denominator: $\quad \frac{1}{2}\times(25+1)=\frac{1}{2}\times 26 = 13$

   2nd denominator: $\quad 25 \times 13 = 325$

   $\frac{2}{25}=\frac{1}{13}+\frac{1}{325}$

2. a. $\dfrac{1}{4}=\dfrac{1}{(4+1)}+\dfrac{1}{4\times(4+1)} \quad = \quad \dfrac{1}{5}+\dfrac{1}{4\times 5} \quad = \quad \dfrac{1}{5}+\dfrac{1}{20}$

   b. $\dfrac{1}{7}=\dfrac{1}{(7+1)}+\dfrac{1}{7\times(7+1)} \quad = \quad \dfrac{1}{8}+\dfrac{1}{7\times 8} \quad = \quad \dfrac{1}{8}+\dfrac{1}{56}$

   c. $\dfrac{1}{10}=\dfrac{1}{(10+1)}+\dfrac{1}{10\times(10+1)} \quad = \quad \dfrac{1}{11}+\dfrac{1}{10\times 11} \quad = \quad \dfrac{1}{11}+\dfrac{1}{110}$

   d. $\dfrac{1}{11}=\dfrac{1}{(11+1)}+\dfrac{1}{11\times(12+1)} \quad = \quad \dfrac{1}{12}+\dfrac{1}{11\times 12} \quad = \quad \dfrac{1}{12}+\dfrac{1}{132}$

3. $\frac{1}{3}$ can be expressed as the sum of four distinct unit fractions several different ways. Some of the ways are shown.

   $\dfrac{1}{3}=\dfrac{1}{4}+\dfrac{1}{12}=\left(\dfrac{1}{5}+\dfrac{1}{20}\right)+\left(\dfrac{1}{13}+\dfrac{1}{156}\right)=\dfrac{1}{5}+\dfrac{1}{13}+\dfrac{1}{20}+\dfrac{1}{156}$

   $\dfrac{1}{3}=\dfrac{1}{6}+\dfrac{1}{6}=\dfrac{1}{6}+\dfrac{1}{12}+\dfrac{1}{12}=\dfrac{1}{6}+\dfrac{1}{12}+\dfrac{1}{13}+\dfrac{1}{156}$

   $\dfrac{1}{3}=\dfrac{3}{9}=\dfrac{2}{9}+\dfrac{1}{9}=\left(\dfrac{1}{5}+\dfrac{1}{45}\right)+\left(\dfrac{1}{10}+\dfrac{1}{90}\right)=\dfrac{1}{5}+\dfrac{1}{10}+\dfrac{1}{45}+\dfrac{1}{90}$

4. $\frac{1}{2} = \frac{1}{3} + \frac{1}{6} = \frac{1}{4} + \frac{1}{12} + \frac{1}{6}$ and $\qquad$ $\frac{1}{2} = \frac{1}{3} + \frac{1}{6} = \frac{1}{3} + \frac{1}{7} + \frac{1}{42}$

5. a. $\frac{1}{2} - \frac{1}{3} = \frac{1}{2\times3} = \frac{1}{6}$

    b. $\frac{1}{4} - \frac{1}{5} = \frac{1}{4\times5} = \frac{1}{20}$

    c. $\frac{1}{7} - \frac{1}{8} = \frac{1}{7\times8} = \frac{1}{56}$

    d. $\frac{1}{9} - \frac{1}{10} = \frac{1}{9\times10} = \frac{1}{90}$

6. $\frac{1}{12} = \frac{1}{3\times4} = \frac{1}{3} - \frac{1}{4}$ and $\qquad$ $\frac{1}{42} = \frac{1}{6\times7} = \frac{1}{6} - \frac{1}{7}$

7. As shown in problem 6, a unit fraction whose denominator is the product of two consecutive numbers can be rewritten as the difference of consecutive unit fractions.

    a. $\frac{9}{10}$. $\frac{1}{1\times2} + \frac{1}{2\times3} + \frac{1}{3\times4} + \cdots + \frac{1}{9\times10}$

    $= \left(\frac{1}{1} - \frac{1}{2}\right) + \left(\frac{1}{2} - \frac{1}{3}\right) + \left(\frac{1}{3} - \frac{1}{4}\right) + \cdots + \left(\frac{1}{9} - \frac{1}{10}\right)$

    $= \frac{1}{1} - \frac{1}{2} + \frac{1}{2} - \frac{1}{3} + \frac{1}{3} - \frac{1}{4} + \cdots - \frac{1}{9} + \frac{1}{9} - \frac{1}{10}$

    $= \frac{1}{1} - \frac{1}{10}$

    $= 1 - \frac{1}{10}$

    $= \frac{9}{10}$

    b. $\frac{5}{11}$. Consider the following:

    $\frac{1}{n} - \frac{1}{n+2} = \frac{n+2}{n(n+2)} - \frac{n}{n(n+2)} = \frac{2}{n(n+2)}$.

    Then $\frac{1}{n(n+2)} = \frac{1}{2}\left(\frac{1}{n} - \frac{1}{n+2}\right)$.

    Substitute the above right member for all expressions in the form $\frac{1}{n(n+2)}$ as in the given expression:

    $\frac{1}{1\times3} + \frac{1}{3\times5} + \frac{1}{5\times7} + \frac{1}{7\times9} + \frac{1}{9\times11}$

    $= \left[\frac{1}{2} \times \left(\frac{1}{1} - \frac{1}{3}\right)\right] + \left[\frac{1}{2} \times \left(\frac{1}{3} - \frac{1}{5}\right)\right] + \left[\frac{1}{2} \times \left(\frac{1}{5} - \frac{1}{7}\right)\right] + \left[\frac{1}{2} \times \left(\frac{1}{7} - \frac{1}{9}\right)\right] + \left[\frac{1}{2} \times \left(\frac{1}{9} - \frac{1}{11}\right)\right]$

    $= \frac{1}{2} \times \left(\frac{1}{1} - \frac{1}{3} + \frac{1}{3} - \frac{1}{5} + \frac{1}{5} - \frac{1}{7} + \frac{1}{7} - \frac{1}{9} + \frac{1}{9} - \frac{1}{11}\right)$

    $= \frac{1}{2} \times \left(\frac{1}{1} - \frac{1}{11}\right)$

    $= \frac{1}{2} \times \left(1 - \frac{1}{11}\right)$

    $= \frac{1}{2} \times \left(\frac{10}{11}\right)$

    $= \frac{5}{11}$

    <u>**Comment:**</u> $\qquad$ Use the above technique for series of the type: $\frac{1}{n(n+d)} + \frac{1}{(n+d)(n+2d)} + \cdots$.

    In such cases, $\frac{1}{n} - \frac{1}{n+d} = \frac{n+d}{n(n+d)} - \frac{n}{n(n+d)} = \frac{d}{n(n+d)}$.

    Then $\frac{1}{n(n+d)} = \frac{1}{d}\left(\frac{1}{n} - \frac{1}{n+d}\right)$.

8. a. $\frac{1}{6}$: $\frac{1}{12}+\frac{1}{12}$; $\frac{1}{7}+\frac{1}{42}$; $\frac{1}{10}+\frac{1}{15}$; $\frac{1}{8}+\frac{1}{24}$; and $\frac{1}{9}+\frac{1}{18}$

    b. $\frac{1}{10}$: $\frac{1}{20}+\frac{1}{20}$; $\frac{1}{11}+\frac{1}{110}$; $\frac{1}{14}+\frac{1}{35}$; $\frac{1}{12}+\frac{1}{60}$; and $\frac{1}{15}+\frac{1}{30}$

    c. $\frac{1}{4}$: $\frac{1}{8}+\frac{1}{8}$; $\frac{1}{5}+\frac{1}{20}$; and $\frac{1}{6}+\frac{1}{12}$

9. Answers may vary. One possible solution for each is given.

    a. $\frac{3}{4} = \frac{2}{4}+\frac{1}{4} = \frac{1}{2}+\frac{1}{4}$

    b. $\frac{5}{6} = \frac{3}{6}+\frac{2}{6} = \frac{1}{2}+\frac{1}{3}$

    c. $\frac{3}{5} = \frac{18}{30} = \frac{15}{30}+\frac{3}{30} = \frac{1}{2}+\frac{1}{10}$

    d. $\frac{2}{7} = \frac{8}{28} = \frac{7}{28}+\frac{1}{28} = \frac{1}{4}+\frac{1}{28}$

10. ***For the Adventurous***

    i. **144.** Given: 1) $\dfrac{1}{12} = \dfrac{1}{12+a} + \dfrac{1}{12+b}$

    By Addition of Fractions: 2) $\dfrac{1}{12} = \dfrac{24+a+b}{(12+a)(12+b)}$

    Product Rule for Proportions: 3) $(12+a)(12+b) = 12(24+a+b)$

    Multiply: 4) $144+12(a+b)+ab = 288+12(a+b)$

    Simplify: 5) $ab = 144$

    Notice that 144 is the square of 12, the denominator of the given unit fraction, that a and b are factors of 144, and that their product is 144.

    ii. Since $ab = 12^2 = (2^2 \times 3)^2 = 2^4 \times 3^2$, 12^2 has $5 \times 3 = 15$ different factors which are shown as entries in the following factor table. The table is explained in section 2.2.

×	1	2	4	8	16
1	1	2	4	8	16
3	3	6	12	24	48
9	9	18	36	72	144

    Since $ab = 144$ and $a \le b$, then (a, b) may have the following pairs of values:
    (1, 144), (2, 72), (3, 48), (4, 36), (6, 24), (8, 18), (9, 16), and (12, 12).

iii. The pairs of values in part *ii* are now substituted in the right member of 1), part i.

$$\frac{1}{12} = \begin{cases} \frac{1}{(12+1)} + \frac{1}{(12+144)} & \text{or} & \frac{1}{13} + \frac{1}{156} \\ \frac{1}{(12+2)} + \frac{1}{(12+72)} & \text{or} & \frac{1}{14} + \frac{1}{84} \\ \frac{1}{(12+3)} + \frac{1}{(12+48)} & \text{or} & \frac{1}{15} + \frac{1}{60} \\ \frac{1}{(12+4)} + \frac{1}{(12+36)} & \text{or} & \frac{1}{16} + \frac{1}{48} \\ \frac{1}{(12+6)} + \frac{1}{(12+24)} & \text{or} & \frac{1}{18} + \frac{1}{36} \\ \frac{1}{(12+8)} + \frac{1}{(12+18)} & \text{or} & \frac{1}{20} + \frac{1}{30} \\ \frac{1}{(12+9)} + \frac{1}{(12+16)} & \text{or} & \frac{1}{21} + \frac{1}{28} \\ \frac{1}{(12+12)} + \frac{1}{(12+12)} & \text{or} & \frac{1}{24} + \frac{1}{24} \end{cases}$$

Notice that $\frac{1}{12}$ can be expressed as a sum of two unit fractions in eight different ways.

4.2 Complex Fractions
Pages 79-81

1. a. $\frac{15}{16}$ b. $\frac{20}{9}$ c. $\frac{16}{27}$ d. $\frac{3}{8}$

2. a. $\frac{16}{15}$ b. $\frac{9}{20}$ c. $\frac{27}{16}$ d. $\frac{3}{2}$

3. a. 2   b. $\frac{5}{3}$ c. $\frac{4}{9}$ d. $\frac{10}{37}$

4. 3

5. $\frac{3}{8}$

6. a. $\frac{3}{10}$ b. $\frac{5}{7}$ c. $\frac{5}{6}$ d. $\frac{3}{5}$

7. a. **5.** $\dfrac{\frac{1}{2} + \frac{1}{3}}{\frac{1}{2} - \frac{1}{3}} = \dfrac{\frac{5}{6}}{\frac{1}{6}} = \dfrac{\frac{5}{6} \times \frac{6}{1}}{\frac{1}{6} \times \frac{6}{1}} = \dfrac{5}{1} = 5$

b. $\dfrac{\mathbf{5}}{\mathbf{18}}.$ $\dfrac{\frac{1}{2} + \frac{1}{3}}{3} = \dfrac{\frac{5}{6}}{3} = \dfrac{\frac{5}{6} \times \frac{1}{3}}{3 \times \frac{1}{3}} = \dfrac{\frac{5}{18}}{1} = \dfrac{5}{18}$

c. $\dfrac{\mathbf{1}}{\mathbf{24}}.$ $\dfrac{\frac{1}{2} - \frac{1}{3}}{4} = \dfrac{\frac{1}{6}}{4} = \dfrac{\frac{1}{6} \times \frac{1}{4}}{4 \times \frac{1}{4}} = \dfrac{\frac{1}{24}}{1} = \dfrac{1}{24}$

8. $\dfrac{53}{210}$. $\quad \dfrac{1}{5} \boxplus \dfrac{1}{7} = \dfrac{\frac{1}{5}+\frac{1}{7}}{2} = \dfrac{\frac{12}{35}}{2} = \dfrac{\frac{12}{35}\times\frac{1}{2}}{2\times\frac{1}{2}} = \dfrac{\frac{12}{70}}{1} = \dfrac{12}{70} = \dfrac{6}{35}$

$\dfrac{1}{3} \boxplus \left(\dfrac{1}{5} \boxplus \dfrac{1}{7}\right) = \dfrac{1}{3} \boxplus \dfrac{6}{35} = \dfrac{\frac{1}{3}+\frac{6}{35}}{2} = \dfrac{\frac{53}{105}}{2} = \dfrac{\frac{53}{105}\times\frac{1}{2}}{2\times\frac{1}{2}} = \dfrac{\frac{53}{210}}{1} = \dfrac{53}{210}$

4.3 Extended Finite Fractions
Pages 81-82

1. a. $\dfrac{10}{33}$. $\qquad \dfrac{1}{3+\frac{1}{3+\frac{1}{3}}} = \dfrac{1}{3+\frac{1}{3+\frac{1}{10}{3}}} = \dfrac{1}{3+\frac{1}{\frac{10}{3}}} = \dfrac{1}{3+\frac{3}{10}} = \dfrac{1}{\frac{33}{10}} = \dfrac{10}{33}$

b. $\dfrac{7}{11}$. $\qquad \dfrac{1}{1+\frac{1}{1+\frac{1}{1+\frac{1}{3}}}} = \dfrac{1}{1+\frac{1}{1+\frac{1}{\frac{4}{3}}}} = \dfrac{1}{1+\frac{1}{1+\frac{3}{4}}} = \dfrac{1}{1+\frac{1}{\frac{7}{4}}} = \dfrac{1}{1+\frac{4}{7}} = \dfrac{1}{\frac{11}{7}} = \dfrac{7}{11}$

c. $\dfrac{8}{3}$. $\qquad 2+\dfrac{1}{1+\frac{1}{2}} = 2+\dfrac{1}{\frac{3}{2}} = 2+\dfrac{2}{3} = \dfrac{8}{3}$

d. $\dfrac{17}{10}$. $\qquad 1+\dfrac{1}{1+\frac{1}{2+\frac{1}{3}}} = 1+\dfrac{1}{1+\frac{1}{\frac{7}{3}}} = 1+\dfrac{1}{1+\frac{3}{7}} = 1+\dfrac{1}{\frac{10}{7}} = 1+\dfrac{7}{10} = \dfrac{17}{10}$

2. a. $\dfrac{1}{2+\frac{1}{3}}$. $\qquad \dfrac{3}{7} = \dfrac{1}{\frac{7}{3}} = \dfrac{1}{2+\frac{1}{3}}$

b. $\dfrac{1}{2+\frac{1}{3+\frac{1}{4}}}$. $\qquad \dfrac{13}{30} = \dfrac{1}{\frac{30}{13}} = \dfrac{1}{2+\frac{4}{13}} = \dfrac{1}{2+\frac{1}{\frac{13}{4}}} = \dfrac{1}{2+\frac{1}{3+\frac{1}{4}}}$

c. $\dfrac{1}{1+\frac{1}{1+\frac{1}{1+\frac{1}{1+\frac{1}{2}}}}}$. $\quad \dfrac{8}{13} = \dfrac{1}{\frac{13}{8}} = \dfrac{1}{1+\frac{5}{8}} = \dfrac{1}{1+\frac{1}{\frac{8}{5}}} = \dfrac{1}{1+\frac{1}{1+\frac{3}{5}}} = \dfrac{1}{1+\frac{1}{1+\frac{1}{\frac{5}{3}}}}$

$= \dfrac{1}{1+\frac{1}{1+\frac{1}{1+\frac{2}{3}}}} = \dfrac{1}{1+\frac{1}{1+\frac{1}{1+\frac{1}{\frac{3}{2}}}}} = \dfrac{1}{1+\frac{1}{1+\frac{1}{1+\frac{1}{1+\frac{1}{2}}}}}$

d. $4 + \dfrac{1}{1 + \frac{1}{2}}$.

$\dfrac{14}{3} = 4 + \dfrac{2}{3} = 4 + \dfrac{1}{\frac{3}{2}} = 4 + \dfrac{1}{1 + \frac{1}{2}}$

4.4 Fractional Parts
Pages 82-83

1. a. **35.** Since $\frac{3}{5}$ of the number is 21, then $\frac{1}{5}$ of the number is $21 \div 3 = 7$, and $\frac{5}{5}$ of the number is $5 \times 7 = 35$. My number is 35.

   b. **49.** Since $\frac{2}{7}$ of the number is 14, then $\frac{1}{7}$ of the number is $14 \div 2 = 7$, and $\frac{7}{7}$ of the number is $7 \times 7 = 49$. My number is 49.

   c. **8.** Since the product of $1\frac{1}{2}$ and the number is 12, then $\frac{3}{2}$ of the number is 12. Since $\frac{3}{2}$ of the number is 12, then $\frac{1}{2}$ of the number is $12 \div 3 = 4$, and $\frac{2}{2}$ of the number is $2 \times 4 = 8$. My number is 8.

   d. **32.** Think of the double of the number as double $\frac{4}{4}$, or $\frac{8}{4}$. Then 56 is added to $\frac{1}{4}$ of the number to produce $\frac{8}{4}$ of the number. Thus, 56 must be $\frac{7}{4}$ of the number. Since 56 is $\frac{7}{4}$ of the number, then $\frac{1}{4}$ of the number is $56 \div 7 = 8$, and $\frac{4}{4}$ of the number is $4 \times 8 = 32$. My number is 32.

   e. **12.** Think of the triple of the number as triple $\frac{2}{2}$, or $\frac{6}{2}$. Then 6 is added to $\frac{5}{2}$ of the number to produce $\frac{6}{2}$ of the number. Thus, 6 must be $\frac{6}{2} - \frac{5}{2} = \frac{1}{2}$ of the number. Since 6 is $\frac{1}{2}$ of the number, then $\frac{2}{2}$ of the number is $2 \times 6 = 12$. The number is 12.

   f. **20.** Think of $3\frac{1}{4}$ times the number as $\frac{13}{4}$ times the number. Then 15 is added to $\frac{13}{4}$ of the number to produce 4 times the number or $\frac{16}{4}$ of the number. Thus, 15 must be $\frac{16}{4} - \frac{13}{4} = \frac{3}{4}$ of the number. Since 15 is $\frac{3}{4}$ of the number, then $\frac{1}{4}$ of the number is $15 \div 3 = 5$, and $\frac{4}{4}$ of the number is $4 \times 5 = 20$. The number is 20.

   Comment: *Each of the above problems 1a-f can also be solved algebraically by using an appropriate equation.*

2. **$20.** Since Dave spent $\frac{2}{5}$ of his money, then $\frac{3}{5}$ of his money was left. Since $12 is $\frac{3}{5}$ of his money, then $\frac{1}{5}$ of his money is $12 \div 3 = 4, and $\frac{5}{5}$ of his money is $5 \times $4 = 20. Dave originally had $20.

3. **30¢.** Since Anne spent $\frac{1}{3}$ of her money, then $\frac{2}{3}$ of her money was left. Therefore, she lost $\frac{1}{2}$ of $\frac{2}{3}$ of her money, which is equivalent to $\frac{1}{3}$ of her money. The 10¢ which she has left is the remaining $\frac{1}{3}$ of her original amount of money. Since 10¢ is $\frac{1}{3}$ of her money, then $\frac{3}{3}$ of her money is $3 \times 10¢ = 30¢$. Anne originally had 30¢.

4. **$\frac{16}{90}$, $\frac{17}{90}$.** Rewrite the two given fractions as equivalent fractions with common denominator: $\frac{1}{6} = \frac{5}{30}$ and $\frac{1}{5} = \frac{6}{30}$. Inserting *two* fractions in an arithmetic sequence between the two given fractions can be accomplished by separating the difference between the two fractions into *three* equal parts. Therefore, multiply each of the equivalent fractions by $\frac{3}{3}$: $\frac{5}{30} = \frac{15}{90}$ and $\frac{6}{30} = \frac{18}{90}$. This gives two fractions, $\frac{16}{90}$ and $\frac{17}{90}$, between the two given fractions. The completed arithmetic sequence is $\frac{15}{90}$, $\frac{16}{90}$, $\frac{17}{90}$, $\frac{18}{90}$.

5. **$\frac{9}{24}$, $\frac{10}{24}$, $\frac{11}{24}$.** Rewrite the two given fractions as equivalent fractions with a common denominator: $\frac{1}{3} = \frac{2}{6}$ and $\frac{1}{2} = \frac{3}{6}$. Inserting *three* fractions in an arithmetic sequence between the two given fractions can be accomplished by separating the difference between the two fractions into *four* equal parts. Therefore, multiply each of the equivalent fractions by $\frac{4}{4}$: $\frac{2}{6} = \frac{8}{24}$ and $\frac{3}{6} = \frac{12}{24}$. This gives three fractions, $\frac{9}{24}$, $\frac{10}{24}$, and $\frac{11}{24}$, between the two given fractions. The completed arithmetic sequence is $\frac{8}{24}$, $\frac{9}{24}$, $\frac{10}{24}$, $\frac{11}{24}$, $\frac{12}{24}$.

6. The sum of the fractions in the farmer's will was not 1, but only $\frac{17}{18}$. That is, $\frac{1}{2} + \frac{1}{3} + \frac{1}{9} = \frac{9}{18} + \frac{6}{18} + \frac{2}{18} = \frac{17}{18}$. With the addition of the eighteenth cow, the children were able to take $\frac{1}{2}$, $\frac{1}{3}$, and $\frac{1}{9}$ of the total, but this was still only $\frac{17}{18}$ of 18 cows, or 17 cows.

5. Geometry and Measurement

5.1 Squares and Rectangles
Pages 84-87

1. a. $6^2 = 36$　　b. $5^2 = 25$　　c. $4^2 = 16$　　d. $3^2 = 9$　　e. $2^2 = 4$　　f. $1^2 = 1$

2. a. $6^2 + 5^2 + 4^2 + 3^2 + 2^2 + 1^2 = 91$
    b. $7^2 + (6^2 + 5^2 + 4^2 + 3^2 + 2^2 + 1^2) = 49 + 91 = 140$
    c. $9^2 + 8^2 + (7^2 + 6^2 + 5^2 + 4^2 + 3^2 + 2^2 + 1^2) = 81 + 64 + 140 = 285$
    d. $10^2 + (9^2 + 8^2 + 7^2 + 6^2 + 5^2 + 4^2 + 3^2 + 2^2 + 1^2) = 100 + 285 = 385$

3. a. 20　　　b. 17　　　c. 18　　　d. 22
    Each column below indicates how the answer to that part was obtained.

Size of Square	Part a	Part b	Part c	Part d
1 × 1	12	12	8	16
2 × 2	6	5	5	–
3 × 3	2	–	4	1
4 × 4	–	–	1	4
5 × 5	+ –	+ –	+ –	+ 1
Totals	**20**	**17**	**18**	**22**

4. a. 1　　　b. 3　　　c. 6　　　d. 10　　　e. 15　　　f. 21
    The pattern is that the total number of rectangles is the sum of all the counting numbers from 1 to the number of squares in the figure.

5. a. 12　　　b. 11　　　c. 9　　　d. 18
    Each column below indicates how the answer to that part was obtained.

Size of Rectangle	Part a	Part b	Part c	Part d
1 × 1	5	5	4	6
1 × 2	4	4	4	7
1 × 3	2	2	–	2
1 × 4	1	–	–	–
2 × 2	–	–	1	2
2 × 3	+ –	+ –	+ –	+ 1
Totals	**12**	**11**	**9**	**18**

5.2 Triangles

1. a. **8.**

Type of Triangle	Listing by Letter	Number
1-part	b, c, d	3
2-part	a-b, b-c, c-d, d-a	4
3-part	—	0
4-part	a-b-c-d	1

The total number of triangles is 3 + 4 + 1 = 8.

b. **8.**

Type of Triangle	Listing by Letter	Number
1-part	a, b, c, d	4
2-part	c-d, b-d	2
3-part	a-d-c, a-d-b	2

The total number of triangles is 4 + 2 + 2 = 8.

c. **10.**

Type of Triangle	Listing by Letter	Number
1-part	a, b, c, d, e	5
2-part	–	0
3-part	a-f-c, a-f-d, b-f-e, b-f-d, c-f-e	5

The total number of triangles is 5 + 5 = 10.

d. **35.**

Type of Triangle	Listing by Letter	Number
1-part	a, b, c, d, e, f, g, h, i, j	10
2-part	a-b, b-c, c-d, d-e, e-f f-g, g-h, h-i, i-j, j-a	10
3-part	a-b-c, c-d-e, e-f-g, g-h-i, i-j-a, j-k-d, j-k-f, b-k-h, b-k-f, d-k-h	10
4-part	—	0
5-part	b-k-f-g-h, d-k-h-i-j, f-k-j-a-b, h-k-b-c-d, j-k-d-e-f	5

The total number of triangles is 10 + 10 + 10 + 5 = 35.

2. a. 1 b. 3 c. 6 d. 10 e. 15 f. 21

The pattern is that the total number of triangles is the sum of all the counting numbers from 1 to the number of small triangles in the figure.

Example:

$1 + 2 + 3 = 6$

3. They are the same. The total number of triangles in these figures can be counted using the same pattern as used in counting the total number of rectangles in the figures of problem 4 on page 87. Some triangles point downward.

4. a. 5 b. 13 c. 27 d. 48

5.3 Circles
Pages 89 – 91

1. a. 2 b. 4 c. 11 d. 16

2.
Number of Straight Cuts	Greatest Number of Pieces of Pie
0	1
1	2
2	4
3	7
4	11
5	16

3. a. The difference between successive numbers in the right-hand column increases by one from line-to-line. That is, the first cut adds 1 to the previous number of pieces, the second cut adds 2 to the previous number of pieces, the third cut adds 3 to the previous number of pieces the fourth cut adds 4 to the previous number of pieces, and the fifth cut adds 5 to the previous number of pieces.

b. **37.** Add three more entries to the table in problem 2.
    $16 + 6 = 22; \quad 22 + 7 = 29; \quad 29 + 8 = 37$
    For 8 straight cuts, the greatest number of pieces of pie is 37.

4. The greatest number of pieces is 7, which is the same as if the pie were round.

5. a. **7 regions.** Three intersecting circles:

    b. Four intersecting circles: 13 regions 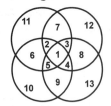   Five intersecting circles: 21 regions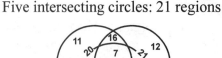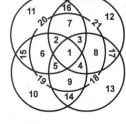

Number of Intersecting Circles	Greatest Number of Regions Formed
1	1
2	3
3	7
4	13
5	21

(differences: +2, +4, +6, +8)

    c. **57.** Add three more entries to the table above.
       21 + 10 = 31;   31 + 12 = 43;   43 + 14 = 57
       The greatest number of regions formed when 8 circles intersect is 57.

6. Cut the wheel of cheese along the dashed lines.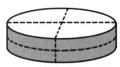

7. a. 0   b. 1   c. 6   d. 10   e. 15
    f. **28.** Every cut intersects each of the preceding cuts. Therefore, eight cuts produce a
       total of 0 + 1 + 2 + 3 + 4 + 5 + 6 + 7 = 28 cuts.

8. a. 1   b. 4   c. 16   d. 25   e. 36
    f. **64.** Every cut intersects each of the preceding cuts and produces one more segment
       than there are cuts. Therefore, each of the eight cuts consists of 8 smaller segments,
       resulting in a total of $8^2 = 64$ smaller segments.

5.4 Perimeter
Pages 92-94

1. a. **The width is 7 m; the length is 14 m.**

   <u>Method 1:</u> Make a table.

width	3	4	5	6	7
length	6	8	10	12	14
perimeter	18	24	30	36	42

   The entries in the last column satisfy the conditions of the problem.

   <u>Method 2:</u> Write and solve an equation.

   $$w + 2w + w + 2w = 42$$
   $$6w = 42$$
   $$\frac{6w}{6} = \frac{42}{6}$$
   $$w = 7$$
   $$2w = 14$$

   The width is 7 m and the length is 14 m.

   b. **The width is 9 m; the length is 12 m.**

   <u>Method 1:</u> Make a table.

width	5	6	7	8	9
length	8	9	10	11	12
perimeter	26	30	34	38	42

   The entries in the last column satisfy the conditions of the problem.

   <u>Method 2:</u> Write and solve an equation.

   $$w + (w + 3) + w + (w + 3) = 42$$
   $$4w + 6 = 42$$
   $$4w + 6 - 6 = 42 - 6$$
   $$4w = 36$$
   $$\frac{4w}{4} = \frac{36}{4}$$
   $$w = 9$$
   $$w + 3 = 12$$

   The width is 9 m and the length is 12 m.

   c. **The width is 8 m; the length is 13 m.**

   <u>Method 1:</u> Make a table.

width	4	5	6	7	8
length	5	7	9	11	13
Perimeter	18	24	30	36	42

   The entries in the last column satisfy the conditions of the problem.

Method 2: Write and solve an equation.

$$w + (2w - 3) + w + (2w - 3) = 42$$
$$6w - 6 = 42$$
$$6w - 6 + 6 = 42 + 6$$
$$6w = 48$$
$$\frac{6w}{6} = \frac{48}{6}$$
$$w = 8$$
$$2w - 3 = 13$$

The width is 8 m and the length is 13 m.

d.. **The width is 3½ m; the length is 17½ m.**

Method 1: Make a table.

width	6	5	4	3
length	30	25	20	15
perimeter	72	60	48	36

The perimeter 42 is halfway between 48 and 36, so try a width that is halfway between 4 and 3, or $3\frac{1}{2}$. If the width is 3, the length is $5 \times 3\frac{1}{2} = 17\frac{1}{2}$, and the perimeter is $3\frac{1}{2} + 17\frac{1}{2} + 3\frac{1}{2} + 17\frac{1}{2} = 42$.
The width is $3\frac{1}{2}$ m and the length is $17\frac{1}{2}$ m.

Method 2: Write and solve an equation.

$$l + \frac{1}{5}l + l + \frac{1}{5}l = 42$$
$$\frac{12}{5}l = 42$$
$$\frac{12}{5}l \times \frac{5}{12} = 42 \times \frac{5}{12}$$
$$l = \frac{210}{12} = 17\frac{6}{12} = 17\frac{1}{2}$$

The width is $3\frac{1}{2}$ m and the length is $17\frac{1}{2}$ m.

2. a. If the perimeter is 10, the sum of the length and the width is 5.

Length	4	3
Width	1	2

There are 2 different rectangles: 4 by 1 and 3 by 2.

If the perimeter is 12, the sum of the length and the width is 6.

Length	5	4	3
Width	1	2	3

There are 3 different rectangles.

If the perimeter is 14, the sum of the length and the width is 7.

length	6	5	4
width	1	2	3

There are 3 different rectangles.

If the perimeter is 16, the sum of the length and the width is 8.

length	7	6	5	4
width	1	2	3	4

There are 4 different rectangles.

If the perimeter is 24, the sum of the length and the width is 12.

length	11	10	9	8	7	6
width	1	2	3	4	5	6

There are 6 different rectangles.

b. If the given perimeter is a multiple of 4, the number of rectangles with different shapes that have the given perimeter is $\frac{1}{4}$ of the perimeter. If the given perimeter is an even number that is *not* a multiple of 4, subtract 2 from the given perimeter; the number of rectangles is then $\frac{1}{4}$ of the result.

c. **No.** If the length is represented by l and the width is represented by w, the perimeter is represented by $2l + 2w$. Since each of the quantities $2l$ and $2w$ are even numbers, their sum is an even number. Therefore, the perimeter has to be even.

3. **2.** Let a, b, and c represent the lengths of the sides of the triangle. Make a table of all combinations of three natural-number measures that have a sum of 10.

a	1	1	1	1	2	2	2	3
b	1	2	3	4	2	3	4	3
c	8	7	6	5	6	5	4	4

Since the sum of the lengths of any two sides of a triangle must be greater than the length of the third side, all but the last two combinations in the table must be eliminated. Only *two* different triangles can have a perimeter of 10: $a = 2$, $b = 4$, $c = 4$ and $a = 3$, $b = 3$, $c = 4$.

4. The perimeter of the given figure, 30 cm, is the sum of the lengths of 10 individual sides of squares. Therefore, the length of just *one* of these sides is $30 \div 10 = 3$ cm.
    a. $12 \times 3 = \mathbf{36\ cm}$ b. $12 \times 3 = \mathbf{36\ cm}$ c. $12 \times 3 = \mathbf{36\ cm}$ d. $14 \times 3 = \mathbf{42\ cm}$

5. a. $\frac{1}{2}$ **unit.**   Since the perimeter of *PQRS* is 1 unit, then the length of one side of *PQRS* is $\frac{1}{4}$ unit, and the perimeter of the shaded region in the diagram at the right is $4 \times \frac{1}{8} = \frac{1}{2}$ unit.

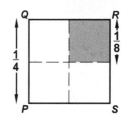

b. **32.** The perimeter of the shaded rectangle is given as 24 m. A second fold of P onto Q creates 4 smaller congruent squares. The sides of the shaded rectangle consist of 6 congruent segments, each labeled n in the diagram. The sum of the six congruent segments is given as 24 m, so the length of one of them is $24 \div 6 = 4$ m. As a result, the length of one side of the square is 8 and the perimeter of $PQRS$ is 8×4 or 32 m.

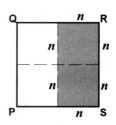

This problem can also be solved by using algebra or by using the strategy shown in part **c**.

c. **24 cm.** Suppose the shorter side of the shaded rectangle has a length of 1 basic unit. Then the length of $\overline{QR}$ is 4 basic units. Thus, the perimeter of the shaded rectangle is $1 + 4 + 1 + 4 = 10$ basic units. Since the perimeter is given as 15, each basic unit is $15 \div 10 = 1.5$. As a result, the length of $\overline{QR}$, 4 basic units, is actually 4×1.5, or 6 cm, and the perimeter of $PQRS$ is $4 \times 6 = 24$ cm.

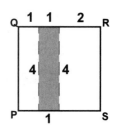

This problem can also be solved by using algebra or the strategy shown in part **b**.

5.5 Circumference
Pages 94-96

1. a. **264 cm.** $C = 2\pi r$
$$\approx 2 \times \tfrac{22}{7} \times 42$$
$$\approx 264 \qquad \text{The wheel travels approximately 264 cm in one turn.}$$

   b. **2083 times.**   5.5 km = 550,000 cm; $550{,}000 \div 264 = 2083\tfrac{1}{3}$.
   The wheel turns approximately 2083 times.

2. **Approximately $3\tfrac{1}{2}$ ft.** Let C represent the *circumference* of the wheel. Then $240 \times C$ represents the distance the wheel travels in 240 turns.
$$\text{Since } 1 \text{ mile} = 5280 \text{ feet:}$$
$$240 \times C = 5280$$
$$C = \tfrac{5280}{240} = 22$$
$$\text{Since } C = 2\pi r:$$
$$2\pi r = 22$$
$$2 \times \tfrac{22}{7} \times r \approx 22$$
$$\tfrac{44}{7} \times r \approx 22$$
$$\tfrac{44}{7} \times r \times \tfrac{7}{44} \approx 22 \times \tfrac{7}{44}$$
$$r \approx \tfrac{7}{2}, \text{ or } 3\tfrac{1}{2}$$

The radius of the wheel is approximately $3\tfrac{1}{2}$ ft.

3. **420 yd.** Note that the two semicircles at the ends have a combined circumference equal to the circumference of one complete circle with diameter equal to 70 yd.

Since $C = \pi \times d$,
$$C \approx \tfrac{22}{7} \times 70$$
$$C \approx 220$$

This circumference, together with the two 100-yd lengths, constitutes the distance around the track. The distance around the track is approximately $220 + 100 + 100 = 420$ yd.

4. a. Counterclockwise   b. Clockwise

   c. **6.** When Gear A makes 3 complete turns, $3 \times 40 = 120$ teeth pass the point of contact with Gear B. Since Gear B has 20 teeth, it will make $120 \div 20 = 6$ complete turns.

   d. **4.** Follow the reasoning employed in part **c**. Since Gear C has 30 teeth, it will make $120 \div 30 = 4$ complete turns.

5. $\tfrac{1}{2}$. Let the circumference of the inner circle $= 2\pi r$. Since the width of the shaded ring is r, the radius of the outer circle is $2r$, and its circumference is $2\pi \times 2r$, or $4\pi r$. The ratio of the circumferences is $\tfrac{2\pi r}{4\pi r}$, or $\tfrac{1}{2}$.

6. **50 in. and 904 in.** In one revolution, the tip of the hour hand travels a path that is equal in length to the circumference of a circle of radius 4 in.
$$C = 2\pi r,$$
$$C \approx 2 \times 3.14 \times 4$$
$$C \approx 25.12$$

In one revolution, the tip of the hour hand travels approximately 25.12 in. The hour hand makes 2 revolutions in a 24-hour period. Therefore, in a 24-hour period, the tip of the hour hand travels *approximately* 2×25.12 in., which is approximately 50 in.

In one revolution, the tip of the minute hand travels a path that is equal in length to the circumference of a circle of radius 6 in.
$$C = 2\pi r,$$
$$C \approx 2 \times 3.14 \times 6$$
$$C \approx 37.68$$

In one revolution, the tip of the minute hand travels about 37.68 in. The minute hand makes 24 revolutions in a 24-hour period. Therefore, in a 24-hour period, the tip of the minute hand travels approximately 24×37.68 in., which is approximately 904 in.

7. **150 cm.**

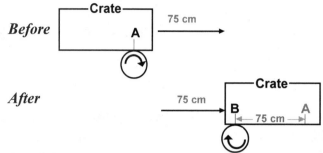

Suppose that *A* is the original point of contact between one cylinder and the crate, and *B* is the point of contact after one complete turn of this cylinder. Then the distance that the cylinder moves along the crate in one complete turn is equal to the circumference of the cylinder, or 75 cm. However, drawing a diagram such as the one above, note that the cylinder also advances an additional 75 cm along the ground. Each point, *A* and *B*, has traveled a total distance of 75 + 75 = 150 cm. The entire crate moves 150 cm for each complete turn of the cylinder.

5.6 *Area of Rectangles and Squares*
Pages 96-98

1. a. The largest rectangular garden that can be enclosed will always be a square with the given perimeter.

   <u>One carton</u>: **36 ft².**
      Perimeter = 1 × 24 = 24 ft
      One side = 24 ÷ 4 = 6 ft
      Area = 6 × 6 = 36 ft²

   <u>Two cartons</u>: **144 ft².**
      Perimeter = 2 × 24 = 48 ft
      One side = 48 ÷ 4 = 12 ft
      Area = 12 × 12 = 144 ft²

   <u>Three cartons:</u> **324 ft².**
      Perimeter = 3 × 24 = 72 ft
      One side = 72 ÷ 4 = 18 ft
      Area = 18 × 18 = 324 ft²

   b. For a given number of cartons, the area of the largest rectangular garden that can be enclosed is 36 times the *square* of the given number of cartons.

   c. <u>32 ft² garden</u>: **One carton.**
      The garden can have one of these sets of dimensions: 32 ft × 1 ft; 16 ft × 2 ft; or 8 ft × 4 ft. The least of the perimeters is for the 8 ft × 4 ft garden: 8 + 4 + 8 + 4 = 24 ft. One carton is the least number needed.

<u>128 ft² garden</u>: **Two cartons.**
A 128 ft² garden can have one of these sets of dimensions: 128 ft × 1 ft; 64 ft × 2 ft;
32 ft × 4 ft; or 16 ft × 8 ft. The least of the perimeters is for the 16 ft × 8 ft garden:
16 + 8 + 16 + 8 = 48 ft. Two cartons is the least number needed.

2. **144 m².** Draw and label a diagram of the pool and
the walk as shown at the right. The area of the walk
is equal to the difference between the areas of the
outer and inner rectangles in the diagram.

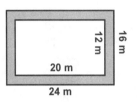

Outer rectangle: A = $l × w$ = 16 × 24 = 384 m²
Inner rectangle: A = $l × w$ = 12 × 20 = 240 m²
Difference: 384 − 240 = 144 m²

The area of the concrete walk is 144 m².

3. a. **325 cm².** Separate the floor into three rectangular
regions as shown at the right. The total area of the
floor is the sum of the areas of the three rectangular regions.

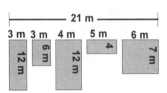

Area = 7 × 20 + 13 × 5 + 10 × 12
= 140 + 65 + 120 = 325 m²

b. **164 m².** Separate the floor into five rectangular regions, as shown at the right. The total area of the floor
is the sum of the areas of the five rectangular regions.

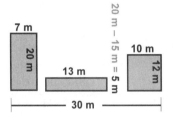

Area = 3 × 12 + 3 × 6 + 4 × 12 + 5 × 4 + 7 × 6
= 36 + 18 + 48 + 20 + 42 = 164 m²

4. **47 ft².** Area of bottom: 3 × 5 = 15 ft²
Area of front and back sides: 2 × (2 × 3) = 12 ft²
Area of left and right sides: 2 × (2 × 5) = 20 ft²

The total area of the plywood needed will be 15 + 12 + 20 = 47 ft²

5. a. $\frac{1}{4}$. Since the area of *PQRS* is 1 unit², then the
length of a side of *PQRS* is 1 unit. The area of the
shaded region in the diagram at the right is then
$\frac{1}{2} × \frac{1}{2} = \frac{1}{4}$ unit².

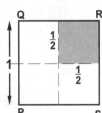

b. **12.** If the area of *PQRS* is 16 cm², then the length of a side of *PQRS* is 4 cm. The area of the shaded region in the diagram at the right is then 4 × 3 = 12 cm².

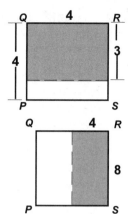

c. **64.** The length of the shaded figure in the diagram at the right is twice its width. Therefore, if the perimeter of the new figure is 24 units, its length is 8 units, and its width is 4 units. Each side of square *PQRS* is 8 units and its area is then 8 × 8 = 64 units².

6. **144 ft².** If the four triangular lawn areas are moved together, as shown in the diagram at the right, they form a square with sides that measure 12 ft. The total lawn area is 12 ft × 12 ft = 144 ft².

7. **2 units².** Draw segment *EG* and *FH*, intersecting at point *O*. Note that the area of triangle *OEF* is half the area of square *OEBF*. Since each side of square *ABCD* measures 2 units, a side of square *OEBF* measures 1 unit, and the area of square *OEBF* is 1 × 1 = 1 unit², the area of triangle *OEF* is $\frac{1}{2}$ of 1, or $\frac{1}{2}$ unit². Square *EFGH* is formed by triangle *OEF* and three triangles congruent to it. The area of the square *EFGH* is 4 × $\frac{1}{2}$ = 2 units².

8. **4 units.** Let *s* represent the length of a side of the square. Then its perimeter is 4 × *s*, and its area is *s* × *s*. Then according to the conditions of the problem, *s* × *s* = 4 × *s*. The only number that makes this a true statement is *s* = 4. The length of a side of the square is 4 units.

9. **No.** Let *s* represent the length of a side of the original square. Then the area of the original square is *s* × *s*, or *s*². If the measure of the side of the new square is now doubled, 2*s* represents the length of a side of the new square. Then the area of the new square is 2*s* × 2*s*, or 4*s*². If each side of a square is doubled, the area is four times as great.

10.

A = B = $\frac{1}{4}$ unit²

Each X = $\frac{1}{16}$ unit²

C = E = $\frac{1}{16}$ unit²

D = F = G = $\frac{1}{8}$ unit²

5.7 Area of Circles
Pages 98-100

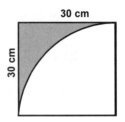

1. **193.5 cm².** The area of the piece of tin that is cut from the square piece of tin is equal to one-fourth of the area of a circle that has a radius of 30 cm. Therefore, we have the following:

Area of square = 30 cm × 30 cm = 900 cm²

$$\text{Area of tin that is cut} = \tfrac{1}{4} \times \pi \times (30 \text{ cm})^2$$
$$\approx \tfrac{1}{4} \times 3.14 \times 900 \text{ cm}^2$$
$$\approx 706.5 \text{ cm}^2$$

Area of scraps ≈ 900 cm² – 706.5 cm²
$$\approx 193.5 \text{ cm}^2$$

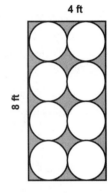

2. a. **6.88 ft².** From the placement of the disks in the given figure, we see that each circle has a diameter of 2 ft and a radius of 1 ft. Therefore, the area of the disks that are cut from the rectangular piece of tin is equal to eight times the area of a circle that has a radius of 1 ft. We then have the following:

Area of rectangle = 8 ft × 4 ft = 32 ft²

$$\text{Area of disks} = 8 \times \pi \times (1 \text{ ft}^2)$$
$$\approx 8 \times 3.14 \times 1 \text{ ft}^2$$
$$\approx 25.12 \text{ ft}^2$$

Area of scraps ≈ 32 ft² – 25.12 ft²
$$\approx 6.88 \text{ ft}^2.$$

b. 1-ft diameter: 4 × 8 = **32 disks.**
2-ft radius: 1 × 2 =   **2 disks.**
6-in. diameter: 8 × 16 = **128 disks.**
8-in. radius: 3 × 6 = **18 disks.**

c. 1-ft diameter: $\approx 32 \text{ ft}^2 - 32 \times \pi \times \left(\tfrac{1}{2} \text{ ft}\right)^2$
$$\approx 32 \text{ ft}^2 - 32 \times 3.14 \times \tfrac{1}{4} \text{ ft}^2$$
$$\approx 32 \text{ ft}^2 - 25.12 \text{ ft}^2$$
$$\approx 6.88 \text{ ft}^2$$

2-ft radius: $\approx 32 \text{ ft}^2 - 2 \times \pi \times (2 \text{ ft})^2$
$$\approx 32 \text{ ft}^2 - 2 \times 3.14 \times 4 \text{ ft}^2$$
$$\approx 32 \text{ ft}^2 - 25.12 \text{ ft}^2$$
$$\approx 6.88 \text{ ft}^2$$

6-in. diameter:
$$\approx 32 \text{ ft}^2 - 128 \times \pi \times \left(\tfrac{1}{4} \text{ ft}\right)^2$$
$$\approx 32 \text{ ft}^2 - 128 \times 3.14 \times \tfrac{1}{16} \text{ ft}^2$$
$$\approx 32 \text{ ft}^2 - 25.12 \text{ ft}^2$$
$$\approx 6.88 \text{ ft}^2$$

8-in. radius:
$$\approx 32 \text{ ft}^2 - 18 \times \pi \times \left(\tfrac{2}{3} \text{ ft}\right)^2$$
$$\approx 32 \text{ ft}^2 - 18 \times 3.14 \times \tfrac{4}{9} \text{ ft}^2$$
$$\approx 32 \text{ ft}^2 - 25.12 \text{ ft}^2$$
$$\approx 6.88 \text{ ft}^2$$

Note: The total area of the scraps in each of the above cases is the same.

3. **One-half.** Consider the situation as pictured in the diagram at the right. The shaded region represents the piece of paper remaining after all scraps have been discarded. The dashed lines separate the original piece of paper into four square regions; clearly, one-half of each of these four regions has been discarded. Therefore, one-half of the entire square has been discarded.

4. **1.34 m².** Note that 1.26 m = 126 cm.
Area of rectangle = 126 cm × 84 cm = 10,584 cm²
Area of window = Area of rectangle + Area of semicircle

$\approx$	10,584 cm² + 2772 cm²	(using $\pi = 3\tfrac{1}{7}$)
$\approx$	13,356 cm²	
$\approx$	1.34 m²	

5. **628 units².** Note that the radius of the outer circle is equal to the width of the ring plus the radius of the inner ring, or 10 units + 5 units = 15 units.

Area of ring = Area of outer circle – Area of inner circle
$$= \quad \pi \times 15^2 \quad - \quad \pi \times 5^2$$
$$= \quad 225\pi \quad - \quad 25\pi$$
$$= \quad 200\pi$$
$$\approx \quad 200 \times 3.14, \quad \text{or } 628 \text{ square units}$$

6. **285,600 yd².** Note that the two semicircles at the ends have a combined area equal to the area of one full circle with diameter equal to 400 yd, or radius equal to 200 yd.

Area of shaded region = Area of square + Area of circle
$$= 400 \text{ yd} \times 400 \text{ yd} + \pi \times (200 \text{ yd})^2$$
$$\approx 160,000 \text{ yd}^2 \quad + \quad 125,600 \text{ yd}^2$$
$$\approx \quad 285,600 \text{ yd}^2$$

7. $\frac{1}{2}$. Note that the area of the shaded region is equal to the area of the large circle minus the area of the two small circles. Let r represent the radius of one of the small circles. Then $2r$ represents the radius of the large circle, and we have the following.

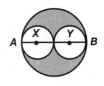

Area of large circle $= \pi \times (2r)^2 = 4\pi r^2$
Area of two small circles $= 2 \times (\pi \times r^2) = 2\pi r^2$
Area of shaded region $= 4\pi r^2 - 2\pi r^2 = 2\pi r^2$

The ratio of the area of the shaded region to the area of the large circle is $2\pi r^2$ to $4\pi r^2$, or $\frac{1}{2}$.

8. a. **1848 ft².** Using a diagram such as the one at the right, note that the goat is able to graze on a piece of land that is shaped like $\frac{3}{4}$ of a circle with a radius equal to the length of the rope, which is 28 ft. Therefore, we have the following.

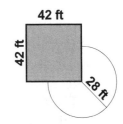

$$\begin{aligned}\text{Grazing Area} &= \tfrac{3}{4} \times \pi r^2 \\ &\approx \tfrac{3}{4} \times \tfrac{22}{7} \times (28 \text{ ft})^2 \\ &\approx \tfrac{3}{4} \times \tfrac{22}{7} \times 784 \text{ ft}^2 \\ &\approx 1848 \text{ ft}^2\end{aligned}$$

The goat can graze on approximately 1848 ft² of land.

b. **7700 ft²** As in part **a**, the goat is able to graze on a piece of land that is shaped like $\frac{3}{4}$ of a circle, with a radius equal to the length of the rope, which is 56 ft. This time, though, a diagram helps to see that the goat can also graze on *two* smaller pieces of land that are in the shape of $\frac{1}{4}$ of a circle with a radius equal to 14 ft, the difference between the length of the rope and the length of a side of the barn. Therefore, we have the following.

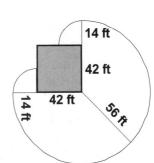

$$\begin{aligned}\text{Large grazing area} &= \tfrac{3}{4} \times \pi \times (56 \text{ ft})^2 \\ &\approx \tfrac{3}{4} \times \tfrac{22}{7} \times 3136 \text{ ft}^2 \\ &\approx 7392 \text{ ft}^2\end{aligned}$$

$$\begin{aligned}\text{Small grazing area} &= 2 \times \tfrac{1}{4} \times \pi \times (14 \text{ ft})^2 \\ &\approx 2 \times \tfrac{1}{4} \times \tfrac{22}{7} \times 196 \text{ ft}^2 \\ &\approx 308 \text{ ft}^2\end{aligned}$$

$$\begin{aligned}\text{Total grazing area} &\approx 7392 \text{ ft}^2 + 308 \text{ ft}^2 \\ &\approx 7700 \text{ ft}^2.\end{aligned}$$

The goat can graze on approximately 7700 ft² of land.

9. **3080 ft²** Using a diagram and the reasoning employed in problem 8, we see that the grazing area can be separated into three distinct parts: $\frac{3}{4}$ of a circle with radius 35 ft, $\frac{1}{4}$ of a circle with radius 14 ft, and $\frac{1}{4}$ of a circle with radius 7 ft.

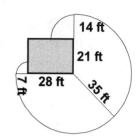

Therefore, we have the following.

$$
\begin{aligned}
\text{Grazing area} \quad &= \tfrac{3}{4} \times \pi \times (35 \text{ ft})^2 \;+\; \tfrac{1}{4} \times \pi \times (14 \text{ ft})^2 \;+\; \tfrac{1}{4} \times \pi \times (7 \text{ ft})^2 \\
&\approx \tfrac{3}{4} \times \tfrac{22}{7} \times 1225 \text{ ft}^2 \;+\; \tfrac{1}{4} \times \tfrac{22}{7} \times 196 \text{ ft}^2 \;+\; \tfrac{1}{4} \times \tfrac{22}{7} \times 49 \text{ ft}^2 \\
&\approx \quad 2887.5 \text{ ft}^2 \quad + \quad\quad 154 \text{ ft}^2 \quad\quad + \quad 38.5 \text{ ft}^2 \\
&\approx \quad\quad\quad\quad\quad\quad\quad\quad 3080 \text{ ft}^2
\end{aligned}
$$

The goat can graze on approximately 3080 ft² of land.

5.8 *Geometric Patterns*
Pages 101-102

1. a. **Five**

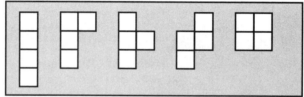

b. If the length of the side of one of the squares measures 1 unit, then the perimeter of each of the first four tetrominoes above is 10, while the perimeter of the last tetromino is 8. Therefore, the square tetromino has the least perimeter.

2. a. **One.** 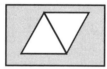 b. **One.**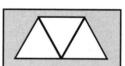

c. **Three.**

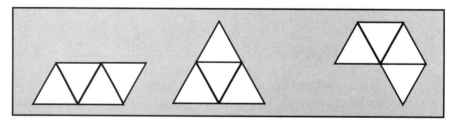

3. **Five.**

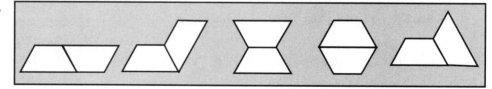

4. a.
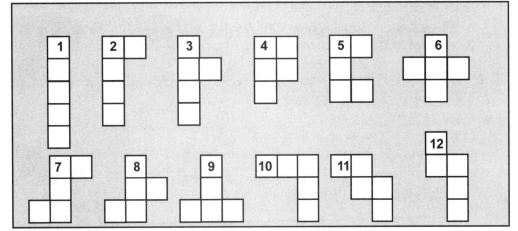

b. Figures 2, 3, 6, 7, 8, 9, 11, and 12 could be folded to make a box with an open top.

c. The following are three possible arrangements of the 12 figures of **4a** above. The number in each figure below refers to a figure in **4a**.

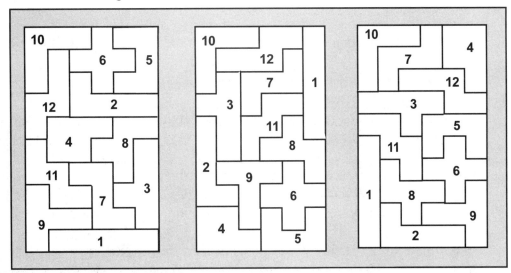

5. **No.** Each domino covers exactly two squares. The 3 by 3 grid contains 9 squares, and $9 \div 2$ is not a whole number.

6. **No.** A checkerboard has 64 squares, usually 32 black squares and 32 colored squares in the alternating arrangement pictured on page 84. Note that each pair of diagonally opposite corner squares is of the same color. If two diagonally opposite corner squares are removed, the numbers of black and colored squares remaining will not be equal to each other. However, given its shape, each domino has to cover one black and one colored square. Furthermore, any whole number of dominoes must cover equal numbers of black and colored squares. Therefore, it is impossible for a whole number of dominoes to cover this board without overlapping.

6. Trains, Books, Clocks, and Things

6.1 Motion Problems
Pages 103-105

1. The trains are separating at the rate of $95 + 105 = 200$ km/h.
   a. **500 km.** At the end of $2\frac{1}{2}$ h, the trains will be $2\frac{1}{2} \times 200 = 500$ km apart.
   b. **1h 45 min.** For the trains to be 350 km apart, the amount of time needed will be $350 \div 200 = 1\frac{3}{4}$ h, or 1 h 45 min.

2. The trains are separating at the rate of $108 - 72 = 36$ km/h.
   a. **111 km.** At 1:05 P.M., the trains will have been traveling for 3 h 5 min, or $3\frac{1}{12}$ h. The trains will be $3\frac{1}{12} \times 36 = 111$ km apart.
   b. **5:30 P.M.** For the trains to be 270 km apart, the amount of time needed will be $270 \div 36 = 7\frac{1}{2}$ h, or 7 h 30 min. The two trains will be 270 km apart at 5:30 P.M. of the same day.

3. **7 mi.** Helen and Kenji approach each other at the rate of $6 + 8 = 14$ mph and meet in $\frac{1}{2}$ h. They were $\frac{1}{2} \times 14 = 7$ mi apart when they started.

4. **2 h.** The distance between the father and son is decreasing at the rate of $72 - 48 = 24$ km/h. They were 48 km apart when the son left home. It will take $48 \div 24 = 2$ h for the son to overtake his father.

5. **6 h.** Given the presence of the current, in this river Lisa can row downstream at the rate of $3 + 1 = 4$ mph and upstream at the rate of $3 - 1 = 2$ mph. Therefore, the 8-mi trip downstream will require $8 \div 2 = 4$ hours. The entire trip takes a total of $2 + 4 = 6$ h.

6. **30 km/h, 60 km/h.** If the trains are 270 km apart and pass each other in 3 h, they were approaching each other at the rate of $270 \div 3 = 90$ km/h. However, 90 km/h is the *sum* of their two rates. Suppose that x represents the rate of the freight train. Then $2x$ represents the rate of the passenger train, and we have the following.

$$x + 2x = 90$$
$$3x = 90$$
$$\frac{3x}{3} = \frac{90}{3}$$
$$x = 30$$

The rate of the freight train is 30 km/h and the rate of the passenger train is $2 \times 30 = 60$ km/h.

7. **4 minutes.**

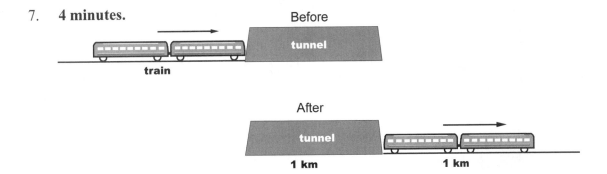

From the diagram, we see that the train must travel a distance of 2 km to clear the tunnel. The train is traveling at the rate of 30 km/h, which is the same as 30 km per 60 min or 1 km per 2 min. It takes the train $2 \times 2 = 4$ min to travel 2 km and clear the tunnel.

8. $\frac{1}{4}$ **mi.** The freight train is passing Leo at a rate equal to the *combined* rates of the passenger and freight trains, or $40 + 20 = 60$ mph. The rate of 60 mph is the same as 60 mi per 3600 seconds. Since 15 sec is $\frac{1}{240}$ of 3600 sec, the train's length is $\frac{1}{240}$ of 60 mi, or $\frac{1}{4}$ mi.

9. **6 seconds.** After the front parts of the trains meet, each train must travel the length of the other train before the rear parts meet and pass. Since each train is $\frac{1}{12}$ mi long, each train must then travel $\frac{1}{12}$ mi. Each train is traveling at the rate of 50 mph, which is the same as 50 mi per 3600 seconds, or 1 mi per 72 seconds. Then to travel $\frac{1}{12}$ mi, each train requires $\frac{1}{12} \times 72 = 6$ seconds. The rear parts of the trains will pass each other 6 seconds after the front parts meet.

10. **40 km.** The trains are approaching each other at the rate of $55 + 65 = 120$ km/h. Since they only need to travel a combined distance of 60 km, they will meet in $\frac{1}{2}$ h. Although the bee reverses its direction frequently, it is flying at a constant rate of 80 km/h. In one hour, the bee flies 80 km. In $\frac{1}{2}$ h the bee flies 40 km.

6.2 Book Problems
Pages 105-107

1. a. **1017.**

Page Numbers	Number of Digits		
1-9	9×1	=	9
10-99	90×2	=	180
100-375	276×3	=	828
	Total	**=**	**1017**

The printer will need a total of 1017 pieces of type.

b. **154.**   Ones place: 38
           Tens place: 40
           Hundreds place: 76
The total number of 3s that the printer will need is $38 + 40 + 76 = 154$.

c. **78.**   Ones place: 38
         Tens place: 40
         Hundreds place: 0
The total number of 4s that the printer will need is $38 + 40 + 0 = 78$.

d. **67.**   Ones place: 37
         Tens place: 30
         Hundreds place: 0
The total number of 8s that the printer will need is $37 + 30 + 0 = 67$.

2.   **170.**   From the solution to problem **1a**, we already know that pages 1 through 99 require $9 + 180 = 189$ pieces of type. Then the remaining pages of this book must require $402 - 189 = 213$ pieces of type. Since each page following page 99 requires 3 pieces of type, there must be $213 \div 3 = 71$ remaining pages, beginning with page 100. The 71 pages will be numbered 100, 101, 102, 103, ... , 170. This book contains 170 pages.

3.   **34 and 35.**   **Method 1:** Begin by finding two perfect squares that bound the product. For example, $30^2 = 900$ and $40^2 = 1600$. We now know that the two page numbers are between 30 and 40. Since the ones digit of the product is 0, one of the page numbers has to be 35. Since 35 is a right-hand page, the facing page is a left-hand page, and its number is 34. Verification: $34 \times 35 = 1190$.

<u>Method 2:</u> The prime factors of 1190 are 2, 5, 7, and 17. Remultiply them to produce a pair of consecutive integers: $2 \times 17 = 34$ and $5 \times 7 = 35$.

4.   **83, 84, 85, 86, 87, 88.**   <u>Method 1:</u> Reason from the average outwards.
Since the pages would be numbered with six consecutive counting numbers, we know that the average of the six page numbers is $513 \div 6 = 85.5$. Therefore, the middle two page numbers are 85 and 86, and the other page numbers are the two numbers immediately preceding 85 and the two numbers immediately following 86. The complete set of page numbers is then 83, 84, 85, 86, 87, and 88.

<u>Method 2:</u> Write and solve an equation.
Since the pages are numbered consecutively, the six page numbers can be represented by n, $n + 1$, $n + 2$, $n + 3$, $n + 4$, and $n + 5$.

We then have the following equations:

$$n+(n+1)+(n+2)+(n+3)+(n+4)+(n+5)=513$$
$$6n+15=513$$
$$6n=498$$
$$\frac{6n}{6}=\frac{498}{6}$$
$$n=83$$

The first page number is 83, followed by 84, 85, 86, 87, and 88.

6.3 *Work Problems*
Pages 107-109

1. **2 h, 6 m.** Working alone, the adult can do $\frac{1}{3}$ of the job in one hour and the child can do $\frac{1}{7}$ of the job in one hour. Working together, the adult and child can do $\frac{1}{3}+\frac{1}{7}=\frac{10}{21}$ of the job in one hour. Since $\frac{10}{21}$ of the job requires one hour, $\frac{1}{21}$ of the job requires $\frac{1}{10}$ of one hour, or 6 min. The entire job will require $21 \times 6 = 126$ min, or two hours six min.

2. **1 h, 20 m.** Working alone, the old-model machine can stamp $\frac{1}{4}$ of the parts in one hour and the new-model machine can stamp $\frac{1}{2}$ of the parts in one hour. (Notice that the exact number of parts is extraneous information.) Working together, the two machines can stamp $\frac{1}{4}+\frac{1}{2}=\frac{3}{4}$ of the parts in one hour. Since $\frac{3}{4}$ of the parts require one hour, $\frac{1}{4}$ of the parts require $\frac{1}{3}$ of one hour, or 20 min. To stamp all the parts then, the two machines will need $4 \times 20 = 80$ min, or one hour twenty minutes.

3. **$1\frac{1}{5}$ days.** Working alone, Laura can do $\frac{1}{3}$ of the job in one day. Eric can do $\frac{1}{4}$ of the job in one day, and Connie can do $\frac{1}{4}$ of the job in one day. Working together, all three can do $\frac{1}{3}+\frac{1}{4}+\frac{1}{4}=\frac{5}{6}$ of the job in one day. Since $\frac{5}{6}$ of the job requires one day, $\frac{1}{6}$ of the job requires $\frac{1}{5}$ of a day. The entire job will require $6 \times \frac{1}{5} = 1\frac{1}{5}$ days.

4. **12 min.** In one minute, water from the faucet will fill $\frac{1}{3}$ of the tub and the open drain will empty $\frac{1}{4}$ of the tub. When both the faucet and the drain are open, $\frac{1}{3}-\frac{1}{4}=\frac{1}{12}$ of the tub will be filled in one minute. Therefore, it will take 12 minutes for the tub to fill completely.

5. **6 days.** Working alone, it would take one worker $9 \times 8 = 72$ days to pave the stretch of road. Therefore, it will take 12 workers $72 \div 12 = 6$ days to do the job working together.

6. **10 days.** The number of individual daily rations that were purchased is $6 \times 15 = 90$. A group of 9 scouts will consume the rations in $90 \div 9 = 10$ days.

7. **8 min.** Working alone, it would take one machine $4 \times 6 = 24$ min to make the copies. 3 machines working together would require $24 \div 3 = 8$ minutes.

8. **40 min.** Working alone, the faster computer can do $\frac{1}{20}$ of the payroll in one minute. Therefore, in $13\frac{1}{3}$ min the faster computer can do $13\frac{1}{3} \times \frac{1}{20} = \frac{2}{3}$ of the payroll. Thus, in $13\frac{1}{3}$ min, the *slower* computer can do $\frac{1}{3}$ of the payroll. To do the entire payroll, the slower computer requires $3 \times 13\frac{1}{3} = 40$ minutes.

6.4 Clock Problems
Pages 109-110

1. a. **10 days.** As discussed on page 109, the clock must gain a total of 720 min before it again shows the correct time. Since it gains 3 min every hour, it will gain 720 min in $720 \div 3 = 240$ h, which is ten days.

   b. **15 days.** This clock needs to *lose* a total of 720 min before it again shows the correct time. Since it loses 2 min every hour, it will lose 720 min in $720 \div 2 = 360$ h, which is fifteen days.

   c. **2700 days.** This clock must gain a total of 720 min = 43,200 sec before it again shows the correct time. Since it gains 2 sec every 3 h, it gains $\frac{2}{3}$ sec every hour. This clock will gain 43,200 sec in $43,200 \div \frac{2}{3} = 64,800$ h, or 2700 days.

2. **2 o'clock and 10 o'clock.** The complete clock face is associated with the 360° of a circle, and each of the 12 hour-intervals around the clock is associated with $360 \div 12 = 30°$. Therefore, the hands of a clock will form an angle that measures 60° at any time when exactly two of these hour-intervals lie between the hands. The only *hours* at which this occurs are 2 o'clock and 10 o'clock.

3. a. **22 times.** The hands of a clock lie directly opposite each other 11 times in each twelve-hour interval, or 22 times each day.

   b. **44 times.** The hands of a clock are perpendicular to each other 22 times in each twelve-hour interval, or 44 times each day.

4. **2:12 A.M., 2:12 P.M., 9:48 A.M., or 9:48 P.M.** In the course of one hour, the hour hand of the clock points to just *five* of the sixty one-minute marks. Therefore, the hour hand points exactly at one of the minute-marks every one fifth of an hour, or every twelve minutes: 1:00, 1:12, 1:24, 1:36, 1:48, 2:00, 2:12, 2:24, and so on through the day. Examining these times, though, we see that at 1:00 there are 4 minute-marks between the hour and minute hands; at 1:12 there are 5 minute-marks between the hour and minute hands; at 1:24 there are 16 minute-marks between the hour and minute

hands; and so on. The only times when the hour and minute hands point exactly to adjacent marks are 2:12 and 9:48. Larry looked at the clock at either 2:12 A.M., 2:12 P.M., 9:48 A.M., or 9:48 P.M.

5. **4 P.M.** **Method 1:** Use reasoning.
Since the time that had elapsed since noon was equal to half the time that remained until midnight, note that the time that had elapsed since noon was also one-third of the total time from noon until midnight. Therefore, the time that had elapsed since noon was one-third of twelve hours, or four hours. The time was 4:00 P.M.

Method 2: Write and solve an equation.
Using the variable t to represent the amount of time that had elapsed since noon, the expression $12 - t$ represents the amount of time that remains until midnight. The information given in the problem can then be translated into the following equation.

$$t = \tfrac{1}{2}(12 - t)$$
$$t = 6 - \tfrac{1}{2}t$$
$$\tfrac{3}{2}t = 6$$
$$\tfrac{3}{2}t \times \tfrac{2}{3} = 6 \times \tfrac{2}{3}$$
$$t = 4$$

The time that elapsed since noon was 4 h, and the time was 4:00 P.M.

6. **540 min.** Each twelve-hour interval contains a 2 in the hour display constantly during the 2nd and 12th hours. This is a total of four hours each day, for $4 \times 60 = 240$ min.

For the remaining twenty hours of the day, there is a 2 in the tens place of the minute display for ten minutes of every hour (from :20 to :29). This is a total of $20 \times 10 = 200$ min.

For the remaining fifty minutes of each of the twenty hours, there is a 2 in the minute display once every ten minutes (:02, :12, :22, :32, :42, and :52), or five minutes every hour. This is a total of $20 \times 5 = 100$ min. There is at least one 2 displayed by the clock for $240 + 200 + 100 = 540$ min of the day.

7. **12:10 P.M.** Sixty actual minutes take only $60 - 6 = 54$ min of time on the slow clock. Then one minute of time on the slow clock takes $\frac{60}{54} = 1\tfrac{1}{9}$ actual min. The slow clock takes 90 of its minutes in going from 10:30 A.M. to 12:00. The *actual* time for this period is $90 \times 1\tfrac{1}{9} = 100$ min, or 1 h 40 min. When the slow clock first shows 12:00, the correct time will be 12:10 P.M.

6.5 Related Problems
Pages 111-114

1. **15.** If we continue with the group of five people discussed on pages 111-112, then the presence of a sixth person requires 5 new handshakes, for a total of $10 + 5 = 15$ handshakes.

2. **45.**

    A   B   C   D   E   F

    B C D E F   A C D E F   A B D E F   A B C E F   A B C D F   A B C D E

    The tree diagram displays a total of $6 \times 5 = 30$ connections, but each handshake has been counted twice. Therefore, there are $30 \div 2 = 15$ distinct handshakes.

3.

Number of People	2	3	4	5	6	7	8
Number of Handshakes	1	3	6	10	15	21	28

4. **45.** The entries in the "Number of Handshakes" column form a pattern of increasing differences, as discussed in Section 1.3. Add two entries to the table in problem 3 to find the number of handshakes that would be exchanged by 10 people.

    1   3   6   10   15   21   28   36   45

    $+2$ $+3$ $+4$ $+5$ $+6$ $+7$ $+8$ $+9$

    If each person shakes hands with each of the others exactly once, ten people would exchange 45 handshakes.

5. **16.** Consider the reasoning employed in the tree diagram. If variable n represents the number of people, then each person shakes hands $(n-1)$ times. However, the expression $n \times (n-1)$ counts each handshake twice, so the total number of handshakes exchanged is $n \times (n-1) \div 2$. Therefore, we are looking for two consecutive numbers whose product is 240, since $240 \div 2 = 120$, the given number of handshakes. Since $10^2 = 100$ and $20^2 = 400$, the numbers are between 10 and 20. Since the ones digit of 240 is 0, one of the numbers must be 15; $240 \div 15 = 16$, so the other number is 16. There are 16 people in the group.

6. **190.** $20 \times 19 \div 2 = 380 \div 2 = 190$. There will be 190 games played altogether.

7. a. 15   b. 21   c. 28   d. 45

    Since these problems are examples of the same mathematical model as used in the handshake problem, the answers here are the same as for the numbers of handshakes exchanged by 6, 7, 8, and 10 people.

8. **10.** Although the five points lie on the same line, the number of segments that can be named is the same as if the points did *not* lie on the same line. There are 10 segments, and they can be listed as follows.

$$\overline{AB} \qquad \overline{AC} \qquad \overline{AD} \qquad \overline{AE}$$
$$\overline{BC} \qquad \overline{BD} \qquad \overline{BE}$$
$$\overline{CD} \qquad \overline{CE}$$
$$\overline{DE}$$

9. **35.** The total number of sides *and* diagonals will be the same as the total number of line segments that can be drawn connecting 10 points that do not lie on a straight line. As discussed in problem **7d**, this number is 45. Ten of these segments form the 10 sides of the decagon. The number of diagonals in a decagon is $45 - 10 = 35$.

10. a. 1   b. 3   c. 6   d. 10   e. 15   f. 21

    The solution of this problem can be related to the solution of the handshake problem in the following manner. Clearly the figure in part **a** contains just one rectangle, so consider the figure in part **b**. Each of the 3 vertical segments of the figure can be assigned a letter as follows.

    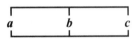

    Note that each pair of these vertical segments determines one rectangle. Therefore, all the rectangles in the figure may be listed as follows.

    > **a, b**   **a, c**
    > **b, c**

    The total number of rectangles is 3, the same as the number of handshakes exchanged among 3 people. The figures in parts **c** through **f** can be related similarly to the numbers of handshakes exchanged among 4, 5, 6, and 7 people.

11. The solution of this problem can be related to the solution of problem 10 in the following manner. Consider the figure in part **a**. Note that the first column of the figure is similar to the figure in part **b** of problem 10, so the first column alone contains 3 rectangles. But each rectangle in the first column also marks a *row* of 3 rectangles, as shown below.

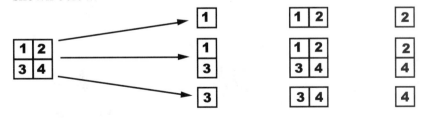

Since there are 3 rows of 3 rectangles, the entire figure contains $3 \times 3 = 9$ rectangles. Following the same reasoning, the figures in parts **b**, **c**, and **d** can be related, respectively, to the figures in parts **c**, **d**, and **e** of problem 10.

a. $3 \times 3 = 9$ b. $6 \times 6 = 36$ c. $10 \times 10 = 100$ d. $15 \times 15 = 225$

12. **1296.** Follow the reasoning employed in problem 11. The total number of rectangles on a 8 by 8 checkerboard is $36 \times 36 = 1296$.

7. Logic

7.1 Cryptarithms
Pages 115-118

1. a. $\begin{array}{r} 9 \\ +1 \\ \hline 10 \end{array}$

    b. $\begin{array}{r} 1673 \\ +9058 \\ \hline 10731 \end{array}$ or $\begin{array}{r} 1453 \\ +9078 \\ \hline 10531 \end{array}$

    c. $\begin{array}{r} 91 \\ +9 \\ \hline 100 \end{array}$

    d. $\begin{array}{r} 9567 \\ +1085 \\ \hline 10652 \end{array}$

    e. $\begin{array}{r} 37 \\ \times 9 \\ \hline 333 \end{array}$

    f. $\begin{array}{r} 125 \\ \times 5 \\ \hline 625 \end{array}$ or $\begin{array}{r} 175 \\ \times 5 \\ \hline 875 \end{array}$

    g. $\begin{array}{r} 2178 \\ \times 4 \\ \hline 8712 \end{array}$

    h. $\begin{array}{r} 142857 \\ \times 3 \\ \hline 428571 \end{array}$ or $\begin{array}{r} 285714 \\ \times 3 \\ \hline 857142 \end{array}$

    i. $\begin{array}{r} 57 \\ \times 13 \\ \hline 171 \\ 57 \\ \hline 741 \end{array}$

    j. $\begin{array}{r} 25 \\ \times 15 \\ \hline 125 \\ 25 \\ \hline 375 \end{array}$

    k. $\begin{array}{r} 513 \\ \times 15 \\ \hline 2565 \\ 513 \\ \hline 7695 \end{array}$

    l. $\begin{array}{r} 7029 \\ \times 519 \\ \hline 63261 \\ 7029 \\ 35145 \\ \hline 3,648,051 \end{array}$

    m. $\begin{array}{r} 21 \\ 45\overline{)954} \\ 90 \\ \hline 54 \\ 45 \\ \hline 9 \end{array}$

    n. $\begin{array}{r} 31 \\ 247\overline{)7657} \\ 741 \\ \hline 247 \\ 247 \end{array}$

    o. $\begin{array}{r} 135 \\ 235\overline{)31725} \\ 235 \\ \hline 822 \\ 705 \\ \hline 1175 \\ 1175 \end{array}$

    p. $(10)^2 = 100$

    q. $(11)^2 = 121$

    r. $\sqrt{10201} = 101$

2. a. $\begin{array}{r} 78 \\ \times 45 \\ \hline 390 \\ 312 \\ \hline 3510 \end{array}$

    b. $\begin{array}{r} 415 \\ \times 82 \\ \hline 830 \\ 3320 \\ 1245 \\ \hline 158530 \end{array}$

    c. $\begin{array}{r} 725 \\ \times 146 \\ \hline 4350 \\ 2900 \\ 725 \\ \hline 105850 \end{array}$

d.
```
      20301
45)913545
    90
    135
    135
      45
      45
```

e.
```
      997
35)34895
   315
   339
   315
   245
   245
```

f.
```
      90809
12)1089708
   108
    97
    96
    108
    108
```

(f.) With only three partial products, *D* and *E* are each 0. Since *AB* × 8 produces a two-digit product, *AB* is 10, 11, or 12. To produce a three-digit product, each of *C* and *F* must be 9 and *AB* cannot be 10 or 11. Therefore, *AB* is 12, *CD8EF* is 90809, and the three partial products from top to bottom are 108, 96, and 108. The numbers immediately above each of the three partial products are 108, 97, and 108, respectively.

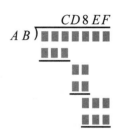

3. a.
```
     364
 ×    27
    2548
     728
    9828
```

b.
```
      286
 ×    826
     1716
      572
     2288
   236236
```

c.
```
      8662
 ×     834
     34648
     25986
     69296
    7224108
```

4.
```
   21514   and    54146
 −  4641        − 6764
   16873         47382
```

5. **2857.** If you choose *A*, *B*, *C*, and *D* to represent the digits of the unknown number, then the problem can be represented by the following cryptarithm.

$$
\begin{array}{r}
14ABCD \\
\times \quad\quad 2 \\
\hline
ABCD14
\end{array}
$$

Solving the cryptarithm, we obtain the following.

$$
\begin{array}{r}
142857 \\
\times \quad\quad 2 \\
\hline
285714
\end{array}
$$

Therefore, the four-digit number is 2857.

7.2 Certainty Problems
Pages 118-120

1. Follow the reasoning employed in the discussion on pages 118-119.
   a. 4   b. 22   c. 22

2. Follow the reasoning employed in the discussion on pages 118-119.
   a. 3   b. 12   c. 10   d. 12

3. **7 checkers.** It is not sufficient to select 4 checkers, since then there is a possibility that you have selected 3 of one color and 1 of the other color. It is also not sufficient to select 5 checkers, since there is a possibility that you have selected 3 of one color and 2 of the other color. Nor is it sufficient to select 6 checkers, since there is still a possibility that you have selected 3 of one color and 3 of the other. However, with the selection of 7 checkers, every possible combination that you could select contains at least 4 checkers of one color. Therefore, to be certain that you have 4 checkers of one color, you must select 7 checkers from the bag.

4. **16 buttons.** If you select 15 buttons, there is still a possibility that you have selected 3 buttons of each of the 5 colors. However, if you add just one more button to the number you select, then you are certain that you have selected at least 4 buttons of one color. Therefore, you need to select 16 buttons.

5. **14 cards.** A standard deck of 52 playing cards contains 4 cards of each of 13 face-values. If you select 13 cards, there is a possibility that each card has a different value. However, if you select one more card, you are then certain you have at least one pair of the same value. Therefore, you need to select 14 cards.

6. **13 people.** If 12 people are gathered together, there is a possibility that each has a birthday that falls in a different month of the year. However, if one more person is added to the group, then there must be at least 2 people of the group who have birthdays that fall in the same month. Therefore, 13 people must be gathered together.

7. **Yes.** There are 365 possible birthdays. If the school had an enrollment of 365 students, there is a possibility that each has a birthday that falls on a different day of the year. The addition of a 366th student would then guarantee that at least 2 students had birthdays that match. Since this school has 400 students, it is certain that at least two of these students have birthdays that fall on the same day of the year.

8. **731 students.** Suppose that the school had an enrollment of $2 \times 365 = 730$ students. Then there is a possibility that each of the 365 possible birthdays is shared by exactly 2 students. However, if one more student were added to this enrollment, then one birthday would have to be shared by 3 students. Therefore, a school must have an enrollment of at least 731 students to be certain that there are three students enrolled whose birthdays fall on the same day of the year.

9. a. **27 people.** There are 26 possible first-name initials. Then if 26 people are gathered together, there is a possibility that each has a different first-name initial. However, if one person were added to this group, then one first-name initial would have to be shared by 2 people. Therefore, 27 people must be gathered together.

   b. **53 people.** Suppose that 2 × 26 = 52 people are gathered together. Then there is a possibility that each of the 26 possible last-name initials is shared by exactly 2 people. However, if one more person were now added to this group, then one last-name initial must be shared by 3 people. Therefore, 53 people must be gathered together.

   c. **677 people.** There are 26 × 26 = 676 possible combinations of first-name and last-name initials. If 676 people were gathered together, there is a possibility that each has a different combination. However, if one more person were added to the group, then one combination must be shared by 2 people. Therefore, 677 people must be gathered together.

10. There are more than 7 million people in New York City. If we subtract the 1 million bald people, then more than 6 million people have hair on their heads. Consider just 1 million of these people. If the biologists are correct, there is a possibility that each of these 1 million people has a different number of hairs on her or his head. With the addition of just one person to this 1 million, two people must have the same number of hairs on their heads. Therefore, since there are more than 6 million people in New York City who have hair on their heads, at least two of these people must have the same number of hairs on their heads.

7.3 *Venn Diagram Problems*
Pages 120-123

1. a. **5 students.** Use a Venn diagram such as the one at the right. Circle *F* represents those students who study French, circle *S* represents those students who study Spanish, and *n* represents the number of students who study both French and Spanish. Label the diagram with the given information, then write and solve an equation.

   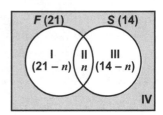

$$\text{I} + \text{II} + \text{III} = 30$$
$$(21 - n) + n + (14 - n) = 30$$
$$35 - n = 30$$
$$n = 5$$

   There are 5 students who study both French and Spanish.

   b. **2 students.** Use a Venn diagram such as the one at the right. Here circle *F* represents those students who passed the first math tests and circle *S* represents those students who passed the second math test. Region IV of the dia-

   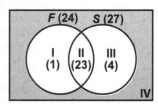

gram then represents those who failed both tests. Since 23 students passed both tests, the value of region II is 23. Since circle F represents 24 students, the value of region I is $24 - 23 = 1$. Since circle S represents 27 students, the value of region III is $27 - 23 = 4$. So $I + II + III = 1 + 23 + 4 = 28$, and the value of region IV is $30 - 28 = 2$. There are 2 students who failed both tests.

c. **7 students.** Use a Venn diagram such as the one at the right. Here circle C represents those students who study chemistry and circle P represents those students who study physics. Region III then represents those students who study physics, but not chemistry. Label the diagram with the given information, then write and solve an equation. (Note that, since circle C represents 14 students, the value of regions I and II together is 14.)

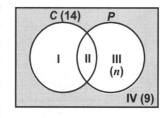

$$\begin{array}{rcl} I + II + III &=& 30 - 9 \\ (I + II) + III &=& 21 \\ (14) + n &=& 21 \\ n &=& 7 \end{array}$$

There are 7 students who study physics but not chemistry.

d. **9 girls.** Use a Venn diagram such as the one at the right. (This is only one of many diagrams that can be drawn to represent this situation.) Here circle M represents those students who play a musical instrument, and a vertical line separates both the rectangle and the circle into separate regions that represent boys and girls. Region IV then represents those girls who do not play a musical instrument. Let n represent the number of girls in this region. Label the diagram, then write and solve an equation.

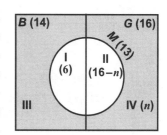

$$\begin{array}{rcl} I + II &=& 13 \\ 6 + (16 - n) &=& 13 \\ 22 - n &=& 13 \\ n &=& 9 \end{array}$$

There are 9 girls who do not play a musical instrument.

2. Use a Venn diagram such as the one at the right. Here circle E represents those students who study English, circle H represents those students who study history, and circle M represents those students who study math. Label the diagram with the given information.

(Continued)

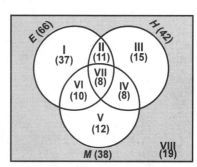

To find the values of regions II, IV, and VI, consider the following simple equations.

II + VII = 19	IV + VII = 16	VI + VII = 18
II + 8 = 19	IV + 8 = 16	VI + 8 = 18
II = 11	IV = 8	VI = 10

Similarly, to find the values of regions I, III, and V, consider these equations.

I + II + VII + VI = 66	III + IV + VII + II = 42	V + VI + VII + IV = 38
I + 11 + 8 + 10 = 66	III + 8 + 8 + 11 = 42	V + 10 + 8 + 8 = 38
I + 29 = 66	III + 27 = 42	V + 26 = 38
I = 37	III = 15	V = 12

Finally, to find the value of VIII, solve one more simple equation.

$$I + II + III + IV + V + VI + VII + VIII = 120$$
$$37 + 11 + 15 + 8 + 12 + 10 + 8 + VIII = 120$$
$$101 + VIII = 120$$
$$VIII = 19$$

a. **12 students.** This is the value of region V. There are 12 students who study math but neither English nor history.

b. **10 students.** This is the value of region VI. There are 10 students who study English and math but not history.

c. **19 students.** This is the value of region VIII. There are 19 students who study none of the three subjects.

3. **38 students.** Use a Venn diagram such as the one at the right. Here circles *A, B,* and *C* represent those students who had read books *A, B,* and *C,* respectively. Label the diagram with the given information, using the method employed in problem 2 to find the values of regions II, IV, VI, I, III, and V. Then the number of students in the class, *n*, is equal to the sum of the values of regions I through VII.

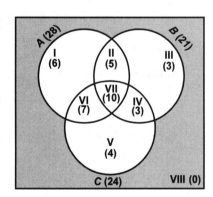

$$n = I + II + III + IV + V + VI + VII + VIII$$
$$n = 6 + 5 + 3 + 3 + 4 + 7 + 10 + 0$$
$$n = 38$$

There were 38 students in the class.

4. Use a Venn diagram such as the one at the right. Here circle SALAD represents those people who ordered salad, circle SOUP represents those people who ordered soup, and circle DESSERT represents those people who ordered dessert. Label the diagram with the given information, using the method discussed in problem 2 to find the values of regions II, IV, VI, I, III, and V.

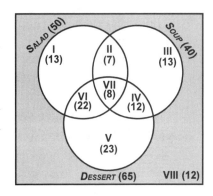

a. **22 people.** This is the value of region VI. There are 22 people who ordered salad and dessert but not soup.

b. **20 people.** The combined values of regions I and II, are 13 + 7 = 20. There are 20 people who ordered salad but not dessert.

c. **13 people.** This is the value of region III. There are 13 people who ordered only soup.

d. **110 people.** The total number of people, n, is equal to the sum of the values of all regions I through VIII.

$$n = \text{I} + \text{II} + \text{III} + \text{IV} + \text{V} + \text{VI} + \text{VII} + \text{VIII}$$
$$n = 13 + 7 + 13 + 12 + 23 + 22 + 8 + 12$$
$$n = 110$$

There were 110 people in all.

5. **7 people.** Use a Venn diagram such as the one at the right. Here circles F, E and S represent those people who visited France, England, and Spain, respectively. Label the diagram with the given information, using the reasoning employed in problem 2 to label the value of region VI as 2. To find the values of the remaining regions, I, II, and IV, study the diagram and consider the following.

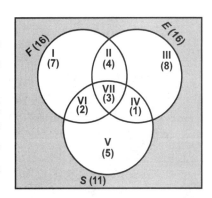

IV + V + VI + VII = 11	II + III + IV + VII = 16
IV + 5 + 2 + 3 = 11	II + 8 + 1 + 3 = 16
IV + 10 = 11	II + 12 = 16
IV = 1	II = 4

$$I + II + VI + VII \qquad = 16$$
$$I + 4 + 2 + 3 \qquad = 16$$
$$I \quad + \quad 9 \quad = 16$$
$$I \qquad\qquad = 7$$

The number of people who visited only France is the value of region I. So, 7 people visited only France.

6. **6 female mice.** Use a Venn diagram such as the one at the right. Here, the left half of the rectangle represents males (M), the right half of the rectangle represents females (F), circle L represents those mice who turned left, and circle T represents those mice who were previously trained. Region IV represents those female mice who were not previously trained and who did not turn left. Using the given information and the reasoning processes discussed in problems 2 through 5, we can label the diagram as shown. Then to find the value of region IV, write and solve a simple equation.

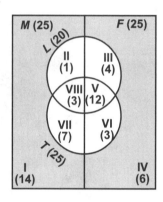

$$IV + III + V + VI \qquad = 25$$
$$IV + 4 + 12 + 3 \qquad = 25$$
$$IV \quad + \quad 19 \quad = 25$$
$$IV \qquad\qquad = 6$$

There are 6 female mice, not previously trained, who did not turn left.

7.4 Whodunits
Pages 124-129

1. Stage 1:   Stage 2:

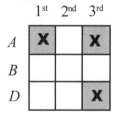
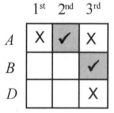

Answer: **Dave plays first base.**

2. Stage 1:
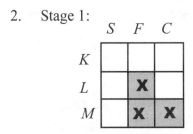

Stage 2:
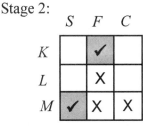

Stage 3:
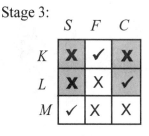

Answer: **Kate had fish, Linda had chicken, and Maya had steak.**

3. Stage 1:
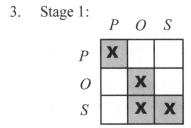

Stage 2:
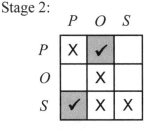

Stage 3:
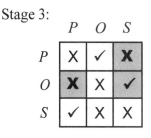

Answer: **Pierce's specialty is orthopedics, Otis's specialty is surgery, and Simmons's specialty is pediatrics.**

4. We assume that two of the first names are female and one is male. This is important in Stage 1, where the information that Clancy is Jacqueline's uncle indicates that Clancy is male and is therefore neither Jacqueline nor Helen. Also enter the information that Helen's name is not Barrow.

Stage 1:
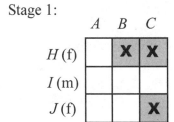

Stage 2:

Stage 3:
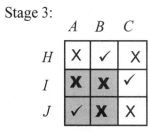

Answer: **The names are Helen Abrams, Irving Clancy, and Jacqueline Barrow.**

5. We assume that two of the first names are female and two are male. Therefore the information that a boy likes blue means that, in Stage 1, we can enter the information that neither Ina nor Jill likes blue. Since one of the girls likes red, we can also enter the information that neither Louis nor Miguel likes red. Furthermore, the statement that no person's name contains the same number of letters as her or his favorite color indicates that Ina does not like red, Jill does not like blue, Louis does not like green, and Miguel does not like orange.

Stage 1:

	R	B	G	O
I	X	X		
J		X		
L	X	X	X	
M	X			X

Stage 2:

	R	B	G	O
I	X	X		
J	✓	X		
L	X	X	X	✓
M	X	✓		X

Stage 3:

	R	B	G	O
I	X	X	✓	X
J	✓	X	X	X
L	X	X	X	✓
M	X	✓	X	X

Answer: **Ina's favorite color is green, Jill's favorite color is red, Louis's favorite color is orange, and Miguel's favorite color is blue.**

6. Note that the information that the rabbit and cat recently gave birth identifies the rabbit and cat as the females and the turtle and dog as the males. Therefore, the information that Mike is a mother allows us to deduce in Stage 1 that Mike is neither the turtle nor dog. The information that Star likes to have *his* back rubbed indicates that Star is male, and therefore is neither the rabbit nor cat. Other statements also allow us to deduce that the rabbit is neither Pete nor Mike, and that Pete is not the dog.

Stage 1:

	S	M	B	P
R (f)	X	X		X
T (m)		X		
D (m)		X		X
C (f)	X			

Stage 2:

	S	M	B	P
R	X	X	✓	X
T		X		
D		X		X
C	X	✓		

Stage 3:

	S	M	B	P
R	X	X	✓	X
T	X	X	X	✓
D	✓	X	X	X
C	X	✓	X	X

Answer: **Star is the dog, Mike is the cat, Butch is the rabbit, and Pete is the turtle.**

7. Note that the word "her" is used in referring to both Ivanov and Malinkov, so both are female. "His" is used in referring to the composer, and "he" is used in referring to the dancer, so both are male. Therefore, we can immediately deduce that neither Ivanov nor Malinkov is the composer or the dancer. Other statements allow us to further deduce that Lebedev is not the dancer and that Malinkov is not the singer.

Stage 1:

	A	C	D	S
I		X	X	
J				
L			X	
M		X	X	X

Stage 2:

	A	C	D	S
I		X	X	
J			✓	
L			X	
M	✓	X	X	X

Stage 3:

	A	C	D	S
I	X	X	X	✓
J	X	X	✓	X
L	X	✓	X	X
M	✓	X	X	X

Answer: **Ivanov is a female singer, Jacobowski is a male dancer, Lebedev is a male composer, and Malinkov is a female architect.**

8. We assume that two of the first names, Dolores and Felice, are female and two are male. Therefore, since Insull is a grandmother, Insull is neither Charles nor Edward. Dolores is an infant, so Dolores cannot be a grandmother; therefore, Dolores cannot be Insull. Also note that Dolores is not Hendricks.

Stage 1:

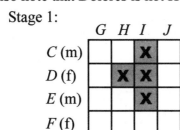

Stage 2:

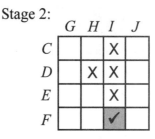

Felice Insull is Jackson's grandmother. But statements in the problem indicate that she is related to neither Charles nor Dolores. Therefore, Jackson's first name must be Edward.

Stage 3:

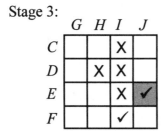

Stage 4:

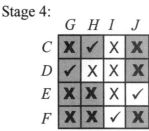

Answer: **The names are Charles Hendricks, Dolores Gold, Edward Jackson, and Felice Insull.**

9. In making a chart for the solution of this problem, note the following. Since Charlotte is younger than both Deborah and Knutsen, Charlotte must be 10 years old. We know that Charlotte is not Knutsen, so Knutsen must be either 11 or 12 years old. Since Lattimer is older than Knutsen, Lattimer must be 12 years old, while Knutsen is 11 years old. Also note that Deborah cannot be Knutsen. The complete chart is shown below.

	J	K	L	10	11	12
C	✓	X	X	✓	X	X
D	X	X	✓	X	X	✓
E	X	✓	X	X	✓	X
10	✓	X	X			
11	X	✓	X			
12	X	X	✓			

Answer: **Charlotte Jones is 10 years old, Deborah Lattimer is 12 years old, and Ethan Knutsen is 11 years old.**

10. In making a chart for the solution of this problem note the following. According to the first names, we assume that two of the students are male and one is female. The third statement indicates that Farelli is female, so Nancy's last name is Farelli. Nancy did not use the hammer or the saw, so she used the wrench. Oliver's last name is not Ellis, so it must be Gross. Then Peter's last name is Ellis. Oliver Gross did not use the hammer, so he must have used the saw while Peter Ellis used the hammer. The complete chart is shown below.

	S	H	W	E	F	G
N	X	X	✓	X	✓	X
O	✓	X	X	X	X	✓
P	X	✓	X	✓	X	X
E	X	✓	X
F	X	X	✓
G	✓	X	X

Answer: **Nancy Farelli used the wrench, Oliver Gross used the saw, and Peter Ellis used the hammer.**

11. **Smith.** Mr. Jones is not the porter's nearest neighbor because his earnings of $50,000 cannot be exactly three times as much as the porter's earnings. Since Mr. Robinson lives in Detroit, Mr. Smith must be the porter's nearest neighbor, and Mr. Jones lives in Chicago. This tells us that the porter's last name is Jones. Since Smith is not the conductor, it follows that Smith is the engineer.

12. **Alice went to China, Betty went to Algeria, and Carolyn went to Bali.** Examining the given statements, notice that, if *ii* and *iii* were *both* false, then both Alice and Carolyn would have gone to Bali. However, this contradicts the given information that each of the three women went to different places. Therefore, either *ii* or *iii* must be true. But notice that *iii* and *iv* cannot both be false, since then Alice would have gone to both Bali and China. Therefore, *iii* must be true, and the other statements are false. Since *ii* is false, Carolyn went to Bali. Since *iv* is false, Alice went to China. It then follows that Betty went to Algeria.

Appendices

Part F

1. Basic Information

2. Angle-Measures in Polygons

3. Pythagorean Theorem

4. Working With Exponents

5. Justifying Some Divisibility Rules

6. Sequences and Series

F

Appendix 1. Basic Information

1.1 Reading Some Common Notations

<u>Numbers</u>: Use "*and*" before a fraction or decimal point.
Read 305¼ as "three hundred five *and one-fourth*"
Read 1001.2 as "one thousand one *and two-tenths*"

Use an ellipsis (three dots: …) to mean "and so forth", with the understanding that an obvious pattern continues.
Read the sequence 2, 4, 6, … as "two, four, six, and so forth without ending."
Read the series $1 + 2 + 3 +$ … as "one plus two plus three, and so forth."
Read the series $1 + 2 + 3 + \cdots + 10$ as "one plus two plus three, and so forth, up to ten."

1.2 Digits

In our base 10 numeration system, a DIGIT can be any one of the ten numerals 0, 1, 2, 3, 4, 5, 6, 7, 8, 9. The number 358 is a three-digit number; its LEAD-DIGIT is 3. The lead-digit of a counting number should not be 0; for instance, 0358 is considered to be a three-digit number.

1.3 Expanded Form of a Number

A counting number may be written in expanded form as follows:

STANDARD FORM   EXPANDED FORM

$$358 \quad = \quad \begin{cases} 300 \ + \ 50 \ + \ 8, \text{ or} \\ 3{\times}100 + 5{\times}10 + 8{\times}1, \text{ or} \\ 3{\times}10^2 + 5{\times}10 + 8{\times}1 \end{cases}$$

1.4 Sets of Numbers

WHOLE NUMBERS = {0,1,2,3, … }

POSITIVE WHOLE or NATURAL or COUNTING NUMBERS = {1,2,3, … }

RATIONAL NUMBERS are numbers that can be written in the form $\frac{a}{b}$ where a and b are whole numbers and b does not equal zero.
Examples: $\frac{7}{15}$, $2\frac{3}{4}(= \frac{11}{4})$, $.9 (= \frac{9}{10}$ or $\frac{90}{100})$ and so forth.

Note that all whole numbers are rational. For example, 3 is a rational number because $3 = \frac{3}{1}$ or $\frac{6}{2}$ and so forth; 0 is rational because $0 = \frac{0}{1}$ or $\frac{0}{2}$ and so forth.

1.5 Fractions

A **COMMON** or **SIMPLE FRACTION** is a fraction in the form $\frac{a}{b}$ where a and b are natural numbers. Note that all common fractions are rational numbers.

A **UNIT FRACTION** is a common fraction with numerator 1. *Examples*: $\frac{1}{4}$, $\frac{1}{17}$.

A **PROPER FRACTION** is a common fraction in which a is less than b. *Examples*: $\frac{2}{5}$ and $\frac{1}{3}$.

An **IMPROPER FRACTION** is a common fraction in which a is greater than or equal to b.

Examples: $\frac{5}{2}, \frac{3}{3}, \frac{7}{1}$.

A **COMPLEX FRACTION** is a fraction whose numerator or denominator (or both) contains a fraction.

Examples: $\dfrac{\frac{2}{3}}{5}$, $\dfrac{5}{\frac{3}{4}}$, $\dfrac{\frac{3}{8}}{\frac{4}{5}}$, $\dfrac{3+\frac{1}{2}}{2+\frac{1}{3}}$

The fraction $\frac{a}{b}$ is **REDUCED TO LOWEST TERMS** if a and b have no common factor other than 1.

1.6 Order of Operations

When computing the value of an expression involving an exponential form or two or more operations, the following priorities must be observed in the order listed:

1. Do computations in parentheses, braces, and brackets first, from innermost to outermost.
2. Evaluate exponential forms, THEN
3. do multiplications and divisions in order from left to right, THEN
4. do additions and subtractions in order from left to right.

Examples:

1.
$$
\begin{aligned}
&5 + 2^3 \times 7 - 32 \\
=\ &5 + \mathbf{8} \times 7 - 32 \\
=\ &5 + \mathbf{56} - 32 \\
=\ &\mathbf{61} \qquad - 32 \\
=\ &\qquad 29
\end{aligned}
$$

2.
$$
\begin{aligned}
&3 + 4 \times \tfrac{(8-6)}{2} \\
=\ &3 + 4 \times \tfrac{2}{2} \\
=\ &3 + \quad \mathbf{4} \\
=\ &\quad 7
\end{aligned}
$$

3.
$$
\begin{aligned}
&3 + 4 \times 8 - \tfrac{6}{2} \\
=\ &3 + \quad \mathbf{32} - \mathbf{3} \\
=\ &\qquad 32
\end{aligned}
$$

4.
$$
\begin{aligned}
&3 + (4 \times 8 - 6) \div 2 \\
=\ &3 + (\ \mathbf{32} - 6) \div 2 \\
=\ &3 + \qquad \mathbf{26} \div 2 \\
=\ &3 + \qquad\qquad \mathbf{13} \\
=\ &\quad 16
\end{aligned}
$$

5.
$$
\begin{aligned}
&9 - 5 - 3 \\
=\ &\quad \mathbf{4} - 3 \\
=\ &\qquad 1
\end{aligned}
$$

6.
$$
\begin{aligned}
&9 - (5 - 3) \\
=\ &9 - \quad \mathbf{2} \\
=\ &\quad 7
\end{aligned}
$$

F

1.7 Average

The AVERAGE or MEAN or ARITHMETIC MEAN of N numbers is obtained by dividing the sum of these N numbers by N.

Example: The average of 2, 5, 8, and 9 is $(2+5+8+9) \div 4 = 24 \div 4 = 6$.

1.8 Some Basic Definitions

Let a and b be natural numbers. We say that **a DIVIDES b**, or, more simply, that **b IS DIVISIBLE BY a** if the remainder is zero when the division $b \div a$ is performed. Equivalently, we say that a is a FACTOR of b and that b is a MULTIPLE of a.

Examples: 3 divides 15; 3 is a factor of 15; 15 is a multiple of 3.
7 does not divide 15; 7 is not a factor of 15; 15 is not a multiple of 7.

A PRIME NUMBER (or PRIME) is a natural number greater than 1 that is divisible only by itself and by 1. Every prime number has exactly two different factors.

Examples: The first eight prime numbers are 2, 3, 5, 7, 11, 13, 17, and 19. Some larger primes are 43, 101, 20147, and 20149. Notice that 2 is the only even prime number, and that 2 and 3 are the only two consecutive whole numbers that are both prime.

A COMPOSITE NUMBER (or COMPOSITE) is a natural number that is the product of 2 or more primes, not necessarily different. Every composite number has three or more factors.

Examples: $18 = 2 \times 3 \times 3$, $35 = 7 \times 5$, $91 = 7 \times 13$, and $25 = 5 \times 5$.

The first eight composite numbers are: 4, 6, 8, 9, 10, 12, 14, and 15. All natural numbers not prime and not 1 are composite.

The number 1 is called a UNIT. It is neither prime nor composite, and is a factor of all natural numbers.

A natural number is said to be FACTORED COMPLETELY when it is expressed as a product of primes.

Example: Since $72 = 2 \times 2 \times 2 \times 3 \times 3$, then $2 \times 2 \times 2 \times 3 \times 3$ represents the complete factorization of 72.

This factorization can be written as $2^3 \times 3^2$ which is called the **PRIME POWER FACTORIZATION** of 72.

The **GREATEST COMMON FACTOR (GCF)** of two natural numbers a and b is the largest natural number that divides both a and b exactly.

Examples: $GCF(12,18) = 6$
$GCF(28,35,91) = 7$

Two natural numbers are RELATIVELY PRIME (or CO-PRIME) and three or more natural numbers are RELATIVELY PRIME (or CO-PRIME) PAIRWISE if the GCF of every pair that can be formed equals 1. Three numbers are RELATIVELY PRIME MUTUALLY if the GCF of the complete set is 1. Any two consecutive numbers such as 95 and 96 are relatively prime.

Examples: 8 and 15 are relatively prime because GCF(8,15) = 1.

16, 27, and 35 are relatively prime pairwise because GCF(16,27,35) = 1.

12, 13, and 14 are relatively prime mutually but not in pairs because GCF(12,14) = 2.

The LEAST COMMON MULTIPLE (LCM) of two natural numbers a and b is the smallest natural number that is divisible by both a and b.

Examples: LCM (9, 12) = 36; LCM (13, 52) = 52.

1.9 Some Common Geometric Terms

Angles: degree-measure, acute, right, obtuse, straight, reflex

Triangles: acute, right, obtuse, scalene, isosceles, equilateral

Quadrilaterals: parallelogram, rectangle, square (a special rectangle), rhombus, trapezoid

Polygons: triangle, quadrilateral, pentagon, hexagon, octagon, decagon, dodecagon

Regular Polygon: A polygon is regular if all sides are congruent and all angles are congruent. *Examples:* square, equilateral triangle.

Area: The number of square units contained in a simple closed region.

Perimeter: The length of the boundary of a simple closed plane figure.

Circumference: The perimeter of a circle.

Congruent Figures: Plane figures that have exactly the same size and shape. If two polygons are congruent, their corresponding sides and angles will have the same measures.

1.10 Some Common Geometric Formulas

PLANE FIGURE	PERIMETER (p); AREA(A)	
(1) Triangle	$p = a + b + c$ $A = \frac{1}{2}b \times h$ or $\frac{1}{2}bh$	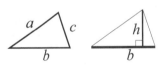
(2) Rectangle	$p = 2l + 2w$ $A = l \times w$ or lw	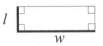
(3) Parallelogram	$p = 2a + 2b$ $A = b \times h$ or bh	
(4) Square	$p = 4 \times s$ or $4s$ $A = s \times s$ or s^2	
(5) Circle	$c = 2\pi r$ $A = \pi \times r \times r$ or πr^2	

SOLID FIGURE	VOLUME (V)	
(1) Rectangular Solid	$V = l \times w \times h$ or lwh	
(2) Cube	$V = s \times s \times s$ or s^3	
(3) Cylinder	$V = \pi \times r^2 \times h$ or $\pi r^2 h$	
(4) Cone	$V = \frac{1}{3} \times \pi \times r^2 \times h$ or $\frac{1}{3} \pi r^2 h$	

1.11 Notes Regarding Answers

After reading a problem, it is helpful to determine exactly what is called for, and to immediately note this at the bottom of the worksheet. For example, suppose a problem requires that the values of A and B be determined. Place "A = ___ and B = ___" in the space where the answer will be given.

Another worthwhile practice is to write the answer in a simple declarative sentence.
Example: "The average speed is 54 miles per hour". This practice usually requires the problem solver to reread the question carefully. Caution: this may not be appropriate in a contest where saving time may be necessary.

Units of measure may or may not be required in an answer. Read the question carefully. Any unit of measure that is included in an answer must be correctly stated. Otherwise the answer is considered to be wrong.

Appendix 2. Angle-Measures in Polygons

2.1 Triangles: Sum of the Angle-Measures

A triangle is shown at the right with a, b, and c representing its angle-measures in degrees. To approximate the sum, you could use a protractor to measure each angle and then estimate the sum.

Assume that a protractor is not available. We can approximate the sum by "cutting off" the angles of the triangle and then by setting angles a and c adjacent to angle b with a common vertex **V**, as shown.

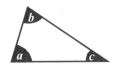

When this is done, we would find that the two exterior sides of the angle *seem to form* what appears to be a straight angle. We then *suspect* that the sum of the angle-measures of any triangle is approximately 180°. Indeed, in the study of Geometry, one learns a proof for the theorem:

> **The sum of the angle-measures of any triangle is 180°.**

Although we will not prove this theorem formally, we will use it to derive additional results in what follows.

2.2 Quadrilaterals: Sum of the Angle-Measures

At the right, quadrilateral *ABCD* is subdivided by diagonal *BD* into two triangles. By so doing, we will be able to use the triangle angle-measure theorem. Observe that the sum of the 6 angle-measures of the two triangles of the quadrilateral is equal to the sum of the 4 angle-measures of the quadrilateral. Therefore:

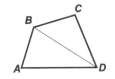

> **The sum of the angle-measures of any quadrilateral is $2 \times 180° = 360°$.**

★ Problems ★

1. Can a quadrilateral have four obtuse angles? Explain.

2. If two angles of a quadrilateral are supplementary angles and the other two angles are congruent, what is the measure of each of the congruent angles?

3. If two angles of a quadrilateral are complementary angles and the third angle has a measure of 115°, what is the measure of the fourth angle?

4. The quadrilateral shown at the right is called a REFLEX QUADRILAT-ERAL because it has an interior angle with a measure greater than 180°. Is the sum of the four angle-measures less than, more than, or equal to 360°? Explain or prove that your answer is correct.

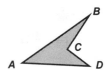

(Solutions are on page 234.)

2.3 Pentagon: Sum of the Angle-Measures

Choose any vertex of pentagon *ABCDE*, say *C*, and draw diagonals from *C* to the non-consecutive vertices, as shown in the diagram. This partitions the pentagon into 3 non-overlapping triangles. The sum of the 9 angle-measures of the 3 triangles is equal to the sum of the 5 angle-measures of the pentagon. Therefore:

> **The sum of the angle-measures of a pentagon is 3 × 180° or 540°.**

Another way to prove the above theorem is to partition pentagon *ABCDE* into a quadrilateral and a triangle. Thus, the sum of the 5 angle measures of the pentagon is equal to the sum of the 4 angle-measures of the quadrilateral and the 3 angle-measures of the triangle, or 360° + 180° = 540°.

2.4 Polygons: Sum of the Angle-Measures

In the table that follows, the columns are titled **Polygon** (the name of the polygon), **Sides** (the number of sides the polygon has), **Triangles** (the smallest number of non-overlapping triangles into which the polygon can be partitioned), **Angle Sum** (the sum of the polygon's angle-measures in degrees).

Polygon	Sides	Triangles	Angle Sum
Triangle	3	1	1 × 180°
Quadrilateral	4	2	2 × 180°
Pentagon	5	3	3 × 180°
Hexagon	6	4	4 × 180°
⋮	⋮	⋮	⋮
n-gon	*n*	*n*−2	(*n*−2) × 180°

Notice in each row that the number of sides is 2 more than the number of triangles into which the polygon can be partitioned. The sum of the angle-measures of any polygon is the product of its number of triangles and 180°. In general:

> **The sum of the measure of the angles of an *n*-sided polygon is (*n*−2) × 180°.**

★ *Problems* ★

1. An octagon is an eight-sided figure. What is the sum of its angle-measures?

2. A REGULAR POLYGON is a polygon all of whose sides are congruent and all of whose angles are congruent. Find the measure of each angle of the following regular polygons:

    (a) nonagon (nine-sided figure)   (b) decagon (ten-sided figure)

    (c) duodecagon (twelve-sided figure)   (d) centigon (100-sided figure)

    (e) milligon (1000-sided figure)

3. Examine the results in problem 2. What happens to the measure of each angle in a regular polygon as its number of sides gets larger?

(Solutions are on pages 234-235.)

2.5 *Exterior Angles of a Pentagon*

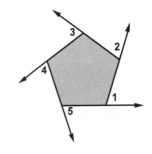

    An EXTERIOR ANGLE of a pentagon is formed by extending one side of the pentagon through a vertex as shown at the right. Each of the pentagon's sides is extended in the same manner to form exterior angles 1, 2, 3, 4, and 5. Notice that the pentagon now has five exterior angles as well as the five original interior angles. We know that the sum of the degree-measures of the interior angles is $3 \times 180°$. Before reading ahead, try to think of a way to find the sum of the angle-measures of the exterior angles. (Note: we could have extended each of the pentagon's sides in the "opposite" direction as well to form 5 other exterior angles.)

    Observe that each exterior angle 1, 2, 3, 4, and 5 is adjacent to an interior angle and that the exterior sides of each pair form a straight angle. Since each exterior angle is the supplement of its adjacent interior angle so the sum of their degree-measures is 180°. The sum of the degree-measures of the five exterior angles and their adjacent interior supplementary angles is $5 \times 180°$. But the sum of the degree-measures of the interior angles is $3 \times 180°$. Therefore the sum of the measures of the five exterior angles is $(5 \times 180°) - (3 \times 180°)$, or $2 \times 180°$, which equals 360°.

> **The sum of the measure of the exterior angles of a pentagon is 360°.**

★ **Problems** ★

1. What is the sum of the degree-measures of the exterior angles of a hexagon?

2. What is the sum of the degree-measures of the exterior angles of an octagon?

3. A regular icosagon is a twenty-sided figure. What is the degree measure of each exterior angle of the regular icosagon?

4. What is the sum of the degree-measures of the exterior angles of a *n*-gon? (see note 2 on page 237.)

5. The measure of an interior angle of a regular polygon is 8 times the measure of an exterior angle. How many sides does the polygon have?

(*Solutions are on page 235.*)

2.6 *Diagonals of a Polygon*

A DIAGONAL of a polygon is a line segment that joins two non-consecutive vertices of the polygon. (The endpoints of the sides of a polygon are the vertices of the polygon.) We wish to determine the number of diagonals that a polygon contains. We begin by observing that a triangle has no diagonals because, for any selected vertex, the other two vertices are consecutive to the selected vertex.

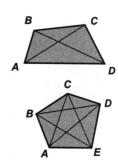

A quadrilateral has two diagonals that connect each pair of opposite vertices.

Notice, that in a pentagon, two diagonals can be drawn from each vertex. The diagram at the right shows the two diagonals that can be drawn from each vertex.

from:	A	B	C	D	E
	∧	∧	∧	∧	∧
to:	C D	D E	E A	A B	B C

Observe that in the schematic above each diagonal has been listed twice. For example, the diagonal from *A* to *D* is listed again as the diagonal from *D* to *A*. Thus, to obtain the number of different diagonals, we must divide the total number of diagonals listed in the schematic by 2. For the pentagon we have: $10 \div 2 = 5$. This result agrees with the diagram shown above.

Consider hexagon *ABCDEF*. Suppose we wish to draw diagonals from vertex *C* to each of the non-consecutive vertices. Relative to *C*, there are 3 such vertices: *A*, *F*, and *E*. Therefore, we can draw three diagonals from each of the 6 vertices of the hexagon. This give us a total of $6 \times 3 = 18$ diagonals. But remember than in the schematic shown above, each diagonal appeared twice. Therefore, the total number of distinct diagonals of a hexagon is $18 \div 2 = 9$. The table below permits us to examine the accumulated data for possible generalization.

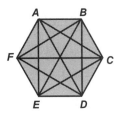

Name of Polygon	Number of Vertices	Number of diagonals from each vertex	Total number of diagonals
Triangle	3	0	$0 = 0$
Quadrilateral	4	1	$4 \times 1 \div 2 = 2$
Pentagon	5	2	$5 \times 2 \div 2 = 5$
Hexagon	6	3	$6 \times 3 \div 2 = 9$
⋮	⋮	⋮	⋮
n-gon	n	$n - 3$	$n \times (n - 3) \div 2$

Notice in each row that the number of vertices of the polygon is 3 more than the number of diagonals from each vertex. Therefore, the total number of diagonals of any polygon is the product of its numbers of vertices and the number of diagonals from each vertex divided by 2. In general, it can be proven that:

> **The total number of diagonals of an *n*-sided polygon is**
> $n \times (n - 3) \div 2.$

★ *Problems* ★

1.   How many different diagonals does an icosagon (twenty-sided polygon) have?

2.   How many different diagonals does a hundred-sided polygon have?

3.   A duodecagon has twice as many sides as a hexagon. Does it have twice as many diagonals as a hexagon? Explain.

4.   Twenty distinct points are placed on a circle. How many different line segments can be drawn if each point is connected to each of the other 19 points? Describe the polygon and the number of diagonals that appear when all of the line segments are drawn.

(Solutions are on page 236.)

2.7 Star-Figures (For the Adventurous)

To begin our study of star-figures we start with a five-pointed star-figure — the most basic star-figure. For convenience, we start with star-figures constructed in circles. First choose any 5 points on a given circle. Connect them according to the following scheme:

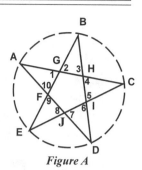

Figure A

Pick a starting point, call it *A*. Label the other points *B*, *C*, *D*, and *E* in clockwise order.

Join *A* to *C* skipping *B*. Join *B* to point *D* skipping *C*. Join *C* to *E* skipping *D*. Join *D* to *A* skipping *E*. Join *E* to *B* skipping *A*. When this process ends in the last point *E* of the clockwise set of points being joined to the second point *B*, the figure closes. If we then erase the circle, the remaining figure is a 5-pointed star-figure as shown in the above diagram.

Observe that the above star-figure has 5 star-triangles, each having a common side with pentagon *FGHIJ*. The angles with vertices at the star points *A*, *B*, *C*, *D*, and *E* are the star-angles of the figure.

Try drawing your own star-figure without using a circle and note that *the results will still be true.*

Suppose eight points are used to make a star-figure. By using the same process as above to connect points, we form the 8-pointed star-figure that is shown at the right. It can also be thought of as two overlapping polygons, each of 4 sides. Observe that the star-figure consists of 8 star-triangles, each having a common side with an octagon.

Suppose seven points are used to make a star-figure. By using the same process as above to connect points, we form the 7-pointed star-figure that is shown at the right. It *cannot* be viewed as two overlapping polygons. Observe that the star-figure consists of 7 star-triangles, each having a common side with a septagon.

Notice that if a star-figure is formed from an even number of points, it will actually consist of two overlapping polygons, but if it is formed from an odd number of points, it will not.

2.8 Star Figures: Sum of the Star Angle-Measures

For simplicity, we will denote "angle 1" by its symbol "∠1". The sum of the angle-measures of the star-triangles in *figure A* on page 232 is $5 \times 180°$. Observe that pentagon *FGHIJ* has 2 sets of exterior angles; one consisting of ∠1, ∠3, ∠5, ∠7, ∠9, and the other consisting of ∠2, ∠4, ∠6, ∠8, ∠10. The sum of the angle-measures of each set of exterior angles is 360°. But both sets of exterior angles are also interior angles of the star-triangles. Therefore the sum of the star-angles equals the difference of the sum of the angle measures of the star-triangles and the sum of the two sets of exterior angles of pentagon *FGHIJ*: $5 \times 180° - 2 \times 360° = 900° - 720° = 180°$.

☆ Problems ☆

1. Find the sum of the angle-measures of the star-angles of a six-point star figure.

2. Complete the following table for star-figures having the following number of star-angles: 5, 6, 8, 9, 10, 12.

    Let N = the number of star-angles in the star-figure.

    S = the angle-degree sum of the star triangles written in the form $N \times 180°$.

    E = the degree-sum of both sets of exterior angles of the related polygon in the interior of the diagram.

    $S - E$ = the degree-sum of the star-angles

N	S	E	S – E
6			
8			
9			
10			
12			

3. Suppose all star-angles of the star-figure are congruent. Compute the degree-measure for each star-angle of a figure of N star-points in the following table:

N	5	6	8	9	10	12
$\dfrac{S-E}{N}$						

4. Suppose a star-figure has N congruent star-angles.
    a. What is the degree-measure of a star-angle in terms of N?
    b. What happens to the degree-measure of a star-angle as N gets larger?

(Solutions are on pages 236-237.)

APPENDIX 2 SOLUTIONS

2.2 Quadrilaterals: Sum of the Angle-Measures
Pages 227-228

1. **No.** The measure of an obtuse angle is greater than 90°. Therefore, the sum of the measures of four obtuse angles is greater than $4 \times 90° = 360°$. This is not possible in any quadrilateral because the sum of its angle measures is always exactly 360°.

2. **90°.** Since the sum of the measures of the supplementary angles is 180°, the sum of the remaining two congruent angles is 180°. Therefore each of the congruent angles has a measure of 90°.

3. **155°.** The sum of the measures of the complementary angles is 90°. To this, add 115°, the measure of the third angle: $90° + 115° = 205°$. Thus the measure of the fourth angle is $360° - 205° = 155°$.

4. **Equal to 360°.** Draw diagonal AC. Since the quadrilateral is now subdivided into two distinct non-overlapping triangles, the sum of its angle-measures is $2 \times 180° = 360°$.

2.4 Polygons: Sum of the Angle-Measures
Pages 228-229

1. **1080°.** An octagon can be subdivided into 6 non-overlapping triangles. Therefore, the sum of its angle-measures is $6 \times 180° = 1080°$.

2. (a) **140°.** Nonagon: sum of angle-measures is $7 \times 180° = 1260°$.
   Each angle has a measure of $1260° \div 9 = 140°$;

   (b) **144°.** Decagon: sum of angle-measures is $8 \times 180° = 1440°$.
   Each angle has a measure of $1440° \div 10 = 144°$.

   (c) **150°.** Duodecagon: sum of angle-measures is $10 \times 180° = 1800°$.
   Each angle has a measure of $1800° \div 12 = 150°$.

   (d) **176.4°.** Centigon: sum of angle-measures is $98 \times 180° = 17640°$.
   Each angle has a measure of $17640° \div 100 = 176.4°$

   (e) **179.64°.** Milligon: sum of angle-measures is $998 \times 180° = 179640°$
   Each angle has a measure of $179640° \div 1000 = 179.64°$.

3. **The measure of the interior angle of a regular polygon increases as the number of sides increases.** Observe that the increases become smaller between successive angle measures. The measures of the angle are less than but seem to get closer and closer to 180°. This is confirmed by looking at the formula for the measure of an angle in a regular n-sided polygon: $[(n-2) \times 180°] \div n$. Notice that $(n-2) \div n$ is always less than 1 but gets closer to 1 as n gets larger and larger. We therefore say that the measure of the interior angle of a regular polygon gets closer to 180° as n gets larger and larger but is always less than 180°.

2.5 *Exterior Angles of a Pentagon*
Pages 229-230

1-2. Let I represent the sum of the interior angle-measures and E the sum of the exterior angle-measures.

1. **360°.** For a hexagon:
    - (1) $E + I = 6 \times 180°$
    - (2) $\phantom{E + {}} I = 4 \times 180°$

    Subtract (2) from (1): (3) $E \phantom{{}+I} = 2 \times 180°$ or 360°

2. **360°.** For an octagon:
    - (1) $E + I = 8 \times 180°$
    - (2) $\phantom{E + {}} I = 6 \times 180°$

    Subtract (2) from (1): (3) $E \phantom{{}+I} = 2 \times 180°$ or 360°

3. **18°.** Each interior angle of a regular icosagon has a measure of $(18 \times 180°) \div 20$ or 162°. Since each exterior angle is the supplement of the interior angle of 162°, each exterior angle is $180° - 162°$ or 18°. (See note 2 on page 237.)

4. **360°.** The sum of an n-sided polygon's interior angle-measures is $(n-2) \times 180°$ or $n \times 180° - 2 \times 180°$. Since the sum of the interior and exterior angle measures is $n \times 180°$, the sum of the exterior angle measures must be $2 \times 180°$ or 360° for any value of n greater than 2.

5. **18 sides.** Let x and $8x$ be the measures of an exterior and an interior angles respectively. Then
    - (1) $x + 8x = 180°$, or
    - (2) $\phantom{x + {}} 9x = 180°$

    Divide both sides of (2) by 9: (3) $x = 20°$
    Let N-gon have n sides: (4) $n \times 20° = 360°$ (Exterior Angle Theorem)
    Divide both sides of (4) by 20°: (5) $n \phantom{{}\times 20°} = 18$

    The polygon has 18 sides.

2.6 Diagonals of a Polygon
Pages 230-231

1. **170.** An icosagon has $\frac{20 \times 17}{2} = 170$ diagonals.

2. **4850.** A hundred-sided polygon has $\frac{100 \times 97}{2} = 4850$ diagonals.

3. **No.** A hexagon has $6 \times (6–3) \div 2 = 9$ diagonals. A duodecagon has $12 \times (12–3) \div 2 = 54$ diagonals. Although a duodecagon has 12 sides, twice as many as the 6 sides of a hexagon, the number of their diagonals are in a ratio of 54:9 or 6:1.

   See note 2 on page 237 for more information on this topic.

4. **190 line segments.** Each of the 20 points can be connected to the remaining 19 points. But remember that the line originating at D and ending at K will be counted again as the line originating at K and ending at D. Thus we must divide the product of 20 and 19 by 2: $\frac{20 \times 19}{2} = 190$ line segments.

   Note: the figure is an icosagon of 20 sides and has a total of $190 – 20 = 170$ diagonals.

2.8 Star Figures: Sum of the Star Angle-Measures
Pages 232-233

1. **180°.** The sum of the angle-measures of the 6 star-triangles is $6 \times 180°$. The sum of the 2 sets of exterior angles is 720° or $4 \times 180°$. Then the sum of the measures of the 6 star-angles is $6 \times 180° – 4 \times 180° = 2 \times 180°$ or 360°. (See the example given in section 8.)

2.

N	S	E	S – E	
5	5 × 180°	4 × 180°	(5–4) × 180° =	**180°**
6	6 × 180°	4 × 180°	(6–4) × 180° =	**360°**
8	8 × 180°	4 × 180°	(8–4) × 180° =	**720°**
9	9 × 180°	4 × 180°	(9–4) × 180° =	**900°**
10	10 × 180°	4 × 180°	(10–4) × 180° =	**1080°**
12	12 × 180°	4 × 180°	(12–4) × 180° =	**1440°**

3.

N	5	6	8	9	10	12
$\frac{S-E}{N}$	36°	60°	90°	100°	108°	120°

4. a. $\dfrac{\left(N\times 180°-4\times 180°\right)}{N}=\dfrac{\left(N-4\right)}{N}\times 180°$

   b. As N gets larger, $\dfrac{N-4}{N}=1-\dfrac{4}{N}$ gets closer to 1, and the degree-measure of each star-angle gets closer to 180°.

Notes

1. A simple method for finding the measure of an interior angle of a regular polygon is to first use the theorem that states that the sum of the exterior angles of an n-gon is 360° to find the measure of each exterior angle. Each interior angle is the supplement of the exterior angle.

    Example: Find the measure of an interior angle of a dodecagon (12-sided polygon). The measure of an exterior angle is $\dfrac{360°}{12}=30°$. The interior angle is the supplement of the exterior angle. Therefore, the measure of the interior angle is $180°-30°=150°$.

2. Is it possible for one polygon to have twice as many diagonals as another polygon? The following proof demonstrates that the answer is "No".

    Suppose the natural numbers n and $2n$ represent the number of sides of the two polygons. Since a polygon must have more than three sides in order to have diagonals, $n>3$. The question may be restated as, "Does any value of n exist for which a $2n$-sided polygon has twice as many diagonals as an n-sided polygon?"

    Proof: Assume that there is a number n for which the $2n$-gon has twice as many diagonals as the n-gon. A n-gon has $\dfrac{n\times(n-3)}{2}$ diagonals; a 2n-gon has $\dfrac{2n\times(2n-3)}{2}$ diagonals. Then:

    (1) $\dfrac{2n\times\left(2n-3\right)}{2}=2\times\dfrac{n\times\left(n-3\right)}{2}$ [Divide both sides of (1) by $\frac{2n}{2}$]

    (2) $2n-3\quad=\quad n-3$ [Subtract $n-3$ from both sides]

    (3) $\quad n\quad\ =\quad 0$

    This proof shows that the only possible solution leads to $n=0$. But $n>3$, so n cannot be 0. Therefore the above assumption is false — that is, *no* value of n exists for which a $2n$-sided polygon has twice as many diagonals as an n-sided polygon.

    The above is an example of an **INDIRECT PROOF**, in which every alternative conclusion is assumed true and then shown to be impossible.

F

Appendix 3.   Pythagorean Theorem

3.1 Pythagoras

Pythagoras of Samos, a Greek of the 6th century B.C., was responsible for the first golden age of mathematics. He was also associated with the origins of Greek philosophy and Greek science including the science of music. He studied the properties of particular numbers, relationships among them, and the mathematical techniques of the Egyptians and the Babylonians. Perhaps the most famous result in all of mathematics carries his name. THE PYTHAGOREAN THEOREM states that in any right triangle, the square of the hypotenuse (the longest side) is equal to the sum of the squares of the remaining two sides (or legs). In the familiar symbolic form:

$$a^2 + b^2 = c^2$$

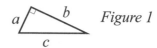 *Figure 1*

where a and b represent the lengths of the legs and c represents the length of the hypotenuse. This relationship among the sides of a right triangle was actually known before the time of Pythagoras.

It is more convenient to hereafter use "side x" instead of "side with length x".

3.2 A Proof of the Pythagorean Theorem

The word THEOREM in mathematics refers very specifically to a statement that is proven. To *prove* the Pythagorean Theorem, it is necessary to show that the relationship is true for *every* right triangle, regardless of shape or size. It is not enough to demonstrate a few special cases, or even thousands or millions of cases. We must show the relationship to be valid for *all* possible cases.

The Pythagorean Theorem has inspired hundreds of different proofs. Here is one of the most famous ones. The proof is accomplished by clever dissection and reassembly. We begin with a square in *Figure 2* that has been assembled from four congruent right triangles (shaded and numbered) and two smaller squares (unshaded) as shown in the diagram. Notice that the side of the large square has length equal to $a + b$.

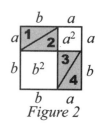
Figure 2

In *Figure 3*, we reassemble the pieces by moving the position of the four congruent right triangles. Notice that the size of the large square remains the same. However, the area of the square covered originally by the two smaller

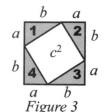
Figure 3

squares (whose areas were a^2 and b^2) must now be replaced by the newly formed area, c^2. Thus, $c^2 = a^2 + b^2$, where c represents the hypotenuse of our original right triangle.

It is important to realize that a, b, and c can represent the sides of *any* right triangle. Thus we have demonstrated that the result is true regardless of the original right triangle. This is, indeed, a genuine proof.

3.3 Pythagorean Triples

Any set of three natural numbers a, b, and c, which satisfy the condition $a^2 + b^2 = c^2$, is called a PYTHAGOREAN TRIPLE or **PT** and is usually written **(a,b,c)**.

For instance, seven examples of Pythagorean Triples are:
$$(3,4,5), \qquad (5,12,13), \qquad (11,60,61), \qquad (8,15,17),$$
$$(20,21,29), \qquad (6,8,10), \quad \text{and} \quad (30,40,50).$$

There are actually an infinite number of PTs. This is easy to demonstrate. For example, (3,4,5) "doubled" produces (6,8,10), and tripled produces (9,12,15), both of which are PTs. So any PT can generate an infinite set of associated PTs by simply multiplying each of the 3 elements of the PT by the same natural number. It can be shown that any number which is a factor of two members of a PT also must be a factor of the third member. Those PTs in which all three integers a, b, and c share no factors other than 1, are called *PRIMITIVE* PYTHAGOREAN TRIPLES (**PPTs**). In general, numbers such as these whose only common factor is 1 usually are called RELATIVELY PRIME.

Notice that (11,60,61) is a PPT because 11, 60, and 61 are relatively prime. However, (6,8,10) is *not* a PPT because 6, 8, and 10 are *not* relatively prime since these three numbers share a common factor of 2.

Examining the seven triples listed above, (3,4,5), (5,12,13), (8,15,17), (20,21,29), and (11,60,61) are PPTs while (6,8,10) and (30,40,50), are NON-PRIMITIVE PTs.

3.4 Table 1: Primitive Triples of Order 1

In this section we consider those special PPTs, (a,b,c), where $b > a$ and $c - b = 1$; that is, the hypotenuse and longer leg are consecutive integers. We will call these triples PRIMITIVE PYTHAGOREAN TRIPLES (**PPTs**) OF ORDER 1.

Observe the numerical differences between each pair of successive numbers in each of the columns. What relationships do you notice? What other relationships can you discover before reading ahead?

a	b	c
3	4	5
5	12	13
7	24	25
9	40	41
⋮	⋮	⋮

Table 1

Here are some things you may have observed:
(1) Each triple consists of relatively prime numbers.
(2) The table has one column of even numbers and two columns of odd numbers.
(3) Each of the even entries in column b is a multiple of 4.
(4) The lengths of the larger leg and the hypotenuse on each line differ by 1.
(5) The numbers in column a are successive odd numbers and increase by the constant 2.
(6) The successive pairs of numbers in each of columns b and c increase by 8, 12, 16, ...
(7) Two of the entries in column b are each divisible by 3 and one entry is divisible by 5.
(8) The product of each triple's two smallest numbers is divisible by 12.
(9) The product of the three numbers in each triple is divisible by 60.

We can increase the number of triples shown in this special table by extending each column according to the pattern of successive number differences in the column, or by using the following formulas for each number triple a, b, and c: if n is an odd number greater than 1, then we can let

$$a = n, \quad b = \frac{n^2 - 1}{2}, \text{ and } c = \frac{n^2 + 1}{2}.$$

Pick any odd number for n and replace n in the three equations. The result will always be a primitive triple in which $c - b = 1$.

★ **Problems** ★

1. Show that each triple in *Table 1* on page 239 satisfies the Pythagorean relationship.

2. Study the pattern of the number-differences in each column and determine the next triple. Is your triple primitive?

3. Can a primitive triple contain three odd numbers? Why or why not?

(Solutions are on page 246.)

3.5 Table 2: Primitive Triples of Order 2

We will refer to the triples in the table at the right as PRIMITIVE PYTHAGOREAN TRIPLES OF ORDER 2. This time we list PPTs where $b > a$ and $c - b = 2$. Compare this table with the one in section 3.4. In what ways are the two tables alike, and also different? Each column of this table can be extended by following the pattern of number differences shown in the column. It can also be extended by using the triple

$$(2n, (n^2 - 1), (n^2 + 1))$$

where n is an even number beginning with 4. Thus $2n$ represents multiples of 4 beginning with 8.

a	b	c
8	15	17
12	35	37
16	63	65
20	99	101
⋮	⋮	⋮

Table 2

The two tables are *alike* in the following respects:

(1) Each triple consists of relatively prime numbers.

(2) Each table has two columns of odd numbers and one of even numbers.

(3) The even numbers are multiples of 4.

(4) There is a constant difference between columns *b* and *c* in each table.

(5) Both third columns consist of odd numbers.

(6) The difference between successive numbers in column *a* of the first table is constant; the same is true in the second table.

(7) In each table the pattern of increasing differences in column *b* is the same as the pattern of increasing differences in column *c*.

(8) Each column can be extended by following its pattern of number-differences.

The two tables are *different* in the following respects:

(1) In the first table columns *a* and *b* contain odd and even numbers respectively. In the second table columns *a* and *b* contain even and odd numbers respectively.

(2) The constant difference between the larger leg and the hypotenuse is different for each table.

(3) In both column *b* and column *c* of the *first* table the differences between successive entries increase by 4 (that is, 8, 12, 16, …), but in the corresponding columns of the *second* table the differences increase by 8 (20, 28, 36, …).

★ *Problems* ★

1. Find the entries for the 5th row of the table on page 240. Determine whether your set of triples are primitive.

2. Show that $[2n, (n^2 - 1), (n^2 + 1)]$ produces Pythagorean Triples for all *n* greater than 1.

(Solutions are on pages 246-247.)

3.6 Triples of the Form (3n,4n,5n)

If each number of the primitive triple (3,4,5) is multiplied by *n*, where *n* is any natural number greater than 1, the result is a *non-primitive* triple which satisfies the Pythagorean relationship $a^2 + b^2 = c^2$. That is, any triple of the form (3*n*, 4*n*, 5*n*) satisfies the condition $a^2 + b^2 = c^2$. Some of these triples are: (6,8,10) for *n* = 2; (9,12,15) for *n* = 3; (15,20,25) for *n* = 5; (18,24,30) for *n* = 6; and so forth. This shows that there are an infinite number of such triples, each of which has the property that the numbers are in the ratio of 3:4:5. We will identify each of these triples as a **(3*n*,4*n*,5*n*) TRIPLE** when *n* is greater than 1.

★ **Problems** ★

1. What primitive triple is related to (21,72,75)?

2. Does $\left(\frac{1}{4}, \frac{1}{3}, \frac{5}{12}\right)$ satisfy the Pythagorean relationship? If so, what primitive triple is related to it?

3. Can a primitive triple contain two even numbers and one odd number? Explain your answer.

(Solutions are on page 247.)

3.7 Order of Primitive Triples

In Table 1 shown in section 3.4, we observed that the difference between the two largest sides of each primitive triple was 1. Because of this feature, we will say that these particular triples are of ORDER 1. Thus, in a right triangle with sides of relatively prime lengths a, b, c, where $a < b < c$ and $c - b = 1$, such triples are said to be PRIMITIVE TRIPLES OF ORDER 1.

In Table 2 shown in section 3.5, the triples are said to be PRIMITIVE TRIPLES OF ORDER 2 because $c - b = 2$.

This might suggest that primitive triples of order 3 exist. But this is not true. The following are some orders that do exist: 1, 2, 8, 9, 18, 25, 32, 49, ... , as shown in the problems for section 3.8. Notice that this sequence contains odd and even numbers. Before reading ahead see if you can detect a pattern.

★ **Problems** ★

1. If you didn't find a pattern in the sequence of numbers of the preceding paragraph, examine just the odd numbers of the sequence. What do you observe? What do you think some other odd-number orders might be?

2. Examine the even numbers of the above sequence. Try to find a pattern. What do you think some other even number orders might be?

3. ***For the Adventurous***:
    Show that primitive triples of order 3 do *not* exist. [Hint: Assume there does exist a primitive triple of relatively prime numbers $(a,b,b+3)$, where $a < b < b+3$ and also $a^2 + b^2 = (b+3)^2$. Show that this assumption leads to a contradiction which implies that the assumption must be false.]

(Solutions are on pages 247-248.)

3.8 Generating Primitive Pythagorean Triples

Babylonians used soft clay tablets and a stylus to impress wedge-shaped marks on the clay. This type of writing is known as cuneiform. After "writing" on the tablets, they were baked in an oven or by the heat of the sun. Many tablets were preserved this way. One particular tablet (Number 322 in the Plimpton collection at Columbia University, circa 1900-1600 B.C.) is particularly noteworthy. It has 15 rows of figures related to Pythagorean triples.

Scholars believe that a missing section of the table showed two natural numbers m and n, where $m > n$, and the triple

$$m^2 - n^2, \ 2mn, \text{ and } m^2 + n^2.$$

As shown in problem 1 on page 244, this triple can be proven to generate Pythagorean triples for all pairs of values under certain conditions. When Pythagoras visited Babylonia 1000 years later than the estimated date of the table, he may have learned of the existence of what we now call Pythagorean triples.

All Primitive Pythagorean Triples can be generated by placing the following restrictions on a, b, and c:

1. c is larger than a or b.
2. $a = m^2 - n^2$
   $b = 2mn$
   $c = m^2 + n^2$

   m and n are natural numbers satisfying the following conditions:

   i. $m > n$. This insures that a is a natural number.
   ii. m and n have no common factor other than 1. Otherwise, a, b, and c would have a common factor other than 1 and (a,b,c) would not be a primitive triple.
   iii. m and n are neither both odd nor both even numbers. Otherwise, a, b, and c would have a common factor of 2 and (a,b,c) would not be a primitive triple.

Example. Let $m = 5$, and $n = 2$.

$$a = 5^2 - 2^2 = 21$$
$$b = 2 \times 5 \times 2 = 20$$
$$c = 5^2 + 2^2 = 29$$
$$a^2 + b^2 = 21^2 + 20^2 = 441 + 400 = 841$$
$$c^2 = 29^2 = 841$$

Since $a^2 + b^2 = c^2$, (a,b,c) is a Pythagorean Triple. It is also primitive because 21, 20, and 29 are relatively prime.

★ *Problems* ★

1. Show that $m^2 - n^2$, $2mn$, and $m^2 + n^2$ will generate Pythagorean Triples.

2. In section 3.7 we examined some odd orders 1, 9, 25, 49, …
   a. Show that m and n can generate orders which are perfect squares.
   b. Show that these orders must include *all* the odd perfect squares.
   c. Why can't these orders be even perfect squares?

3. In section 3.7 we examined some even orders 2, 8, 18, 32, …
   a. Show that m and n can generate orders which are doubles of perfect squares.
   b. Show that these orders must include the doubles of *all* perfect squares.

4. Must the order of every PPT be either an odd perfect square or twice a perfect square? Explain your answer.

(Solutions are on page 248.)

3.9 Some Additional Facts

1. ***Euclid's Proof on the Infinitude of Pythagorean Triples***
   Euclid of Alexandria lived about 300 B.C. and is famous as a Geometer. His book *Elements* is considered to be the most influential textbook ever written, and is one of the most historically significant works in mathematics. The essence of this proof is given in modern terminology. Initially, the listing of the squares of the natural numbers was given and then the differences between successive pairs of squares, as shown in the following table:

Differences between consecutive square numbers.

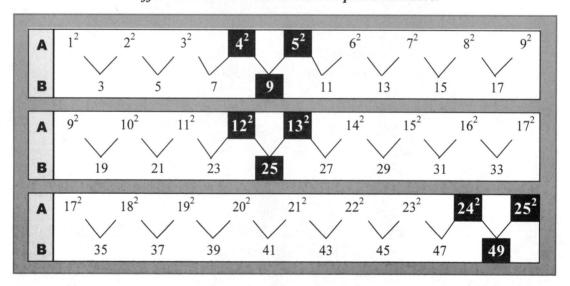

Each difference shown in the continued row B is equal to the difference of the two squares directly above in row A. Observe that some of the entries in row B (9, 25, and 49) are themselves perfect squares. Such triples satisfy the condition for being a Primitive Pythagorean Triple because the condition that the difference of two consecutive squares is equal to a third square is equivalent to the Pythagorean condition.

Since the table can be extended indefinitely, the number of square odd numbers that are in row B is infinite, and the infinitude of the Primitive Pythagorean Triples is thus proven.

2. If (a, b, c) is a Pythagorean Triple, one of the triple is divisible by 3, one is divisible by 5, the product of the two legs is always divisible by 12, and the product of the three sides is always divisible by 60.

3. Table 3 of Pythagorean triples is one in which the two smaller values of each triple differs by one. Shown are the five smallest sets of values of such triples. Reading down any column, notice how quickly the difference between successive rows becomes very large.

a	b	c
3	4	5
20	21	29
119	120	169
696	697	985
4059	4060	5741

Table 3

APPENDIX 3 SOLUTIONS

3.4 Table 1: Some Primitive Triples
Pages 239-240

1. Show that each triple satisfies $a^2 + b^2 = c^2$.

Row	a	b	c	a^2	$+$	b^2	$=$	c^2
1	3	4	5	9	+	16	=	25
2	5	12	13	25	+	144	=	169
3	7	24	25	49	+	576	=	625
4	9	40	41	81	+	1600	=	1681

2. **(11,60,61).** Reading downward, column a increases by 2. Therefore, $a = 11$ in row 5. The pattern of increases for column c is the same as that for column b. For each pair of successive numbers beginning at the top of columns b and c, the pattern of increases is 8, 12, 16, 20, ... Therefore in row 5, $b = 40 + 20 = 60$ and $c = 41 + 20 = 61$. The triple is (11,60,61), which is a primitive triple.

3. If a and b are odd numbers, their squares are also odd numbers and the sum of those squares is an even number. Therefore the square of c must be an even number. It then follows that no Pythagorean Triple, either primitive or non-primitive, can consist of three odd numbers.

3.5 Table 2: More Primitive Triples
Pages 240-241

1. **(24,143,145).** Reading downward, column a increases by 4. Thus, $a = 24$ in row 6. The pattern of increases for column c is the same as that for column b. For each pair of successive numbers beginning at the top of columns b and c, the pattern of increases is 20, 28, 36, 44, ... Therefore in row 6, $b = 99 + 44 = 143$ and $c = 101 + 44 = 145$.

We must show that (24,143,145) is a Pythagorean Triple. $a^2 = 24^2 = 576$; $b^2 = 143^2 = 20449$; $c^2 = 145^2 = 21025$. Since $576 + 20449 = 21025$, $a^2 + b^2 = c^2$.

To show that 24, 143 and 145 are relatively prime, observe that 143 and 145 are consecutive odd numbers and as such are relatively prime. The only factors of 24 we need to consider are 2 and 3. Neither of these is a factor of 143 or 145. Therefore, 24, 143, and 145 are relatively prime. (24, 143, 145) is a primitive triple.

2. We need to compare the left side of $(2n)^2 + (n^2 - 1)^2 = (n^2 + 1)^2$ to the right side.
    (1) Left side: $(2n)^2 + (n^2 - 1)^2 = (4n^2) + (n^4 - 2n^2 + 1) = n^4 + 2n^2 + 1$
    (2) Right side: $(n^2 + 1)^2 = n^4 + 2n^2 + 1$

Since both sides of the equation are equal to the same expression for any value of n, the equation produces Pythagorean Triples.

3.6 Triples of the Form (3n, 4n, 5n)
Pages 241-242

1. **(7,24,25).** Since the sum of the digits of each number of the triple is 3 or a multiple of 3, each number of the triple is divisible by 3 (has a factor of 3). That is, $21 = 7 \times 3$, $72 = 24 \times 3$, and $75 = 25 \times 3$. Thus, $(21,72,75)$ is related to the primitive triple $(7,24,25)$.

2. **Yes; (3,4,5).** Does $\left(\frac{1}{4}\right)^2 + \left(\frac{1}{3}\right)^2 = \left(\frac{5}{12}\right)^2$?
    $$\left(\frac{1}{4}\right)^2 + \left(\frac{1}{3}\right)^2 = \left(\frac{1}{4} \times \frac{1}{4}\right) + \left(\frac{1}{3} \times \frac{1}{3}\right) = \frac{1}{16} + \frac{1}{9} = \frac{25}{144}$$
    $$\left(\frac{5}{12}\right)^2 = \frac{5}{12} \times \frac{5}{12} = \frac{25}{144}$$
    Therefore, $\left(\frac{1}{4}\right)^2 + \left(\frac{1}{3}\right)^2 = \left(\frac{5}{12}\right)^2$

    If we multiply each of the given numbers in the triple by the least common multiple of the denominators, the result will be a triple of natural numbers. Since LCM $(4,3,12) = 12$, the given triple is related to $\left(12 \times \frac{1}{4}, 12 \times \frac{1}{3}, 12 \times \frac{5}{12}\right)$. This is equivalent to $(3,4,5)$.

3. **No.** A primitive triple cannot contain two even numbers since all members of the triple must be relatively prime. Two even numbers are each divisible by 2 and therefore not relatively prime. It can be shown that if a Pythagorean triple has two even numbers, then the third number must also be even.

3.7 Order of Primitive Triples
Page 242

1 **81, 121, 169, …** The odd numbers in the order list 1, 2, 8, 9, 18, 25, 32, and 49 are 1, 9, 25, and 49 which are squares of consecutive odd numbers. Some other odd squares are 81, 121, and 169.

2. **50, 72, 98, …** The even numbers of the above order list are 2, 8, 18, and 32. This list can be written as 1×2, 4×2, 9×2, and 16×2. Observe that the first number in each product is a square number. Some other even orders are 25×2, 36×2, and 49×2.

3. ***For the Adventurous***
    Assume that there is a PPT of order 3.
    Let a, b, and $b + 3$ be the triple of order 3 where $0 < a < b < b+3$.

$$
\begin{aligned}
1) \quad a^2 + b^2 &= (b + 3)^2 \\
2) \quad a^2 + b^2 &= b^2 + 6b + 9 \\
3) \quad a^2 &= 6b + 9 \\
4) \quad a^2 &= 3(2b + 3)
\end{aligned}
$$

Thus, 3 is a factor of a. Then $(2b + 3)$ must furnish another 3 as a factor of a^2. This can occur only if 3 is a factor of b.

If 3 is a factor of b, it is also a factor of $b + 3$. Then the triple is not primitive. We then conclude that primitive triples of order 3 do not exist.

3.8 Generating Primitive Pythagorean Triples
Pages 243-244

1. Does $(m^2 - n^2)^2 + (2mn)^2 = (m^2 + n^2)^2$?

$$
\begin{aligned}
(m^2 - n^2)^2 + (2mn)^2 &= (m^4 - 2m^2n^2 + n^4) + (4m^2n^2) \\
&= (m^2 + 2mn + n^2) \\
&= (m^2 + n^2)^2
\end{aligned}
$$

Since the left side of the equation can be rewritten as the right side, then the equation produces PTs.

2. a. The order is $c - b$. Choose $b = 2mn$. Then $c - b = (m^2 + n^2) - 2mn = (m - n)^2$. Since $m - n$ can represent any natural number, $c - b = (m - n)^2$ is a perfect square.

   b. Since one of m and n is odd and the other even, $m - n$ represents any odd number. Then $(m - n)^2$ is odd. Thus the orders include all the odd perfect squares.

   c. Since $m - n$ is odd, $(m - n)^2$ cannot be even. The order $c - b = (m - n)^2$ cannot be an even perfect square.

3. a. The order is $c - b$. Choose $b = (m^2 - n^2)$. Then $c - b = (m^2 + n^2) - (m^2 - n^2) = 2n^2$. Therefore, $c - b = 2n^2$ can generate orders which are doubles of perfect squares.

   b. Since n can be any natural number, $c - b = 2n^2$ generates orders which include the doubles of all perfect squares.

4. **Yes.** The only expressions that generate orders are $(m - n)^2$ and $2n^2$.

References
Archibald, Ralph, *Theory of Numbers*, Merrill, 1970
Beiler, Albert H., *Recreations in the Theory of Numbers*, Dover Publications, 1966
Boyer, Carl B., *A History of Mathematics*, Revised by Merzbach, Uta C., Wiley & Sons, 1991
Loomis, Elisha S., *The Pythagorean Proposition*, NCTM, 1990
Singh, Simon, *Fermat's Enigma*, Walker & Company, 1997
Swetz, Frank J. and Kao, T.I., *Was Pythagoras Chinese?*, Penn State University Press, 1977

Appendix 4. Working With Exponents

4.1 Reading Exponents and Powers

Sometimes a number is used as a factor several times, as in $6 \times 6 \times 6 \times 6 \times 6 \times 6 \times 6$. A short way to write this last expression is to use the symbol 6^7. This is read as "six to the seventh power." In this example, the 6 (the factor that repeats) is called the *base* and the small 7 (which tells us how many times the factor repeats) is called the *exponent*. In general we read b^n as "b to the nth power." The form b^n is called the *exponential form*. **In this appendix we will restrict bases and exponents to the counting numbers, except where noted.**

When the exponent is 2 or 3, we may read the power in several ways. For example, 9^2 may be read as "nine to the second power" or "nine square" or "nine squared." Similarly, 7^3 is read as "seven to the third power" or "seven cube" or "seven cubed."

When a number is written with no exponent, then the exponent is understood to be 1. Thus $5 = 5^1$, $6 = 6^1$, and so forth.

4.2 Multiplying Powers of the Same Base

The expression $3^4 \times 3^2$ means $(3 \times 3 \times 3 \times 3) \times (3 \times 3)$ which equals $3 \times 3 \times 3 \times 3 \times 3 \times 3$. The last expression may be written in exponential form as 3^6. Compare this exponent with the original exponents. Notice that the exponent 6 is equal to the sum of the original exponents 4 and 2. We express this in the following form: $3^4 \times 3^2 = 3^{4+2} = 3^6$.

> **First Rule of Exponents:** $b^r \times b^s = b^{r+s}$

Caution: Remember that to use this rule, the bases must be the same!

Example: $2^3 \times 2^1 \times 2^2 = 2^6$. Notice that this actually says that $8 \times 2 \times 4 = 64$.

★ *Problems* ★

1. Show that $(5b^4) \times (6b^3) = 30b^7$.

2. What is the value of n when:
   a. $8^5 \times 8 = 8^n$ b. $7^n \times 7^n \times 7^n \times 7^n = 7^{12}$ c. $4^{2n} \times 4^3 = 4^{11}$

3. Multiply and simplify $\left(3a^2b^2\right) \times (4ab) \times \left(5a^3b^4\right)$

4. Multiply and simplify $\left(\frac{1}{2}p^2r^2\right) \times \left(\frac{2}{3}p^3r\right) \times \left(\frac{3}{5}p^3s\right)$

(*Solutions are on page 254.*)

4.3 Dividing Powers of the Same Base

The division $5^7 \div 5^3$ may also be written in the form $\dfrac{5^7}{5^3}$ which is equal to

$$\frac{5 \times 5 \times 5 \times 5 \times 5 \times 5 \times 5}{5 \times 5 \times 5} = 5 \times 5 \times 5 \times 5.$$

The last expression may be written in exponential form as 5^4. Compare this exponent with the original exponents. Notice that the exponent 4 is equal to the difference of the original exponents 7 and 3. We express this in the following form: $5^7 \div 5^3 = 5^{7-3} = 5^4$.

Second Rule of Exponents: $b^r \div b^s$ **or** $\dfrac{b^r}{b^s} = b^{r-s}$, **provided that** $r > s$.

Caution: Remember that to use this rule, the bases must be the same!

Example: $3^5 \div 3^2 = 3^{5-2} = 3^3$.

★ *Problems* ★

1. Express $4^3 \div 4$ as a power of 2.

2. Express $(7^8 \times 7) \div (7^2 \times 7^4)$ as a power of 7.

3. Simplify $d^3 e^4 f^5 \div d\, e^2 f^3$.

4. Simplify $\left(\dfrac{5^2 a^5}{3b}\right) \times \left(\dfrac{3^3 b^3}{5a^2}\right)$.

5. Simplify $\left(\dfrac{8^3 p^4}{5^2 r^2}\right) \times \left(\dfrac{5^3 r^6}{8p}\right)$.

(Solutions are on page 254.)

4.4 The Zero Power of b

Let us extend our rule for division of powers of the same positive base to the case where the exponents are equal. For example $5^3 \div 5^3$ would equal 5^{3-3}, which is 5^0. What can such an exponent mean? Clearly $5^3 \div 5^3$ must equal 1 because any natural number divided by itself must equal 1. So it must be true that $5^0 = 1$. In general, $b^r \div b^r = b^{r-r} = b^0$, which logically must be 1.

> **Definition:** $b^0 = 1$ for any $b \neq 0$.

Example: $(8^7 \times 8^2) \div (8^4 \times 8^5) = 8^9 \div 8^9 = 8^0 = 1$.

★ *Problems* ★

1. Simplify $(5^5 \times 5) \div (5^0 \times 5^6)$.

2. Simplify $12^3 \times 12 \times 12^0 \times 12^2$.

(Solutions are on page 255.)

4.5 Powers of Powers

Suppose we wish to find a power of a power as in the case $(b^2)^3$. Read this as "the third power of b square" or as "the cube of b square". Then $(b^2)^3$ equals $(b^2) \times (b^2) \times (b^2)$. This can be written more simply as $b^2 \times b^2 \times b^2$ which is equal to $b^{2+2+2} = b^6$. Notice that exponent 6 is equal to the product of the original exponents 2 and 3. This same result follows if we write $(b^2)^3$ as $(b \times b)^3 = (b \times b) \times (b \times b) \times (b \times b) = b \times b \times b \times b \times b \times b = b^6$.

> **Third Rule of Exponents:** $(b^r)^s = b^{r \times s} = b^{rs}$ for any $b > 0$.

Example: $(10^2)^4 = 10^8$. Notice that this says that $100 \times 100 \times 100 \times 100 = 100,000,000$.

★ *Problems* ★

1. Simplify $(9^5)^7 \div (9^7)^5$.

2. Simplify $(5 \times a^3)^2$.

3. Compare $5 \times (a^3)^2$ with the result in problem 2.

4. Show why $(a^2 \times b^5)^3 = a^6 \times b^{15}$.

(Solutions are on page 255.)

4.6 Fermat's "Little" Theorem

Pierre de Fermat (1601-1665) was a French lawyer and mathematician. He communicated with many mathematicians relative to his discoveries in algebra, geometry, probability, calculus, and number theory. French academicians consider him to be one of the discoverers of Calculus. However his chief interest was number theory. The following example is related to one of his many discoveries.

What is the remainder when 3^{20} is divided by 7?

We will look for a pattern by examining the sequence of remainders associated with 3^1, 3^2, 3^3, 3^4, and so forth.

Remainders when 3^N is divided by 7												
Power	3^1	3^2	3^3	3^4	3^5	3^6	3^7	3^8	3^9	3^{10}	3^{11}	3^{12}
Remainder	3	2	6	4	5	1	3	2	6	4	5	1

Shortcut: A remainder can be obtained by multiplying the preceding remainder by 3 and then dividing the result by 7. For example, to obtain the remainder for 3^5, take the preceding remainder for 3^4 and multiply it by 3. Divide the product by 7. The remainder is 5. Enter it in the table under 3^5.

Notice that when 1 occurs as a remainder, the set of remainders appears to repeat in the same order until 1 occurs again, and will continue to repeat in this manner as the sequence of powers is extended. So we expect the remainders for 3^6, 3^{12}, 3^{18}, and so forth to be 1. Since $3^{20} = 3^{18} \times 3^2$, 3^{20} has the same remainder as 3^2. Therefore 3^{20} has a remainder of 2 when divided by 7.

In the following table, we explore the effect 7 has when it divides powers of other number bases. We do not include 7 or a multiple of 7 as a base because the remainder is 0 when such bases are divided by 7.

Remainders When a^N is Divided By 7												
a	a^1	a^2	a^3	a^4	a^5	a^6	a^7	a^8	a^9	a^{10}	a^{11}	a^{12}
1	1	1	1	1	1	1	1	1	1	1	1	1
2	2	4	1	2	4	1	2	4	1	2	4	1
3	3	2	6	4	5	1	3	2	6	4	5	1
4	4	2	1	4	2	1	4	2	1	4	2	1
5	5	4	6	2	3	1	5	4	6	2	3	1
6	6	1	6	1	6	1	6	1	6	1	6	1
8	1	1	1	1	1	1	1	1	1	1	1	1
9	2	4	1	2	4	1	2	4	1	2	4	1
10	3	2	6	4	5	1	3	2	6	4	5	1
11	4	2	1	4	2	1	4	2	1	4	2	1
12	5	4	6	2	3	1	5	4	6	2	3	1
13	6	1	6	1	6	1	6	1	6	1	6	1

Observations

1. Notice that a^7 has a remainder of a when $a < 7$, and a remainder of $a - 7$ when $7 < a < 14$.
2. Observe that each entry in the a^6 and a^{12} columns is 1 for all values of a relatively prime to 7.
3. When 1 occurs as a remainder in a row, 1 marks the end of a group of remainders that will repeat in the same order for higher powers of the base in the same row.

One form of Fermat's "Little" Theorem is related to the 2nd observation:

> a^{n-1} **has a remainder of 1 when divided by** n, **where** n **is prime and** a **is relatively prime to** n.

★ *Problems* ★

1. What is the remainder when 4^8 is divided by 7?

2. What is the remainder when 3^{100} is divided by 13?

3. What is the remainder when 3×1776^2 is divided by 5?

4. ***For the Adventurous:***
   When $3n^2$ is divided by 5, where n is any natural number, can the remainder be 4? Explain.

5. What is the remainder when $2^{37} \times 2^{23} \div 2$ is divided by 5?

(Solutions are on pages 255-256.)

Appendix 4:   Solutions

4.2 Multiplying Powers of the Same Base
Page 249

1. **$30b^7$.** $(5b^4) \times (6b^3) = 5b^4 \times 6b^3$
    $$= 5 \times 6 \times b^3 \times b^4 \quad \text{(regrouping)}$$
    $$= 30b^{3+4} \quad \text{(First Rule)}$$
    $$= 30b^7 \quad \text{(simplifying)}$$

2. *a.* $n = 6$ b. $n = 3$ c. $2n + 3 = 11$
    $$2n = 8$$
    $$n = 4$$

3. **$60a^6b^7$.** Regroup: $\left(3a^2b^2\right) \times \left(4ab\right) \times \left(5a^3b^4\right)$
    $$= (3 \times 4 \times 5) \times (a^2 \times a \times a^3) \times (b^2 \times b \times b^4)$$
    $$= 60a^6b^7$$

4. **$\frac{1}{5} p^8 r^3 s$.** Regroup: $\left(\frac{1}{2}p^2r^2\right) \times \left(\frac{2}{3}p^3r\right) \times \left(\frac{3}{5}p^3s\right)$
    $$= \left(\frac{1}{2} \times \frac{2}{3} \times \frac{3}{5}\right) \times \left(p^2 \times p^3 \times p^3\right) \times \left(r^2 \times r\right) \times s$$
    $$= \frac{1}{5}p^8r^3s$$

4.3 Dividing Powers of the Same Base
Page 250

1. **4^2.** $4^3 \div 4 = 4^3 \div 4^1 = 4^{3-1} = 4^2 = (2^2)^2 = 2^4$

2. **7^3.** $(7^8 \times 7) \div (7^2 \times 7^4) = 7^9 \div 7^6 = 7^{9-6} = 7^3$

3. **$d^2e^2f^2$.**   Regroup: $d^3e^4f^5 \div de^2f^3 = \dfrac{d^3}{d} \times \dfrac{e^4}{e^2} \times \dfrac{f^5}{f^3} = d^{3-1}e^{4-2}f^{5-3} = d^2e^2f^2$

4. **$45a^3b^2$.** Regroup: $\left(\dfrac{5^2a^2}{3b}\right) \times \left(\dfrac{3^3b^3}{5a^2}\right) = \left(\dfrac{5^2}{5}\right) \times \left(\dfrac{3^3}{3}\right) \times \left(\dfrac{a^5}{a^2}\right) \times \left(\dfrac{b^3}{b^2}\right) = 5 \times 3^2 a^3 b^2 = 45a^3b^2$

5. **$320p^3r^4$.** Regroup: $\left(\dfrac{8^3p^4}{5^2r^2}\right) \times \left(\dfrac{5^3r^6}{8p}\right) = \left(\dfrac{8^3}{8}\right) \times \left(\dfrac{5^3}{5^2}\right) \times \left(\dfrac{p^4}{p}\right) \times \left(\dfrac{r^6}{r^2}\right) = 8^2 \times 5p^3r^4 = 320p^3r^4$

4.4 The Zero Power of b
Page 251

1. **1.** $(5^5 \times 5) \div (5^0 \times 5^6) = 5^6 \div 5^6 = 5^{6-6} = 5^0 = 1$

2. **12^6.** $12^3 \times 12 \times 12^0 \times 12^2 = 12^{3+1+0+2} = 12^6$

4.5 Powers of Powers
Page 251

1. **1.** $(9^5)^7 \div (9^7)^5 = 9^{35} \div 9^{35} = 9^{35-35} = 9^0 = 1.$

2. **$25a^6$.** $(5 \times a^3)^2 = (5 \times a^3) \times (5 \times a^3) = 5 \times 5 \times a^3 \times a^3 = 25a^6.$

3. In problem 2, the exponent 2 acts on both 5 and a^3.
   In problem 3 the exponent 2 acts only on a^3.
   $5 \times (a^3)^2 = 5a^6.$

4. **$a^6 \times b^{15}$.** $(a^2 \times b^5)^3 = (a^2 \times b^5) \times (a^2 \times b^5) \times (a^2 \times b^5)$
   $= a^2 \times a^2 \times a^2 \times b^5 \times b^5 \times b^5$
   $= (a^2)^3 \times (b^5)^3$
   $= a^6 \times b^{15}$

4.6 Fermat's "Little" Theorem
Pages 252-253

1. **3.** According to Fermat's Little Theorem, $4^{7-1} = 4^6$ has a remainder of 1 when 4^6 is divided by 7. Since $4^8 = 4^6 \times 4^2$, 4^8 has the same remainder as $4^2 = 16$ when divided by 7. Then 4^8 has a remainder of 1×2 or 2 when 4^8 is divided by 7.

2. **3.** **Method 1:** According to Fermat's Little Theorem, 3^{13-1} or 3^{12} has a remainder of 1 when divided by 13. Then, $(3^{12})^8 = 3^{96}$ has a remainder of 1. Since $3^{100} = 3^{96} \times 3^4$, the remainder of 3^{100} when divided by 7 is 1×3 or 3.

   Method 2: Observe that 3^3 has a remainder of 1 when divided by 13. Then $(3^3)^{33} = 3^{99}$ has a remainder of 1 when divided by 13. Since $3^{100} = 3^{99} \times 3$, then 3^{100} has a remainder of 3 when divided by 13.

   Method 3: This problem can also be solved by making a table of remainders of the powers of 3 when divided by 13 to find a pattern of remainders. See page 256.

Remainders when 3^n is divided by 13									
Power of 2	3^1	3^2	3^3	3^4	3^5	3^6	3^7	3^8	3^9	$\cdots$
Remainder	3	9	1	3	9	1	3	9	1	$\cdots$

The pattern of remainders 3, 9, 1 repeats endlessly. Observe that each of 3^3, 3^6, 3^9, ... have a remainder of 1 when divided by 13. Then 3^{99} has a remainder of 1 when divided by 13, and 3^{100} has a remainder of 3 when divided by 13.

3. **3.** $1776^2 = 1776 \times 1776$. When multiplied out, the units digit is 6. Then, when multiplied by 3, the units digit is 8. When 8 is divided by 5, the remainder is 3. Therefore, when 3×1776^2 is divided by 5, the remainder is 3.

4. ***For the Adventurous:***
    No. The first row in the table below contains the first ten perfect squares. The second row contains the remainders when each is divided by 5. The third row contains the entries of the second row multiplied by 3. The fourth row contains the remainders when the second row is divided by 5.

A Table Based on the First Ten Perfect Squares										
n^2	1	4	9	16	25	36	49	64	81	100
$n^2 \div 5$: Remainders	1	4	4	1	0	1	4	4	1	0
$3 \times$ Row 2	3	12	12	3	0	3	12	12	3	0
$3n^2 \div 5$: Remainders	3	2	2	3	0	3	2	2	3	0

Each group of ten perfect squares, 11^2 through 20^2, 21^2 through 30^2, 31^2 through 40^2, and so forth, will produce the same second row as the group 1^2 through 10^2. Then multiplying any perfect square by 3 and then dividing by 5 produces the remainders 0, 2, or 3, only. Therefore, the remainder *cannot* be 4.

5. **3.** $2^{37} \times 2^{23} \div 2 = 2^{37 + 23 - 1} = 2^{59}$.

Remainders when 2^n is divided by 5												
Power of 2	2^1	2^2	2^3	2^4	2^5	2^6	2^7	2^8	2^9	2^{10}	2^{11}	2^{12}	$\cdots$
Remainder	2	4	3	1	2	4	3	1	2	4	3	1	$\cdots$

Observe that the remainders 2, 4, 3, and 1 recur in groups of 4 in order. Then, when divided by 5, 2^{60} has a remainder of 1 and 2^{59} has a remainder of 3.

Appendix 5: Justifying Some Divisibility Rules

The following discusses further and provides some justifications for the tests of divisibility developed on pages 65-76.

★ In this appendix, the word ***number*** always refers to a natural number.

★ A ***theorem*** is a mathematical statement or rule that can be proven based on given assumptions and previously proven theorems.

5.1 Simple Divisibility Theorems

If a number ends in 0, 2, 4, 6, or 8, it is divisible by 2.

If a number ends in 0 or 5, it is divisible by 5.

If a number ends in 25, 50, 75, or 00, it is divisible by 25.

If a number ends in 00, it is divisible by 4 and 25, or by 2^2 and 5^2.

If a number ends in 000, it is divisible by 8 and 125, or by 2^3 and 5^3.

If a number ends in 0000, it is divisible by 16 and 625, or by 2^4 and 5^4.

5.2 Basic Divisibility Principles

Let a, b, and c be natural numbers and either $b + c = a$ or $b - c = a$.

> **DIVISIBILITY PRINCIPLE 1 (DP1)**
> **If b and c are each divisible by d, then a is divisible by d.**
>
> **DIVISIBILITY PRINCIPLE 2 (DP2)**
> **If a and b are each divisible by d, then c is divisible by d.**

5.3 Divisibility by 2^n

Question: Is the number 538,672 divisible by 8?

Rewrite the given number as the sum $538{,}000 + 672$. Observe that the first addend ends in 000 — that is, it is a multiple of 1000 — and is therefore divisible by 8. Notice that the second addend is also divisible by 8 since $672 \div 8 = 84$. Since both addends are divisible by 8, the given number is divisible by 8 by **DP1**.

<u>Comment:</u> The above procedure shows how to use the last three digits to determine if a number is divisible by 2^3. The validity of extending this method to any power of 2 can be proven.

> ***Theorem:*** **If a number ends in n zeros, the given number is divisible by 2^n.**

> ***Theorem:*** **If the last n digits of a given number form a number divisible by 2^n, then the given number is also divisible by 2^n.**

5.4 Divisibility by 9

Let ABCD represent a four-digit number. The left-hand digit A is called the *lead digit* of the number. In this discussion, the lead digit may not be zero.

Suppose the number's digit-sum, A + B + C + D, is divisible by 9. Prove that the number ABCD, itself, is divisible by 9.

Proof:

Rewrite ABCD as   (1) $1000A + 100B + 10C + D$
which equals   (2) $\underline{999A} + A + \underline{99B} + B + \underline{9C} + C + D$
Regroup (2)   (3) $[999A + 99B + 9C] + [A + B + C + D]$

Notice that each term in $[999A + 99B + 9C]$ is divisible by 9 and that their sum is divisible by 9 by **DP1**. The digit-sum $[A + B + C + D]$ was initially assumed to be divisible by 9. Therefore, *ABCD* is divisible by 9 by **DP1.**

Comment: The above proof shows that any four-digit number whose digit-sum is divisible by 9 will also result in the number itself being divisible by 9. Furthermore, it can be shown that any *n*-digit number whose digit-sum is divisible by 9 will also result in the number itself being divisible by 9.

> **Theorem:** If the digit-sum of a natural number is divisible by 9, then the given number is divisible by 9.

Suppose we interchange the parts of this theorem, as stated below. We get a new statement that may or may not be true. The new statement is called the CONVERSE of the original theorem. Because we will prove it true, it will become a new theorem.

> **Theorem:** If a natural number is divisible by 9, then the digit-sum of the given number is divisible by 9.

Proof of the converse:

Let ABCD be a four-digit natural number divisible by 9. We now prove that the digit-sum $A + B + C + D$ is also divisible by 9.

Rewrite ABCD as   (1) $1000A + 100B + 10C + D$
Which equals   (2) $\underline{999A} + A + \underline{99B} + B + \underline{9C} + C + D$
Regroup (2).   (3) $(999A + 99B + 9C) + (A + B + C + D)$

Notice that each term in $(999A + 99B + 9C)$ is divisible by 9. Then their sum is divisible by 9 by **DP1**. The number ABCD was initially assumed to be divisible by 9. Therefore, the digit-sum $(A + B + C + D)$ is divisible by 9 by **DP2.**

Comment: The preceding proof can be extended to show that if any *n*-digit number is divisible by 9, then its digit-sum is also divisible by 9.

In the first proof on page 258, we demonstrated that if the digit-sum of a number was divisible by 9. then the number itself was divisible by 9. A similar procedure can establish the principles that if the digit-sum of any number is divisible by 3, then the number is also divisible by 3, and its converse. Therefore it follows that:

> ***Theorem:*** **If the digit-sum of a natural number is divisible by 3, then the given number is divisible by 3.**
>
> ***Theorem:*** **If a natural number is divisible by 3, then the digit-sum of the given number is divisible by 3.**

5.5 Divisibility by 11

Vocabulary introduced on page 73 helps us to describe a pattern of sums and differences. In the four-digit number ABCD, we refer to B and D as "odd-place" digits, and to A and C as "even-place" digits. Assume that the difference of the sums of the odd-place digits and even-place digits, $(B + D) - (A + C)$, is equal to 0 or to a multiple of 11.

We now prove that the given number, ABCD, is divisible by 11.

Proof:

Rewrite *ABCD* as   (1) $1000A + 100B + 10C + D$.

Rewrite (1) by associating each addend with the closest multiple of 11.

       (2) $(1001A - A) + (99B + B) + (11C - C) + D$

Regroup (2) as   (3) $[1001A + 99B + 11C] + [(B + D) - (A + C)]$

The first set of terms in (3), $[1001A + 99B + 11C]$, are each divisible by 11. Therefore their sum is divisible by 11 by **DP1**. The difference of the sums in the next set of terms, $[(B + D) - (A + C)]$, was assumed to have a value of 0 or a multiple of 11. Therefore *ABCD*, the sum of all terms in (3), is a multiple of 11 by **DP1**.

The above proof can be extended to any natural number of *n* digits.

> ***Theorem:*** **If the sum of the odd-place digits and the sum of the even-place digits of a given natural number differ by 0 or by a multiple of 11, the given number is divisible by 11.**

5.6 Divisions Producing Same Remainders

Suppose that a and b are two different natural numbers with $a > b$. Let d be a natural number that divides each of a and b, leaving the same remainder in each case. Prove that the largest value of d is $a - b$.

Proof:

Let r be the remainder in each case and let q_1 and q_2 be the two different quotients. Then the following occur:

$$(1) \quad a = q_1 d + r$$
$$(2) \quad b = q_2 d + r$$

By subtracting the members of equation (2) from the members of (1), we get

$$(3) \quad a - b = q_1 d - q_2 d$$

Rewrite (3) as

$$(4) \quad a - b = (q_1 - q_2) \times d.$$

Equation (4) shows that d is a factor of $a - b$. The largest possible factor of $a - b$ is $a - b$ itself. Therefore, the largest possible value of d is $a - b$. Observe that in this case, $q_1 - q_2$ has its smallest possible value, 1.

> **Theorem:** The largest number that divides each of a and b, leaving the same remainder in each case, is $a - b$.

Example: What is the largest number that divides each of 394 and 475, leaving the same remainder in each case?

Let $a = 475$, and $b = 394$. Then the largest number to divide each of 475 and 394, leaving the same remainder in each case is $475 - 394 = 81$.

Notice that when 475 and 394 are each divided by 81, the remainder in each case is 70. Notice also that the quotients are 5 and 4 respectively and their difference is $5 - 4 = 1$. In this example, equations (1) and (2) above become:

$$(1) \quad 475 = 5 \times 81 + 70$$
$$(2) \quad 394 = 4 \times 81 + 70$$

Furthermore, all other divisors leaving the same remainder in each case are factors of 81. If 475 and 394 are each divided by 27, the remainder is 16; if by 9, the remainder is 7; if by 3, the remainder is 1; and if by 1, the remainder is 0.

When the remainders in both divisions are zero, then $a - b$ itself is actually the Greatest Common Factor of each of a and b. For example, the largest number that divides both 36 and 48, leaving the same remainder in each case, is their difference, 12. Since the remainder in each division is 0, 12 is the Greatest Common Factor of 48 and 36.

★ *Appendix 5 Problems* ★

1. Is the number 9,571,272 divisible by   a. 4?   b. 8?   c. 16?   d. 3?   e. 9?

2. What is the smallest natural number that must be added to 123,456 so that the result is divisible by 25?

3. What is the smallest natural number divisible by 9 that is greater than 35,462?

4. For how many different values of A is 375A9392 divisible by 16?

5. What replacement for the digit B makes 32B0B6 divisible by 9?

6. What is the smallest 3-digit natural number divisible by 12 if all three digits are the same?

7. For what value of B is the six-digit number 123B28 divisible by 24?

8. What replacements of the digits A and B make the number A5413B divisible by 72?

9. What replacements of A and B make the 3-digit number A4B divisible by 11?

10. Replace the missing digit in each of the following so that the number is divisible by 11.
    a. 83■   b. 36■9   c. 59■12   d. ■0918

11. List all four-digit numbers divisible by 44 if the digits are 1, 2, 3, and 4, not necessarily in that order.

12. What is the largest number that divides each of 47 and 36, leaving the same remainder?

13. What is the largest number that divides each of 57 and 38, leaving the same remainder?

14. What is the largest number that divides each of 95, 78, and 61, leaving the same remainder in each case?

15. What is the largest number that divides each of 225, 201, and 189, leaving the same remainder in each case?

(*Solutions are on pages 262-263.*)

Appendix 5 Solutions
Page 261

1. a. **Yes.** Since 72 is divisible by 4, so is 9,571,272.

    b. **Yes.** Since 272 is divisible by 8, so is 9,571,272.

    c. **No.** Since 1272 is not divisible by 16, neither is 9,571,272.

    d. **Yes.** Since the sum of the digits, 33, is divisible by 3, so is 9,571,272.

    e. **No.** Since the sum of the digits, 33, is not divisible by 9, neither is 9,571,272.

2. **19.** If 19 is added to 56, then the given number will end in 75, making it divisible by 25.

3. **35,469.** If the sum of the digits, 20, is increased by 7, the resulting sum, 27, will be divisible by 9. Therefore, the number 35,462 should be increased by 7 to 35,469.

4. **10.** Since 9392 is divisible by 16, any of the ten digits may replace A.

5. **8.** The digit-sum is $11 + 2B$. If the digit-sum is 18, B is not a whole number. Then the digit-sum is 27, $2B = 16$ and $B = 8$. The number is 328,086.

6. **444.** Divisibility by 12 implies divisibility by 3 and by 4. If all three digits are the same the number is a multiple of 111. All multiples of 111 are also multiples of 3. The least three-digit multiple of 4 that has three digits the same is 444. The number itself is 444.

7. **5.** Divisibility by 24 implies divisibility by 8 and by 3. The sum of the digits of 123B28 is $16 + B$, which is divisible by 3. Therefore B is 2 or 5 or 8. Since 528 is divisible by 8 but 228 and 828 are not, B is 5. The number is 123,528.

8. **A = 8 and B = 6.** Any number divisible by 72 is divisible by both 9 and 8. Thus 13B is divisible by 8 and $B = 6$. The number A54136 has a digit-sum of $19+A$, which equals 27. The value of A is 8 and the number is 854136.

9. **(4,0), (3,1), (2,2), (1,3); (9,6), (8,7), (7,8), or (6,9).** The sum of A and B must be either 4 or 15, but A cannot be 0. The multiples of 11 are 440, 341, 242, 143, 946, 847, 748, and 649.

10. a. 83**6**   b. 36**1**9   c. 59**3**12   d. **6**0918

11. **3124 and 4312.** The ones digit is even. To be divisible by 4, the last two digits must be 24, 32, or 12. To be divisible by 11, the sum of the odd digits must be 5, as must the sum of the even digits. 4312 and 4312 are the only ones that satisfy both conditions.

12. **11.** $47 - 36 = 11$. The divisor is 11 and the remainder is 3.

13. **19.** $57 - 38 = 19$. The divisor is 19 and the remainder is 0.

14. **17.** $95 - 78 = 17$ and $78 - 61 = 17$. The GCF of 17 and 17 is 17. The divisor is 17 and the remainder is 10.

15. **12.** $225 - 201 = 24$ and $201 - 189 = 12$. The GCF of 24 and 12 is 12. The divisor is 12 and the remainder is 9.

Appendix 6. Sequences and Series

This Appendix is an extension of the material introduced on pages 37-51, *Number Patterns*. We say that a SEQUENCE of numbers is an ordered list of numbers. The numbers in the sequence are called the TERMS of the sequence. The terms are identified by their ORDER (position) in the sequence.

It is helpful for the reader to have some background in algebra.

6.1–6.2 SEQUENCES

6.1 Arithmetic Sequences [A.S.]

The reader should review Addition Patterns in Part C section 1.1 on pages 38-42. In that section, ordered sequences of numbers were formed by adding a common difference to the preceding number. Such addition patterns are called ARITHMETIC SEQUENCES (A.S.).

Example: 2, 5, 8, 11, ... , 20 is an A.S. where 2 is the FIRST TERM and 3 is the COMMON DIFFERENCE which is added to each of the preceding numbers until the LAST TERM 20 is reached. The three dots (...) denote that the indicated pattern continues.

We now continue our discussion in more general terms. Suppose an A.S. of n terms has a first term a and a common difference of d. Then the A.S. becomes a, $a + 1d$, $a + 2d$, $a + 3d$, and so forth as shown in the table below.

Term number	1	2	3	4	5	...	n
Term of A.S.	a	$a + d$	$a + 2d$	$a + 3d$	$a + 4d$	...	$a + (n-1)d$

Before reading ahead, study the above table and try to find a relationship between the term number and the term itself.

Observe that the number of ds which are added to a in a term of A.S. is 1 less than the term number. For example, the 17th term of an A.S. will be represented by $a + 16d$. The common difference of an A.S. equals *any term* after the first term minus the *preceding term*.

If the nth term of an A.S. is represented by l, then:

$$l = a + (n - 1) \times d$$

Example: Find the 31st term of the A.S. 2, 5, 8, …

Given: $a = 2$, $d = 3$, $n = 31$

$$l = a + (n - 1) \times d$$
$$l = 2 + (31 - 1) \times 3$$
$$l = 2 + \quad 30 \quad \times 3$$
$$l = \quad 92$$

The 31st term of the A.S. is 92.

★ **Problems** ★

1. If $a = 3$, $d = 5$, and $n = 10$, find the value of l in this A.S.
2. Find the 41st term of the A.S. 10, 14, 18, …

(Solutions are on page 273.)

6.2 Geometric Sequences [G.S.]

The reader should review Multiplication Patterns in part C section 1.2 on pages 42-44.

In that section another type of ordered sequence was formed by multiplying each term except the first term by a fixed number called the common ratio r. Such multiplication patterns are called GEOMETRIC SEQUENCES (G.S.).

Example: 3, 6, 12, 24, 48, … , 384 is a G.S. where 3 is the FIRST TERM and 2 is the fixed number r called the COMMON RATIO which is used to multiply each preceding number until the LAST TERM 384 is reached.

We now continue our formal discussion in more general terms. Suppose a G.S. of n terms has a first term of a and a common ratio of r. Then the G.S. becomes a, $a \times r$, $a \times r \times r$, $a \times r \times r \times r$, and so forth. It is convenient to display the terms of the G.S. in exponential form as shown in the table that follows.

Term number	1	2	3	4	5	…	n
Term of the G.S.	a	ar^1	ar^2	ar^3	ar^4	…	ar^{n-1}

Before reading ahead, study the above table and try to find a relationship between the number of a term and the term itself.

Observe that for any term of the sequence that the exponent of r is 1 less than the number of the term. Thus, the 17th term of a general G.S. is ar^{16}.

The common ratio (multiplier) of a G.S. is equal to the quotient of any term after the first divided by the preceding term.

If the last term of a G.S. is l, then

$$l = ar^{n-1}$$

Notice that it is possible for certain sequences to be both Arithmetic and Geometric Sequences as in the case 5, 5, 5, 5, 5 where $d = 0$ or $r = 1$.

★ Problems ★

1. If $a = 2$, $r = 3$, and $n = 6$, what is the value of l ?

2. Find the 8th term of $\frac{1}{8}, \frac{1}{4}, \frac{1}{2}, \ldots$

3. What number term is 384 in the example on page 265?

(Solutions are on page 273.)

6.3–6.5   SERIES

Although the mathematics of sequences is remarkably rich and quite fascinating, we will be primarily concerned with finding *sums* of the terms of certain special sequences. We will refer to the sum of the terms of a sequence as a SERIES.

Our basic goal is the development of workable methods for computing the sum of n terms of an Arithmetic or Geometric Series.

6.3 Arithmetic Series

We begin with an illustrative example:

Find the sum of the first 43 terms of the Arithmetic Sequence 2, 5, 8, ...

Notice that $a = 2$, $d = 3$, and $n = 43$.
The 43rd term is obtained using the formula $l = a + (n - 1) \times d$.
The 43rd term is: $2 + (42) \times 3 = 128.$

Therefore, we will compute the sum (1) S = 2 + 5 + 8 + $\cdots$ + 122 + 125 + 128.

To do this, we employ a clever trick and rewrite S in reverse order.

(2) $S = 128 + 125 + 122 + \cdots + 8 + 5 + 2$

Thus

(1) $S = 2 + 5 + 8 + \cdots + 122 + 125 + 128$
(2) $S = 128 + 125 + 122 + \cdots + 8 + 5 + 2$

Adding (1) and (2) yields:

(3) $2S = 130 + 130 + 130 + \cdots + 130 + 130 + 130$
where 130 occurs 43 times as an addend.

Therefore (4) $2S = 130 \times 43$

and (5) $S = \frac{130 \times 43}{2}$

$S = 2795$

The sum of the first 43 terms of the Arithmetic Sequence 2, 5, 8, ... , 128 is 2795.

We now apply this procedure to the general case to find the sum of the first n terms of an A.S. whose first term is a, common difference is d, and n^{th} term is $a + (n-1) \times d$. We can represent the sum S as

(1) $S = a + [a + 1d] + [a + 2d] + \cdots + [a + (n-1)d]$

For convenience, let the letter $l = a + (n-1) \times d$. Observe that if we represent the last term by l, then we can represent the next to last term by $l - d$, the term before that by $l - 2d$, and so forth. Reversing (1) we get

(2) $S = l + [l - 1d] + [l - 2d] + \cdots + [l - (n-1)d]$

Adding (1) and (2) yields:
(3) $2S = [a + l] + [a + l] + [a + l] + \cdots + [a + l]$, where $[a + l]$ occurs n times.
(4) $2S = [a + l] \times n$ or $2S = n \times [a + l]$

(5)
$$S = \frac{n \times (a + l)}{2}$$

Equation (5) is a formula for finding the sum of an Arithmetic Series where a, n, d, and l are obtainable. Remember, $l = a + (n-1) \times d$

Example: Find the sum of the Arithmetic Series $1 + 2 + 3 + 4 + \cdots + 25$

Observe that $a = 1$, $d = 1$, $n = 25$ and $l = 25$.

$$S = \frac{n \times (a + l)}{2}$$

F

$$S = \frac{25 \times (1+25)}{2}$$

$$S = 25 \times 13$$

$$S = 325$$

The sum of the Arithmetic Series $1 + 2 + 3 + 4 + \cdots + 25$ is 325.

★ *Problems* ★

Find the sum of each of the indicated Arithmetic Series in problems 1-6.

1. The first term is 3 and the 12th and last term is 47.

2. $5 + 8 + 11 + \ldots,$ to 16 terms

3. All of the consecutive odd numbers from 1 to 49 inclusive.

4. $2 + 3.5 + 5 + \ldots;$ 21 terms

5. $\frac{1}{3} + 2\frac{2}{3} + 5 + \ldots;$ 15 terms

6. $1 + 2 + 3 + \ldots;$ n terms

(Solutions are on pages 273-274.)

6.4 Finite Geometric Series

Compute the sum of the first 10 terms of the G.S. 1, 3, 9, 27, ...

Notice that $a = 1$, $r = 3$, and $n = 10$. The 10th term is obtained using the formula $l = ar^{n-1}$. The 10th term is 1×3^9. Therefore we need to compute $S = 1 + 3 + 9 + \cdots + 1 \times 3^9$. For convenience, we rewrite S as $1 + 3 + 3^2 + 3^3 + \cdots + 3^9$ [equation (1)].

For Geometric Series, we employ another clever trick. We multiply S and each term of the series by 3, the value of the common ratio r.

This yields $3S = 3 + 3^2 + 3^3 + \cdots + 3^9 + 3^{10}$ [equation (2)].

Thus   (2) $3S = \quad 3 + 3^2 + 3^3 + \cdots + 3^9 + 3^{10}$
and   (1) $S = 1 + 3 + 3^2 + 3^3 + \cdots + 3^9$

Subtracting (1) from (2) yields:

(3) $2S = 3^{10} - 1,$ or

$$(4) \qquad S = \frac{3^{10} - 1}{2}$$

We apply this procedure to the general case to find the sum of the first n terms of a Geometric Series whose first term is a, common ratio is r, and nth term is ar^{n-1}.

$$(1) \qquad \text{Let } S = a + ar + ar^2 + \cdots + ar^{n-1}$$

Multiply S by r to obtain:

$$(2) \qquad rS = ar + ar^2 + \cdots + ar^{n-1} + ar^n$$

Subtracting (1) from (2) yields:

$$(2) \qquad rS = \qquad ar + ar^2 + \cdots + ar^{n-1} + ar^n$$
$$(1) \qquad \underline{S = a + ar + ar^2 + \cdots + ar^{n-1}}$$
$$(3) \qquad rS - S = ar^n - a$$

$$(4) \qquad (r-1)S = ar^n - a$$

$$(5) \qquad \boxed{S = \frac{ar^n - a}{r - 1}}$$

Equation (5) may also be written in the equivalent form

$$(5a) \qquad \boxed{S = \frac{a - ar^n}{1 - r}}$$

Equations (5) and (5a) are equivalent formulae for finding the sum of a Geometric Series when a, n, and r are known.

Example: Find the sum of the Geometric Series $1 + 2 + 2^2 + 2^3 + \cdots + 2^9$

Observe that $a = 1$, $r = 2$, and $n = 10$.

$$S = \frac{ar^n - a}{r - 1}$$

$$S = \frac{1 \times 2^{10} - 1}{2 - 1}$$

$$S = 2^{10} - 1$$

$$S = 1023$$

The sum of the Geometric Series $1 + 2 + 2^2 + 2^3 + \cdots + 2^9$ is 1023.

★ **Problems** ★

Find the sum of each of the following Geometric Series.

1. $1 + 3 + 9 + \cdots + 729$

2. $5 + 25 + 125 + \cdots + 3125$

3. $4 + 2 + 1 + \frac{1}{2} + \ldots$;   8 terms

4. $1 + x + x^2 + x^3 + \ldots$;   7 terms

5. $4 - 2 + 1 - \frac{1}{2} + \ldots$;   10 terms

(Solutions are on pages 275-276.)

6.5 Infinite Geometric Series [I.G.S.]

When the number of terms of a Geometric Series increases without bound, we call such a series an *Infinite Geometric Series*.

For an Infinite Geometric Series such as $1 + 2 + 4 + 8 + \ldots$, the sum grows larger and larger. This will always be true if the common ratio r is greater than 1. In such a case where the sum grows larger without bound as the number of terms increases, we say that the series *diverges.*

However, it is possible to find the "sum" of certain Infinite Geometric Series such as $1 + \frac{1}{2} + \frac{1}{4} + \frac{1}{8} + \ldots$ (Note that r is a positive number less than 1; $r = \frac{1}{2}$)

Indeed, if r is between -1 and 1, or equivalently $|r| < 1$, then we are able to obtain the sum of an Infinite Geometric Series. In such a case, we say that the series *converges.*

Let us consider the Geometric Series.

$$S = 1 + \frac{1}{2^1} + \frac{1}{2^2} + \frac{1}{2^3} + \cdots + \frac{1}{2^n}.$$

Notice that $a = 1$, $r = \frac{1}{2}$, and there are $n + 1$ terms.

We will increase the value of n and observe what happens to S.
Note that the value of $\left(\frac{1}{2}\right)^{n+1}$ will vary.

By formula 5a, $S = \dfrac{a - ar^n}{1 - r}$

$$S = \frac{1 - \left(\frac{1}{2}\right)^{n+1}}{1 - \frac{1}{2}}$$

$$S = 2 \times \left[1 - \left(\tfrac{1}{2}\right)^{n+1}\right]$$

Let us examine values for $\left(\frac{1}{2}\right)^{n+1}$.

(1) If $n = 9$: $\left(\frac{1}{2}\right)^{10} = \frac{1}{1024}$. This is less than .001.

(2) If $n = 19$ $\left(\frac{1}{2}\right)^{20} = \left(\frac{1}{1024}\right)^2$. This is less than $(.001)^2 = .000001$.

(3) If $n = 39$: $\left(\frac{1}{2}\right)^{40} = \left(\frac{1}{2}\right)^{20} \times \left(\frac{1}{2}\right)^{20}$. This is less than $(.000001)^2 = .000000000001$.

In the expression for the sum, look at $1 - \left(\frac{1}{2}\right)^{n+1}$. Notice that as n increases, $\left(\frac{1}{2}\right)^n$ decreases and becomes closer and closer to zero. Consequently, $1 - \left(\frac{1}{2}\right)^{n+1}$ gets closer and closer to 1. The sum S gets closer and closer to 2×1. We then say that this Infinite Geometric Series *converges* to 2. Thus, the sum is said to be 2.

In general, for an Infinite Geometric Series where $|r| < 1$, it can be shown that the series converges to a sum S where

$$\boxed{S = \frac{a}{1 - r}}$$

The above equation is a simple formula for the sum of an infinite series when $|r| < 1$.

Thus, if we allow the Geometric Series on page 270 where $a = 1$ and $r = \frac{1}{2}$ to continue indefinitely, we may use this formula to compute S as follows:

$$S = \frac{1}{1 - \frac{1}{2}}$$

$$S = \frac{1}{\frac{1}{2}}$$

$S = 2$ Therefore, the series converges to 2. Its sum is 2.

⭐ **Problems** ⭐

In each of the following Infinite Geometric Series, compute the sum..

1. $4 + 2 + 1 + \ldots$

2. $\frac{1}{4} + \frac{1}{16} + \frac{1}{64} + \ldots$

3. $\frac{1}{5} - \frac{1}{5^2} + \frac{1}{5^3} - \ldots$

4. $\frac{1}{n} + \frac{1}{n^2} + \frac{1}{n^3} + \ldots$ (Assume $|n| > 1$)

5. Express $.777\ldots$ as an equivalent fraction $\frac{a}{b}$ where a and b are natural numbers.
   (Hint: $.777\ldots = .7 + .07 + .007 + \ldots$)

6. Express $.242424\ldots$ as an equivalent fraction $\frac{a}{b}$ where a and b are natural numbers.
   (Hint: $.242424\ldots = .24 + .0024 + .000024 + \ldots$)

7. Express $5.213213213\ldots$ as a mixed number.

8. Find the sum of the Infinite Geometric Series where $a = 3$, and $r = \frac{1}{3}$. Write the first six terms of this series.

9. Find the first term of the Infinite Geometric Series whose common ratio is $\frac{1}{6}$ and whose sum is $\frac{9}{5}$.

10. Find the common ratio if $S = 25$ and $a = 10$.

(Solutions are on pages 276-277.)

Appendix 6:   Solutions

6.1 Arithmetic Sequences
Pages 264-265

1. **48.** $l = a + (n-1)d$, where $a = 3$, $n = 10$ and $d = 5$.
   $l = 3 + (10 - 1) \times 5$
   $l = 3 + \quad (9) \quad \times 5$
   $l = 48$

2. **170.** $l = \quad a + (n-1)d$, where $a = 10$, $n = 41$, and $d = 4$.
   $l = 10 + (41 - 1) \times 4$
   $l = 10 + \quad (40) \quad \times 4$
   $l = 170$

6.2 Geometric Sequences
Pages 265-266

1. **486.** $l = ar^{n-1}$, where $a = 2$, $r = 3$, and $n = 6$.
   $l = 2 \times 3^{6-1} = 2 \times 3^5 = 2 \times 243 = 486$

2. **16.** $l = ar^{n-1}$, where $a = \frac{1}{8}$, $r = 2$, and $n = 8$.
   $l = \frac{1}{8} \times 2^{8-1} = \frac{1}{8} \times 2^7 = \frac{1}{8} \times 128 = 16$

3. **8.** $l = ar^{n-1}$, where $a = 3$, $r = 2$, and $l = 384$.
   $384 = 3 \times 2^{n-1}$
   $128 = \quad 2^{n-1}$
   $2^7 = \quad 2^{n-1}$
   $7 = n - 1$
   $n = 8$

F

6.3 Arithmetic Series
Pages 266-268

1. **300.** $S = \frac{n}{2}(a + l)$
   $S = \frac{12}{2}(3 + 47)$
   $S = 6 \times 50 = 300$

2. **440.** $l = a + (n-1)d$ for $n = 16$, $a = 5$, and $d = 3$.
   $l = 5 + (16 - 1) \times 3 = 5 + 45 = 50$

$S = \frac{n}{2}(a + l)$ for $n = 16$, $a = 5$, and $l = 50$.

$S = \frac{16}{2}(5 + 50)$

$S = 8 \times 55 = 440$

3. **625.** $l = a + (n - 1)d$ for $l = 49$, $a = 1$, and $d = 2$.

$49 = 1 + (n - 1) \times 2$

$48 = (n - 1) \times 2$

$24 = n - 1$

$n = 25$

$S = \frac{n}{2}(a + l)$ for $n = 25$, $a = 1$, and $l = 49$.

$S = \frac{25}{2}(1 + 49)$

$S = 25 \times 25 = 625$

4. **357.** $l = a + (n - 1)d$ for $n = 21$, $a = 2$, and $d = 1.5$.

$l = 2 + (21 - 1) \times 1.5 = 2 + 20 \times 1.5 = 2 + 30 = 32$

$S = \frac{n}{2}(a + l)$ for $n = 21$, $a = 2$, and $l = 32$.

$S = \frac{21}{2}(2 + 32)$

$S = 21 \times 17 = 357$

5. **250.** $l = a + (n - 1)d$ for $n = 15$, $a = \frac{1}{3}$, and $d = 2\frac{1}{3}$.

$l = \frac{1}{3} + (15 - 1) \times \frac{7}{3} = \frac{1}{3} + 14 \times \frac{7}{3} = \frac{99}{3} = 33$

$S = \frac{n}{2}(a + l)$ for $n = 15$, $a = \frac{1}{3}$, and $l = 33$.

$S = \frac{15}{2}\left(\frac{1}{3} + \frac{99}{3}\right)$

$S = \frac{15}{2} \times \frac{100}{3} = 250$

6. $\dfrac{n(n+1)}{2}$ **or** $\dfrac{n^2 + n}{2}$. $l = a + (n - 1)d$ for $n = n$, $a = 1$, and $d = 1$

$l = 1 + (n - 1)1 = n$

$S = \frac{n}{2}(a + l)$ for $n = n$, $a = 1$, and $d = 1$.

$S = \frac{n}{2}(1 + n)$

$S = \dfrac{n^2 + n}{2}$ or $\dfrac{n(n+1)}{2}$

6.4 Finite Geometric Series
Pages 268-270

1. **1093.** $\quad l = ar^{n-1}$, where $a = 1$, $r = 3$, and $l = 729$.

$$729 = 1 \times 3^{n-1}$$
$$3^6 = 3^{n-1}$$
$$6 = n - 1$$
$$n = 7$$

$$S = \frac{ar^n - a}{r - 1} \quad \text{for } a = 1, r = 3, \text{ and } n = 7.$$

$$S = \frac{1 \times 3^7 - 1}{3 - 1}$$

$$S = \frac{2187 - 1}{2} = 1093$$

2. **3095.** $\quad l = ar^{n-1}$, where $a = 5$, $r = 5$, and $l = 3125$.

$$3125 = 5 \times 5^{n-1}$$
$$5^5 = 5^n$$
$$n = 5$$

$$S = \frac{ar^n - a}{r - 1} \quad \text{for } a = 5, r = 5, \text{ and } n = 5.$$

$$S = \frac{5 \times 5^5 - 5}{5 - 1}$$

$$S = \frac{15625 - 5}{4} = 3095$$

3. $7\frac{31}{32}$. $\quad$ Since $-1 < S < 1$, use $S = \dfrac{a - ar^n}{1 - r}$, where $a = 4$, $r = \frac{1}{2}$, and $n = 8$.

$$S = \frac{4 - 4 \times \left(\frac{1}{2}\right)8}{1 - \frac{1}{2}}$$

$$S = \frac{4 - \frac{1}{64}}{\frac{1}{2}} = \frac{\frac{255}{64}}{\frac{1}{2}} = \frac{\frac{255}{64} \times 64}{\frac{1}{2} \times 64} = \frac{255}{32} = 7\frac{31}{32}$$

4. $\dfrac{x^7 - 1}{x - 1}$. $\quad$ Use $S = \dfrac{ar^n - a}{r - 1}$ where $a = 1$, $r = x$, and $n = 7$.

$$S = \frac{1x^7 - 1}{x - 1} = \frac{x^7 - 1}{x - 1}$$

F

5. $2\frac{85}{128}$.   Use $S = \dfrac{a - ar^n}{1-r}$ where $a = 4$, $r = -\frac{1}{2}$, and $n = 10$.

$$S = \frac{4 - 4\left(-\frac{1}{2}\right)^{10}}{1 - \left(-\frac{1}{2}\right)}$$

$$S = \frac{4 - 4\left(\frac{1}{1024}\right)}{1 + \frac{1}{2}}$$

$$S = \frac{4 - \frac{1}{256}}{\frac{3}{2}}$$

$$S = \frac{4 \times 256 - \frac{1}{256} \times 256}{\frac{3}{2} \times 256}$$

$$S = \frac{1024 - 1}{384}$$

$$S = \frac{1023}{384} = 2\frac{255}{384} = 2\frac{85}{128}$$

6.5 Infinite Geometric Series
Pages 270-272

1. **8.**   Use $S = \dfrac{a}{1-r}$ where $a = 4$ and $r = \frac{1}{2}$.

$$S = \frac{4}{1 - \frac{1}{2}} = \frac{4}{\frac{1}{2}} = 8$$

2. $\frac{1}{3}$.   Use $S = \dfrac{a}{1-r}$ where $a = \frac{1}{4}$ and $r = \frac{1}{4}$.

$$S = \frac{\frac{1}{4}}{1 - \frac{1}{4}} = \frac{\frac{1}{4}}{\frac{3}{4}} = \frac{1}{3}$$

3. $\frac{1}{6}$.   Use $S = \dfrac{a}{1-r}$ where $a = \frac{1}{5}$ and $r = -\frac{1}{5}$.

$$S = \frac{\frac{1}{5}}{1 - \left(-\frac{1}{5}\right)} = \frac{\frac{1}{5}}{1 + \frac{1}{5}} = \frac{\frac{1}{5}}{\frac{6}{5}} = \frac{1}{6}$$

4. $\dfrac{1}{n-1}$. Use $S = \dfrac{a}{1-r}$ where $a = \dfrac{1}{n}$ and $r = \dfrac{1}{n}$.

$$S = \dfrac{\frac{1}{n}}{1-\frac{1}{n}} = \dfrac{\frac{1}{n}}{\frac{n-1}{n}} = \dfrac{1}{n-1}$$

5. $\dfrac{7}{9}$. Use $S = \dfrac{a}{1-r}$ where $a = .7$ and and $r = .1$.

$$S = \dfrac{0.7}{1-0.1} = \dfrac{.7}{.9} = \dfrac{7}{9}$$

6. $\dfrac{8}{33}$. Use $S = \dfrac{a}{1-r}$ where $a = .24$ and and $r = .01$.

$$S = \dfrac{0.24}{1-0.01} = \dfrac{.24}{.99} = \dfrac{8}{33}$$

7. $\mathbf{5\dfrac{71}{333}}$. Use $S = \dfrac{a}{1-r}$ where $a = .213$ and and $r = .001$.

$$S = 5 + .213213213\ldots$$

$$S = 5 + \dfrac{0.213}{1-0.001} = 5 + \dfrac{.213}{.999} = 5\dfrac{71}{333}$$

8. $\mathbf{4\dfrac{1}{2}}$. Use $S = \dfrac{a}{1-r}$ where $a = 3$ and and $r = \dfrac{1}{3}$

$$S = \dfrac{3}{1-\frac{1}{3}} = \dfrac{3}{\frac{2}{3}} = 4\dfrac{1}{2}$$

The first six terms are $3, 1, \dfrac{1}{3}, \dfrac{1}{9}, \dfrac{1}{27}, \dfrac{1}{81}$.

9. $\mathbf{1\dfrac{1}{2}}$. Use $S = \dfrac{a}{1-r}$ where $S = \dfrac{9}{5}$ and and $r = \dfrac{1}{6}$.

$$\dfrac{9}{5} = \dfrac{a}{1-\frac{1}{6}}$$

$$a = \dfrac{9}{5} \times \dfrac{5}{6} = \dfrac{3}{2}$$

10. $\dfrac{3}{5}$.   Use $S = \dfrac{a}{1-r}$ where $S = 25$ and and $a = 10$.

$$25 = \dfrac{10}{1-r}$$
$$25 - 25r = 10$$
$$15 \quad\quad = 25r$$
$$r = \dfrac{15}{25} = \dfrac{3}{5}$$

F

Index

Index

Boldfaced italicized listings indicate definitions.

A

Acting out the problem   28-29
Addition patterns   38-41
Age problems   33, 54
Algebra, use of   31-33, 92-94, 212-216,
    237, 240, 248, 249, 258-260, 265-272
Alphametrics   *see Cryptarithms*
Angle measures   227-237
    exterior   229-230, 233, 236-237
    in pentagons   228
    in polygons   228-229, 237
    in quadrilaterals   227-228
    in star-figures   233
    in triangles   227, 228
Area   *225*
    formulas   225
    of circles   98-100, 225
    of rectangles and squares   96-100, 225
Arithmetic
    sequence   *39, 264,* 38-41, 264-265
    series   *266,* 22-23, 49-51, 266-268
Average   *224*

Backwards, working   29-31
Basic information   222-226
Book problems   *see Digit problems*

C

Calculators, use of   11
Calendar problems   23, 41, 67
Card Trick Problem, the   52-56
Carrying out the plan   3, 4-5
Certainty problems   118-120
Census Taker Problem, the   54
Chalkboard, use of   9
Changing your point of view   33-34
Characteristics of good problems   8

Checkerboard Problem, the   84-86, 114
Chicken-Cow Problem, the   18-19
Choosing problems   7
Circles
    area   *225*, 98-100
    circumference   *225*, 94-96
    regions   90-91
Clock Problems   109-110
Coin problems   2, 19, 33, 36
Combinatorics and Probability   *118*, 16-19,
    36
Combined divisibility tests   74-76
Completely factored   *224*, 54-62
Composite numbers   *224*
Complex fractions   *223*, 79-81
Computers, use of   11
Congruent figures   *225*
Consecutive numbers   33, 56, 65, 69
Consecutive unit fractions   78-79
Counterfeit Coin Problem, the   36
Creating problems   7
Cryptarithms   115-118

Definitions, basic   222-226
Diagonals and chords   *230*, 22-23, 34,
    112-114, 230-231, 237
Diagrams
    drawing   14-15
    tree   *17*, 55, 58, 62, 112
    Venn   *120*, 120-123
Dice problems   18-19, 36
Digit problems   *222*, 65, 69-75, 105-107,
    115-118
Divisibility   *65, 224*, 65-76, 257-263
    combined   74-76
    principles   67-68, 75-76, 257

tests of divisibility
for 2 65-66, 69, 74-75, 257
for 3 70-71, 74, 259
for 4 69, 74, 257
for 5 65-66, 74, 257
for 7, 11, and 13 75-76
for 8 68-69, 75, 257
for 9 70-71, 74-75, 258-259
for 10 65-66
for 11 71-76, 259
for 16 68-69
for 100 65-66
for powers of 2 68-69, 257
for powers of 10 66
Divisions producing same remainder
58-60, 252-253, 260-261
Dominoes 17, 101-102
Drawing a picture or diagram 14-15
Duplicated sheets, use of 10

E

Elapsed time 109-110
Ellipsis, Use of 222
Equation, writing a 31-33, 92-94, 121-123,
237, 240, 248, 249, 258-260, 265-272
Euclid's algorithm 58-60
Evaluating problems 8
Even numbers 66
Even-place digits 73, 259
Exercise vs. problem *2*
Experimenting 26-27
Exponents *249*, *see Powers*
Exponential form *249*
Extended finite fractions 81-82
Extending problems 8

F

Factorial *56*
Factor *52*, *224*, 52-64
complete *224*, 58-62
greatest common (GCF) *57*, *224*,
57-60, 64
prime *54*, 54-56, 58, 76, 224
tree *17*, 55, 58, 62, 112

Farmer's Will Problem, the 83
Fermat's "Little" Theorem 252-253
Fibonnaci sequence 47-48
Figurate numbers 44-46
Finding a pattern 22-23
Flow chart 30-31
Formulas, geometric 225-226
Four 4s Problem, the 25
Four-step method of problem solving, 3-6
Fractional parts 82-83
Fractions *223*, 77-83
complex 79-81
extended finite 81-82
unit 77-79

G

Gauss, Karl Friedrich 49-50
Geometric formulas 225-226
Geometric patterns 42-44
Geometric sequence *265*, 42-44, 265-266
terms of a *39*, 42-44, 265-266, 268-270
Geometric series *266*, 268-272
Goldbach's conjectures 57
Greatest common factor (GCF) *57*, *224*,
57-60, 64
Guess and check 24-25

H

Handshake Problem, the 111-113
Helping students 11
Hexagonal numbers *46*
How to Solve It 3

I

Indirect proof 237

L

Language of a problem 3
Lead-digit of a number 222
Least common multiple (LCM) *61*, *225*,
60-64
List, make a 16-17, 57-58, 61, 88, 106,
111-114, 118

Logic problems   36, 124-129
Looking back   5-6

M

Magic square   25
Mathematical cryptagrams   *see Cryptarithms*
Motion problems   103-105
Multiples   *224*, 60-64
    common   61
    least common (LCM)   *61*, *225*, 60-64
Multiplication patterns   42-44

N

Nets   *35*
Nonroutine word problems   7
Number bracelet   49
Number cubes   18, 20
Numbers
    even   *66*
    Fibonnaci   *47*, 48
    figurate   44-46
    forms of   222
    hexagonal   *46*
    odd   *66*
    pentagonal   *46*
    prime   *54*, *224*, 54-62, 76
        relatively   *60*, *225*, 61, 239
    rectangular   *46*
    sets of   222
    square   *see Perfect squares*
    triangular   *45*, 44-45, 111-114

O

Odd numbers   *66*
Odd-place digits   73, 259
Oral presentation, use of   10
Order of a term of a sequence   *39*
Order of a Pythagorean Triple   *242*, 239-245
Order of operations   81, 223
Organized list, making an   16-17, 57-58,
    61, 88, 106, 111-114, 118
Overhead projector, use of   9-10

P

Parts, fractional   82-83
Pascal's Triangle   *48*
Patterns
    addition   38-41
    and sums   49-51
    finding   22-23
    multiplication   42-44
    unusual   46-49
Pentagonal Numbers   *46*
Pentominoes   *102*
Perfect squares   *53*, 22, 45-47, 86, 238,
    244, 245, 248, 249
Perimeter   *225*, 92-94
Picture, drawing a   14-15
Plan, carrying out a   3, 4-5
Planning how to solve a problem   4
Point of view, changing your   33-34
Polya, George   3
    four step method   3-6
Polygon
    angle measure of a   227-237
    diagonals of a   *230*, 230-231, 237
    exterior angles of a   *229*-230, 233, 237
    regular   *225*, *229*, 237
PowerPoint presentation   9-10
Powers   *249*, 249-256
    dividing   250
    multiplying   249
    powers of   251
    reading   249
    zero   *43*, 251
Presenting problems   9-10
Prime numbers   *54*, *224*, 54-62, 76, 239
    factors   *54*, 54-62, 76, 224
    relatively   *60*, *225*, 61, 239
Prime Power Factorization   *54*, *224*, 54-62
Probability and combinatorics   16-19, 36
Problems   *2*
    age   33, 54
    book   105-107
    calendar   23, 41, 67
    certainty   118-120
    characteristics of good   8

Boldfaced italicized listings indicate definitions.

choosing 7
chords and diagonals 22-23, 34, 112-114
clock 109-110
coin 2, 19, 33, 36
creating 7
evaluating 8
extending 5-6, 8
language of 3
logic 36, 124-129
motion 103-105
nonroutine 7
presenting 9-10
routine word 7
strategies in solving *see Strategies*
understanding 3
vs. exercises *2*
work 107-109
Problems, well-known
Card Trick, the 52-56
Census Taker, the 54
Checkerboard, the 84-86, 114
Chicken and Cow, 18-19
Counterfeit Coin, the 36
Farmer's Will, the 83
Four 4s, the 25
Handshake, the 111-113
Magic Square, the 25
Pascal's Town 48
Pythagorean
Theorem 238-248
triples *239*, 239-245
generating 240, 243-244
infinitude of 244-245
nonprimitive 241-242
Primitive *239*, 239-245
order of 242-245

R

Reasonableness of answers 5
Rectangles
area *225*, 96-100
counting regions 84-87, 114
perimeter *225*, 92-94

Rectangular numbers *46*
Regular polygons *225*, *229*, 237
Related problems 20-23, 111-114
Relatively prime numbers *60*, *225*, 61, 239
Remainders 58-60, 252-253, 260-261
Rhind papyrus 77
Routine word problems 7
Rule for a sequence 40

S

Sequence *39*, *264*, 38-51, 222
and series 38-51, 264-277
arithmetic *39*, *264*, 38-41, 264-265
Fibonacci 47-48
geometric *265*, 42-44, 265-266
order of a term *39*
rule for a 40
term of a *39*, 42-44, 264-270
Series *266*
arithmetic 22-23, 49-51, 266-268
geometric 268-272
Sets of numbers 222
Simpler related problem, solving a 20-21, 38-47
Square numbers *see Perfect squares*
Squares
area *225*, 96-98
counting 84-87
perimeter *225*, 92-94
Standard form of a number *222*
Strategies, problem solving 4-5, 8, 13-36
acting out the problem 28-29
changing your point of view 33-34
drawing a picture or diagram 14-15
experimenting 26-27
finding a pattern 22-23
guessing and checking 24-25
making an organized list 16-17, 57-58, 61, 88, 106, 111-114, 118
making a table 18-19, 22-23, 38-44, 47, 52, 56, 61, 63, 65, 66, 69, 70, 84-86, 88, 90, 91, 93, 97, 113, 122, 124-129, 228, 231, 233, 239, 240, 244, 245, 252, 264, 265

miscellanea   35-36
solving a simpler problem   20-21, 38-47
working backwards   29-31
writing an equation   31-33, 93-94
Sum
of an arithmetic series   *266*, 22-23, 49-51, 266-268
of a geometric series   268-272
Sums, patterns and   49-51

Table, making a   *see Strategies (making a table)*
Tangram   98
Teaching techniques   9-11
chalkboard   9
duplicated sheets   10
helping students   11
oral presentation   10
overhead projector   9-10
Term of a sequence   *39*, 42-44, 264-270
order of a   *264*, *39*
Terminal zeros   *54*, 56
Tests for divisibility   *see Divisibility tests*
Tetrominoes   102
Textbook, using a   7
Tree diagram   *17*, 55, 58, 62, 112
Triangles
area of   *225*
counting   87-89
perimeter of   *225*, 94

Triangular numbers   *45*, 44-45, 111-114
Trominoes   101-102

Understanding the problem   3
Unit fraction principle   78
Unit fractions   *223*, 77-79
consecutive   *78*
Unusual patterns   46-49
Use of an ellipsis   222

Variables, use of   31-33, 92-94, 121-123, 237, 240, 248, 249, 258-260, 265-272
Venn diagrams   *120*, 120-123
Volume formulas   226

Whodunits   124-129
Word problems, routine   7
Work problems   107-109
Working backwards   29-31
Writing an equation   31-33, 93-94

Zero exponent   *43*, 251
Zeros, terminal   *54*, 56

Boldfaced italicized listings indicate definitions.

HOST YOUR OWN TOURNAMENT

OUR TOURNAMENT PROGRAM

A TOURNAMENT IS A ONE-DAY LOCAL OR REGIONAL EVENT FOR STUDENTS IN GRADES 4 - 6 OR 6 - 8. IT PROVIDES A FACE-TO-FACE TEAM COMPETITION FOR AS MANY TEAMS AS YOUR VENUE CAN ACCOMMODATE, AND COULD PROVIDE AN EXCITING CULMINATION TO THE SCHOOL YEAR OR AN EXCITING KICK-OFF FOR A NEW YEAR.

THE TOURNAMENT YOU SET UP BEARS YOUR ORGANIZATION'S NAME - IT'S YOUR TOURNAMENT! RECENT TOURNAMENTS HAVE BEEN SPONSORED BY SCHOOL DISTRICTS, COLLEGES, PROFESSIONAL ORGANIZATIONS, AND AFTER-SCHOOL ENRICHMENT PROGRAMS.

A DETAILED TOURNAMENT HANDBOOK IS PROVIDED TO ENABLE YOUR SCHOOL, DISTRICT OR ORGANIZATION TO SUCCESSFULLY LAUNCH ONE OF THESE FAST-GROWING EVENTS.

PAYMENT OF THE ANNUAL FEE ENABLES YOU TO GIVE THE TOURNAMENT YOUR OWN NAME, DECIDE WHO WILL BE INVITED, AND WHEN IT WILL BE HELD!

FREQUENTLY ASKED QUESTIONS

How do I register for a Tournament?

Simply fill out a Tournament Agreement form (available in this packet and also on line) and send it to our office for approval. Once it's approved (approval is based upon whether there is another Tournament running too close to the area you are requesting), you will be asked to submit fees and you will receive the Tournament Handbook. If you want to get an idea of the numbers of Math Olympiad teams in your proposed region, give us a call.

What information is contained in the handbook?

The handbook contains detailed instructions and valuable suggestions for running a successful event. Included are: schedules (for before the date and on the actual date), sample table arrangements, areas of responsibility and detailed instructions for your committee members (only 3 - 4 heads of committees make this endeavor work very well), and sample correspondence forms (including publicity letters for before and after the tournament, press releases, and team registration forms).

How is the tournament different from the monthly Mathematical Olympiad Contests?

Although the problems on the Tournaments are similar to those on the contests, there are some major differences. The competition is divided into three parts. Each team of 5 students will take a 10-question individual contest. That is followed up by another 10-question *team* event, where only one set of answers is submitted for each team. Finally, in the event of any ties (individuals or teams), there is a set of tiebreaker problems.

What does it mean when we say, "It's YOUR Tournament?"

The name that you give your tournament will appear in a 2-inch high masthead on top of every page (we provide the template for you to use). This tournament represents your group and provides many benefits, including promoting your reputation for excellence, strengthening your organization, generating publicity, or if desired, producing revenue.

What does the sponsoring organization have to do to get ready?

The sponsoring organization decides what fee (if any) to charge to teams, chooses a site, invites schools, prints and packages the contests, and buys awards. Our handbook will guide you through every step.

How will the teams get their results?

Every student and team will know where they stand in the Tournament by the end of the event. Scoring is done by a few volunteers during the event. An electronic spreadsheet is provided on which you will enter individuals' scores. That spreadsheet will rank the results, so that you will be able to have an awards program on the same day!

Are solutions to the problems included?

There is review time for all questions built into the suggested schedule. A set of Power Point® slides is included to use on that day, so that the person reviewing the answers has little to do, but explain strategies and answer questions.

Is it necessary that the students at the tournament have participated in the monthly Math Olympiad Contests?

No, in fact many sponsoring organizations use this as a way to get more schools in their area involved in Math Olympiads. Your tournament may be administered anytime from April through December of the same school year.

What if I still have other concerns or questions?

We are always available to help you or answer any other questions you may have. Just call or e-mail us.